78

Adaptations
as Imitations

Adaptations as Imitations

Films from Novels

James Griffith

DELAWARE

Newark: University of Delaware Press
London: Associated University Presses

Associated University Presses
440 Forsgate Drive
Cranbury, NJ 08512

Associated University Presses
16 Barter Street
London WC1A 2AH, England

Associated University Presses
P.O. Box 338, Port Credit
Mississauga, Ontario
Canada L5G 4L8

The paper used in this publication meets the requirements
of the American National Standard for Permanence of Paper
for Printed Library Materials Z39.48–1984.

Library of Congress Cataloging-in-Publication Data

Griffith, James John, 1951-
    Adaptations as imitations : films from novels / James Griffith.
        p.   cm.
    Includes bibliographical references and index.
    ISBN 0–87413–633–4 (alk. paper)
    1. Film adaptations. I. Title.
PN1997.85.G66   1997
791.43'6—dc21
                                                                    97–3543
                                                                    CIP

PRINTED IN THE UNITED STATES OF AMERICA

*Dedicated to my parents
and to Kathy*

Contents

Preface

I suppose this study began when I first started reading seriously. Films were already a source of enjoyment, and when I read novels for the same pleasure, I "filmed" them. That is, I did what I think many readers do: imagine the novel's action in pictures, even "casting" the roles; my imagination may have gone only a bit further with mental notes about editing and camera angles.

Given this habit of reading, I later found the theoretical commentaries on film adaptations to be faulty. The common critical assumption held that good novels were beyond the capabilities of film, but I had already "seen" some of these movies, and they worked quite well. This book commits to paper what I hope will defend and justify my imagination—and the imagination of those filmmakers who have committed their visions of novels to celluloid.

Early help came from Mr. Charles Eisele and Brother John Plumpe at Vianney High School; the former made me appreciate and want to write clear prose, and the latter taught the first class I ever took that studied film. Then, an off-hand remark by Daniel Greenblatt at the University of Missouri encouraged me to think about combining the two pursuits of English and film studies.

Once I formally undertook the work, answers to questions, useful suggestions, and other forms of assistance came from several sources. Amy R. Weissbrod kindly allowed me to examine some cutting continuities owned by MGM. At Houghton Mifflin, Teresa Buswell helpfully expedited a permissions request regarding *Deliverance*, and Faith Barbato, of Harper Collins, accomplished the same in regard to *To Kill a Mockingbird*. Cartha Sexton, at an early stage of the project, provided excellent typing. The Ohio State University College of the Humanities blessed me with the Hayon Award, and I thank them and Yehiel Hayon, who established the award in memory of his parents; the money that accompanied the award went into a VCR, a necessary instrument of film criticism today. Jerry W. Carlson of DePaul University, and Dennis Aig, Lisa Kiser, and Tom Hendricks—all of Ohio State University—came up with solutions or pointed me toward the right resources. James Phelan did the same and, as Chair of the OSU English Department, also offered valuable help in the form of access to copying services. Robert Wagner read a version of the manuscript, and represented best what has been lost in the closing of OSU's Department of Photography and Cinema. Marlene Longenecker and Steven Fink aided me by arranging for relevant teaching assignments, and the students in those sections of Introduction to Fiction, American and English Literature and Film, and Studies in Narrative: Hitchcock and Kubrick all pushed me to rethink and refine my positions.

I owe thanks to some conference organizers and editors for other "tryouts" of my work. James Phelan and the Sixth Annual Conference in the Humanities on Narrative Poetics gave me an opportunity to preview ideas about point of view in film, and Mark Shale and the Institute of Liberal Studies Conference on Science and Culture allowed me the same chance in regard to my work on Kubrick's *2001*. Shorter versions of my chapters on *The Natural* and *Deliverance* appeared earlier ("Say It Ain't So: *The Natural*," *Literature/Film Quarterly* 19 [1991]: 157–63; and "Damned if You Do, and Dammed if You Don't: James Dickey's *Deliverance*," *Post Script* 5.3 [1986]: 47–59), and I thank the editors, James M. Welsh and Gerald Duchovnay respectively, for their consideration at the time and for their permitting me to use the material here again.

In the later stages, I obviously owe a great debt to Jay L. Halio, Chair of the Board of Editors at the University of Delaware Press, and to the anonymous reader for the Press whose kind response so strongly shared my interests. Julien Yoseloff, Director, and all the cast and crew at the Associated University Presses—notably Christine A. Retz and Don Kalbach—capably saw the project through editing and on to the premiere.

Throughout the project, I have enjoyed the company of two scholars and gentlemen. James L. Battersby and Morris Beja have been excellent directors in my complicated role of literary/film theorist/critic; their contributions can only have enhanced the book, but like the hottest directors, their star power should not be diminished by association if my work performs poorly at the box office of popular and critical opinion.

Finally, however, I turn to those to whom I owe my greatest obligation for love and support, and to whom I dedicate this book: they saw that I got started, and she saw that I got finished.

Adaptations
as Imitations

Introduction

As a question becomes more complicated and involved, and extends to a greater number of relations, disagreement of opinion will always be multiplied, not because we are irrational, but because we are finite beings, furnished with different kinds of knowledge, exerting different degrees of attention, one discovering consequences which escape another, none taking in the whole concatenation of causes and effects, most comprehending but a very small part; each comparing what he observes with a different criterion, and each referring it to a different purpose.

—Samuel Johnson, *The Adventurer*, No. 107

Howland Owl:	"What's a-matter? Don't like the answers you get here? Try a bran' new question . . ."
Churchy La Femme:	"Nothin' doin'! My question's okay. . . . You think of some new answers."

—Walt Kelly

Daniel Blum's *A Pictorial History of the Silent Screen* contains a still from IMP's 1914 production of *Jane Eyre*. Irving Cummings as Rochester stands in the center of the frame arm in arm with his bride-to-be, Jane, played by Ethel Grandin. They and their guests appear startled by an interruption of the wedding, but the intruder is not Mason, as in Charlotte Brontë's novel; rather, the insane Mrs. Rochester (played by a Miss Hazeltone) has come forward to show who occupies Rochester's mind and attic.[1] Brontë has two consecutive scenes that effectively block Jane from marrying and cause her to leave Thornfield: at the church, where Mason interrupts the wedding by charging that Rochester still has a wife, and in the attic at Thornfield, where Rochester admits as much but shows her to be more like a "clothed hyena" than a woman.

This film version, a four-reeler of about an hour's length,[2] collapses the two scenes, apparently obviating the need for Mason's character. Apropos of the nearly axiomatic discussions of adaptations, we could say that this film exemplifies the typical diluting of the novel's impact by shortening and simplifying the action. I would never argue that the film's one scene is not shorter than the novel's two. I would question, however, whether the film simplifies the action and impact. Certainly, the film as a whole may be simplified—it may be barely recognizable as Brontë's story—but to frustrate Jane and send her from Thornfield, the action here seems adequate. In other words, despite the infidelity to the original, the film preserves the dramatic effect of the shocking discovery.

Of course, by focusing on this one action, I have only raised, not settled, the issue of adapting novels to the screen. Novels have often been brought to the screen, so the possibility of attempting adaptations cannot concern us as an issue; on the other hand, the possibility of faithfully transferring a work from one medium to another remains an issue. Great novelists have joined this debate since nearly the beginning of film production. Tolstoy was excited by the cinema because it seemed capable of surpassing written effects:

> It is a direct attack on the old methods of literary art. . . . But I rather like it. This swift change of scene, this blending of emotion and experience—it is much better than the heavy, long-drawn-out kind of writing to which we are accustomed. It is closer to life.[3]

But, speaking of Tolstoy's *Anna Karenina*, Virginia Woolf cites what she believes to be an insurmountable limitation of the silent adaptation:

> The alliance is unnatural. Eye and brain are torn asunder ruthlessly as they try vainly to work in couples. . . . For the brain knows Anna almost entirely by the inside of her mind—her charm, her passion, her despair. . . . All this, which is accessible to words, and to words alone, the cinema must avoid.[4]

Many novels, as the critical literature attests, meet the attack Tolstoy mentions and emerge unbeaten in the battle over which is "closer to life." Nonetheless, Woolf's assertion that some written works are beyond adaptation to the screen has virtually become a given of film criticism. One typical view of adaptations holds that they are the products of businessmen, not artists. Francis Levy suggests that adapting "literary" novels is good business because these "difficult" and "artistic" works offer the "originality, diversity of appeal and allure to top talent"—not to mention the then current success of Milos Forman's version of Ken Kesey's *One Flew Over the Cuckoo's Nest*. Richard Corliss once wrote that "the Seventies saw the end of Hollywood's reliance on plays and novels as fodder for its movies" and that "the power has certainly shifted from studio boss to writer and director, or writer-director," a conclusion backed up with statistics on Academy Award nominations and winners. Only ten years later, though, Oscar statistics pointed to different conclusions: novels may not appeal to as wide an audience as films, "but Hollywood has always relied on the tried, never mind true. Besides, originals can be pricey these days. . . . Whether from mild intellectual adventure or bottom-line conservatism, Hollywood has lately been raiding the bestseller list."[5] And in the nineties, the work of directors such as James Ivory demonstrates that success—measured in reviews, awards, and box office—need not begin with a shrewd purchase of a title off the bestseller list; in fact, the release of some adaptations (for instance, *Howard's End*, *The Remains of the Day*, *Like Water for Chocolate*, and *The Age of Innocence*) these days will confer bestseller status on a novel rather than exploit such status.

Whether or not the acquisition of a novel's film rights makes good business sense, quantity does not necessarily affect quality. If we can set aside the quantitative, business judgments, I think we can examine the more interesting aspect of the issue: Is it true that some or all novels cannot be adapted to film faithfully, adequately preserving the novel's style, plot, and effects? Levy refers to the adage, "Great literature seldom makes great movies. But very good pulp makes very good movies" (see, below, the discussion of Béla Balázs, perhaps the earliest to promulgate this truism); yet he also notes that new audiences and techniques are allowing innovations that are "stretching the possibilities of film form itself."[6] My critical sensibilities lean toward the excitement of Tolstoy, who saw unlimited possibilities; but the history of film criticism has mostly followed Woolf's sense of limited possibilities: the filmmaker can frustrate Jane Eyre's marriage, but *Jane Eyre* will frustrate the filmmaker in the end.

The Theoretical Treatment of Adaptations
Up to Bluestone

Béla Balázs is the first film theorist to deal with the subject directly. Well known theorists who were his contemporaries did not address the issue of adaptations at length. The Gestalt theories of Hugo Münsterberg and Rudolf Arnheim and the formalist theories of Vachel Lindsay, Lev Kuleshov, V. I. Pudovkin, and Sergei Eisenstein set out, in part, to establish film as an independent art; therefore, they go to some length to separate it from other arts, particularly theater. These theorists hardly mention adaptations, but if they treated the issue in depth, they would most likely still be concerned with distinguishing the material and technical attributes of literature and film—attributes that would seemingly render adaptations difficult if not impossible by definition. As for attributes novels and film share, even Eisenstein's "Dickens, Griffith, and the Film Today" does not go beyond demonstrating how Dickens, in his narrative techniques, developed a nascent type of montage; Eisenstein does not then say how such shared capabilities might affect the issue of adaptation.[7] These writers might agree that a novel could be adapted to the screen when the filmmaker transforms it through the techniques that, they variously believe, define film form (for example, montage or the "foregrounding" of cinema's technical limitations). The process would probably severely alter the original novel, but that should be beside the point for the filmmaker: without adherence to these formal principles, these theorists would say the entire enterprise is worthless as film anyhow. Of course, such treatment hardly makes referring to a novel worthwhile in the first place.

Balázs is the first important theorist to discuss the issue directly, and he makes explicit some of what is implicit in so much early formalist thinking. Balázs's willingness to raise the issue of adaptations strikes me as characteristic of his desire to develop a formalist theory of film that can embrace a wider range of work than is allowed by his fellow theorists. So, whereas Arnheim bemoans the coming of sound—and every other technical innovation to follow—Balázs writes of the expressive possibilities in sound, color, the narrated film, and three-dimensional film. The Russian writers define the art as fundamentally one of montage editing. Balázs says that montage gives meaning to the film, but he also attempts to show how editing causes audience "identification" with the image and allows for the subtler "microdrama" of realism; and leaving editing aside, he sees the expressive possibilities in the "panorama" or long-take, shots—all of which goes well beyond the "make-it-strange" aesthetics of the Russians.[8]

Of course, rather than being more inclusive, Balázs may simply be too eclectic and even self-contradictory. For instance, I think Balázs tries too hard to make "identification" central to the audience's familiar involvement in the film's "microdrama":

> In the cinema the camera carries the spectator into the film picture itself. We are seeing everything from the inside as it were and are surrounded by the characters of the film. They need not tell us what they feel, for we see what they see and see it as they see it. . . . Herein lies the psychological act of "identification."[9]

This passage confuses point of view with identification. The point of view, in film as in written fiction, may not be attached to a particular character; however, if the point of view is that of one character, the reader-viewer need not take on that character's ideas or values—that is, need not *identify* with him or her.

J. Dudley Andrew notes another problem with this concept: "Spectator identification and delusion are seen here in a positive light whereas they work against the concepts of defamiliarization and of art as formal technique, which Balázs struggled to establish." Andrew states that Balázs's apparently contradictory stance grows out of a good Marxist avoidance of extremes: formalist technique should be used to shape the content gathered from the world around us, but should not be indulged in for its own sake.[10] His tendency to compromise between two positions also muddles the thinking on adaptations.

The compromise stems from his desire to account for adaptations on the screen—they cannot be ignored since it is "accepted practice"—whereas his formalist theory, which equates form and content, would seem to disallow adaptations on principle.

> The theoretical reason on which the opposition to adaptation is based is that there is an organic connection between form and content in every art and that a certain art form always offers the most adequate expression for a certain content. Thus the adaptation of a content to a different art form can only be detrimental to a work of art, if that work

of art was good. In other words, one may perhaps make a good film out of a bad novel, but never out of a good one.

This connection between form and content, he adds, is an "undeniably correct thesis." The possibility of adaptations, then, depends on a clarification of what "content" means:

> There can be no doubt that it is possible to take the subject, the story, the plot of a novel, turn it into a play or a film and yet produce perfect works of art in each case—the form being in each case adequate to the content. How is this possible? It is because, while the subject, or story, of both works is identical, their *content* is nevertheless different. It is this different *content* that is adequately expressed in the changed form resulting from the adaptation.
>
> ... [T]he raw material of reality can be fashioned into many different art forms. But a "content" which determines the form, is no longer such raw material.[11]

The reductive terminology traps him. "Form" equals "art form," which equals medium, so a change from page to screen necessarily changes form; then, if form equals content also, content changes too. To escape with the possibility of adaptation intact, Balázs must force a distinction between story or plot (not the same thing, I believe) and content-form.

The adaptations Balázs points to include Shakespeare's use of old tales for his plays, but these examples raise equivocations on the term "adaptation." The question arises, for instance, whether *Romeo and Juliet* is an adaptation of the story familiar in several languages or of the Arthur Brooke poem that came out about thirty years before the play. Furthermore, is the musical *West Side Story* an adaptation of the same story? Is the film an adaptation of the story too, or of the Broadway hit? The term "adaptation" is slippery here, for surely any artist can try to "adapt" a story to a medium (Brooke's poem), a finished work to another medium (Shakespeare's play), or a finished work to another context (the contemporary musical version). Most commonly, though, the term denotes the attempt to adapt a finished work to another medium. Balázs tells us that this sort of adaptation is not possible, but that the story's events can be retold on the screen—a conclusion that seems fairly obvious to me. Balázs allows that adaptations are possible, but his definition of adaptation excludes the most common sense of the word as used in film criticism—an unsatisfactory compromise.

I admire Balázs's attempt to overcome a significant limitation in a formalism that defines a medium and then deductively proscribes, at least by implication, what many artists persist in trying to do. Even so, I do not think Balázs really overcomes such limits, and, unfortunately, his conclusions have been the basis of most writing on adaptations ever since.

Perhaps the best known—and, to that extent, the most important and influential—book on the subject is George Bluestone's *Novels Into Film*. At one point, he anticipates semiotic terminology when he distinguishes the "institutional approach" (that is, the conventional code) that the novel or film each employ in its own way.[12] However, as a theorist, his formalism emphasizes the reader's or viewer's response to the novel or film, as in his discussion of the physical and psychological differences in our perception of time while reading a novel or viewing a film. This theoretical hat is the one Bluestone wears most often and the one he tips to Balázs.

Like Balázs, Bluestone views the material and technical features of film as the basis of its aesthetics, but he also agrees with Balázs that such aesthetics must not forget film's narrative function. Bluestone parts with Balázs slightly when he moves the discussion from the work itself to the reader-viewer's affective response to that work. "And between the percept of the visual image and the concept of the mental image lies the root difference between the two media." Bluestone's thesis has its basis in the same distinction between media that Balázs emphasizes: those who argue over an adaptation's fidelity to a novel fail to realize "that mutations are probable the moment one goes from a given set of fluid, but relatively homogeneous, conventions to another; that changes are *inevitable* the moment one abandons the linguistic for the visual medium."[13] As his thesis would indicate, Bluestone thinks this difference becomes critically important in an audience's possible responses:

> Perceptual knowledge is not necessarily different in strength; it *is* necessarily different in kind. The rendition of mental states—memory, dream, imagination—cannot be as adequately represented by film as by language. . . . The film, by arranging external signs for our visual perception, or by presenting us with dialogue, can lead us to infer thought. But it cannot show us thought directly.[14]

From these premises logically follow other important and insurmountable differences: "The novel has three tenses; the film has only one," which echoes Balázs's statement that "pictures have no tenses. They show only the present—they cannot express either a past or a future tense";[15] furthermore, "the novel renders the illusion of space by going from point to point in time; the film renders time by going from point to point in space." With such theoretical affinity, Bluestone can hardly surprise us by arriving at Balázs's conclusion:

> What happens, therefore, when the filmist undertakes the adaptation of a novel, given the inevitable mutation, is that he does not convert the novel at all. What he adapts is a kind of paraphrase of the novel— the novel viewed as raw material. He looks not to the organic novel, whose language is inseparable from its theme, but to characters and incidents which have somehow detached themselves from language and, like the heroes of folk legends, have achieved a mythic life of their own.[16]

Despite initial appearances, the latter half of this reference demonstrates that Bluestone shares with Balázs the same notion of "raw material," as becomes clearer when he cites Balázs's study on the same page. Like Balázs, then, even though Bluestone obviously admits the possibility of adapting novels to the screen, he does so only in the sense that both can tell the same story.

In his discussions of six adaptations (*The Informer, Wuthering Heights, Pride and Prejudice, The Grapes of Wrath, The Ox-Bow Incident,* and *Madame Bovary*), Bluestone consistently refuses to denigrate the filmmakers' efforts by using the novels as standards: "One can, if he wishes, argue with alterations which change the novelist's intention and meaning. But the final standard, the one to which we must always revert, is whether, regardless of thematic, formal, and medial mutations, the film stands up as an autonomous work of art."[17] Even though he points out the nearly complete excision of the second half of *Wuthering Heights* and the substitution of an uplifting ending for the despair that closes *The Grapes of Wrath*, Bluestone acknowledges the success—both financial and critical—of these films.

I find it significant that he considers the financial matters, for commercialism seems to qualify his theoretical stance. If he begins by separating percept and concept, Bluestone nonetheless finishes by adding, "An art whose limits depend on a moving image, *mass audience, and industrial production* is bound to differ from an art whose limits depend on language, a limited audience and individual creation."[18] The commercial pressures in filmmaking are undeniable, but the question remains whether Bluestone fully accounts for them in his theory. Given the sample he examines, Bluestone could inductively reach his conclusions about the process of changing novels for the screen. However, if financial and political exigencies affect the process, can one deductively conclude that these financial and political concerns necessarily apply in aesthetic decisions?

Anybody viewing films such as *Wuthering Heights* and *The Grapes of Wrath* and hundreds more adaptations that make severe alterations might be expected to draw conclusions similar to those of Bluestone—and Balázs before him. Abundant and obvious evidence fills the study conducted by Lester Asheim and reported in his dissertation (to which Bluestone refers often) and then summarized in a series of articles. Asheim's method is to make objective, quantitative comparisons between twenty-four "classic" or "standard" novels and their film adaptations; his purpose is thereby to correct impressionistic criticism in this field. Overall, he concludes that the movie industry aims at an audience of underestimated intelligence, but he sees audience demands and limitations of the medium that also motivate changes from book to film. Some statements remind us of Balázs and anticipate Bluestone:

> One of the ways through which the film version can render subtleties intelligible is to be explicit rather than implicit, specific rather than general. In part, this is a characteristic of presentation which arises out of the medium itself, since the visual depiction of an action is more explicit and specific than indirect exposition concerning it.[19]

For Asheim, however, this statement reflects a quantitative fact, not a qualitative judgment. It becomes one of thirty-nine basic findings in six categories: "Imposition of the Technology of Film Production" (for example, verbal form must be rendered visually, which requires condensation); "Considerations of the Artistic Uses of the Medium" (for example, films emphasize action, always present an omniscient point of view, can maintain description); "Recognition of the Limitations and Interests of the Audience" (for example, plot and characterization are both simpler and more glamorous, and endings are affirmative if not happy);

"Requirements of the Star System" (for example, stars' roles gain importance whereas supporting roles tend toward stereotype); "Deference to Pressures Outside the Industry and the Medium"— that is, the Production Code—(for example, despite the emphasis on action, films launder violence and sex, punish evil, and never criticize or ridicule certain religious or social values); and "Attempts to Remain Faithful to the Novel" (for example, adaptations usually maintain the broader outlines of the story and characterization—and the title).[20]

Generally, these statements can follow from the implications of Balázs's theory, and they certainly fit the lines of Bluestone's argument. Again, though, Asheim's conclusions measure observable fact. When he says that adaptations simplify the novels in such a way as to avoid challenging the minds of the audience, he is not leveling insults at the filmmakers; rather, he is noting a fact of Hollywood production. He does once complain that the movie's own "excellence is in itself a fault, for the audience that knows only the film and not the book is presented with a 'falsified' interpretation which leaves no clues that would permit it to reconstruct the original 'truth'";[21] nevertheless, such opinions are the exception in his work.

Bluestone takes these facts and uses them to support a formalist view similar to that of Balázs. A problem arises because, whereas most of Asheim's thirty-nine conclusions are relative to commercial concerns, Bluestone uses them to support aesthetic theories. Bluestone mentions commercial pressures, but he persists in treating the differences between film and book as necessary properties of their respective media.[22]

The question becomes whether such a formalist theory may be deductively applied to films made without the various commercial constraints Asheim discusses. Only at the end of his study does Bluestone mention changes that were occurring when he was sending his book to press. Along with technological advances, the most notable change may be Otto Preminger's defiance of the Production Code with the release of *The Man With the Golden Arm*; nevertheless, Bluestone mentions no possible contradictions of his conclusions, whereas he does hope for an innovative cinema that "will, at last, assert its independence from the traditional arts."[23]

As I mentioned before, the early film theorists were struggling to establish film as an art worthy of serious consideration on its own terms, defending it against the condescension accorded a mass entertainment. Understandably, a traditional formalism must have offered the seemingly most suitable path, and their studies worked variations on the sort of neoclassical definitiveness found in Lessing's *Laocoön*:

> If it be true that painting employs wholly different signs or means of imitation from poetry,—the one using forms and colors in space, the other articulate sounds in time,—and if signs must unquestionably stand in convenient relation with the thing signified, then signs arranged side by side can represent only objects existing side by side, or whose parts so exist, while consecutive signs can express only objects which succeed each other, or whose parts succeed each other, in time.
>
> Objects which exist side by side, or whose parts so exist, are called bodies. Consequently bodies with their visible properties are the peculiar subjects of painting.
>
> Objects which succeed each other, or whose parts succeed each other in time, are actions. Consequently actions are the peculiar subjects of poetry.[24]

If "painting" and "poetry" were changed to "film" and "novel," the formulation would nearly match that of Balázs or Bluestone.

The Theoretical Heritage of Bluestone

Theorists coming after Bluestone, even when they challenged earlier formalists, nonetheless often found similar answers to the questions about adaptations. In France, Jean Mitry echoes Balázs when he attacks the notion that adaptations work like translations:

> The means of expression *in being different* would express different things—not the same things in different ways. . . . We talk as if adaptation were a matter of translation, like passing from one language to another, when in fact it is a matter of passing from one *form* to another, a matter of transposition, of reconstruction.

From this premise, Mitry can draw conclusions that then agree with Bluestone's central distinction between concept and percept:

> Time in the novel is constructed with words. In the cinema it is constructed with actions. The novel *creates* a world while the cinema

puts us in the presence of a world which it organizes according to a certain continuity. *The novel is a narrative which organizes itself in a world; the film, a world which organizes itself in a narrative.*[25]

Under the circumstances, Mitry can encourage filmmakers to use novels only "as a point of departure, as an inspiration" for their personal vision. Nevertheless, Mitry allows that occasionally a filmmaker adheres to the letter of the novel, an adaptation that should produce no more than an "illustration" of the original, and yet produces "a valuable *reflection* of the original";[26] he puts David Lean's adaptations of Dickens's works in this category, but the exception, as they say, is supposed to prove the rule.

Another theorist promulgating this rule, with another few exceptions, is Siegfried Kracauer. In the phenomenological *Theory of Film*, he rejects formalist theories and attempts to show that film, whose "basic properties are identical with the properties of photography. . . is uniquely equipped to record and reveal physical reality and, hence, gravitates toward it."[27] Kracauer still thinks in terms of form and content, but he argues that content is preeminent. As Andrew perceptively notes, Kracauer sets out on a scientific enterprise, but wants to avoid the abstractions of science *and* aesthetics that have gone before.[28] On the issue of adaptations, then, although Kracauer sees both the novel and film as attempting to "feature the flow or stream of life"—an "affinity" that is, in his terms, definitively photographic, hence cinematic— they usually do not "focus on the same aspects of it": film uses "material phenomena from which its emotional and intellectual contents merge," whereas the novel develops "a mental continuum" whose components often "elude the grasp of the cinema." If Kracauer offers the possibility of adapting a few novels (*The Grapes of Wrath* stands out as his exceptional case) that involve sufficient "psychophysical correspondences,"[29] his theoretical framework still cannot accommodate most adaptations even though it changes the emphasis in the form-content dichotomy.

Edward Murray reaches almost the same conclusion:

Although it is both possible and desirable for the novelist and filmmaker each to suggest the objective and subjective realms as co-existing . . . it is also true that the basic difference between page and screen imposes strict limits on the power of each to convey certain kinds of material. Because he employs a linguistic medium, the novelist is uniquely privileged to explore thoughts and feelings, to discriminate among various sensations, to show the complex interpenetration of past and present, and to handle large abstractions.

Murray admits that producers' greed makes worthy adaptations difficult, but he insists that the technical differences are "of equally decisive importance."[30]

In *Reflections on the Screen*, George Linden goes further into the psychology of the viewer's response and develops its implications beyond the form-content framework. This approach takes him away from the film and into the theater, for he becomes more concerned with the process of viewing than with that of creating. Linden's version of the concept-percept division focuses on the writer's voice that can be understood by the singular reader, but cannot be easily translated by the camera for the mass audience:

> Because of the inevitable differences of the two media, however, the narrative line of the novel becomes transformed by the film into plot. But plot is merely a subplan in movies. Plot in film is but an element in theme. Thus, the director must be able to translate the novelist's verbal value system—his tone or stance—into a visual theme if he is to capture the novel. Theme expresses the artist's view of the nature of existence.[31]

Linden's usage of "plot" and "theme" may lead one astray, (and "point of view," "style," and "tone" may be the roads not taken), but he still arrives at the popular destination: the conclusion that novels can do something on the mental level that films must transmute into physical action or observable imagery.

Charles Eidsvik's thoughts on the issue (in, happily, clearer prose) develop more fully the implications of this approach that focuses on the viewer's psychological response. For him, narrative is a game of pretend, of "what if," and filmed narrative is fundamentally—and uniquely in the dark theater—a game of voyeurism. By emphasizing the theatrical setting for the audience, he makes the irreconcilable difference between novel and film one of object as opposed to event: "Art objects such as poems, paintings, and novels are meant to be experienced at leisure and kept for a long time. Art events are meant to be experienced dramatically without viewer intervention and to speak to their own moments in history." Of course, by now the wide circulation of video cassettes that can be viewed at leisure and kept for a long time must put these ideas in new light, but that aside, Eidsvik's stance on adaptations is inevitable: "The film critic cannot take literary or art criticism as a model or expect of films what he would of novels, paintings or poems."[32] The division between object and event is just as final as that between concept and percept.

As a scientific study of signs, semiotics should also define barriers between a medium of words and one of sounds and images. Christian Metz stakes out the territories in much the same way as Bluestone does: "A concept is signified; a thing is expressed. . . . There is *more than one difference* between expression and signification: One is natural, the other conventional; one is global and continuous, the other divided into discrete units; one is derived from beings and things, the other from ideas."[33] That is, one is pictures, the other is words. But, if cinema is not a language system, it is a sort of language capable of narrative: "It is not because the cinema is language that it can tell such fine stories, but rather it has become language because it has told such fine stories." This shared capability for narrative forms the usual basis for the semiological study of adaptations.[34]

In this vein, Harold Toliver views narrative as an artistic shape given to an already conventionally structured nature. But, since "the mode of thought and experience . . . depends on the method of presentation," written narrative will not be the same as filmed narrative: "Films thus add to narration—or may add to narration—the impact of the unnameable and subtract some of the controls of grammar; they may add the mutely pictorial beauty or stark reality of objects and the inarticulate sensation of change as a camera reports it."[35]

Frank McConnell begins with a compatible distinction and develops a theory of complementary narrative capabilities. In *The Spoken Seen*, he characterizes film as "photographed replicas of human figures moving on a screen" and literature as "artificial representations of vocal sounds marshalled on a page"; neither, he insists, is preeminent as narrative art.[36] In *Storytelling and Mythmaking*, McConnell imitates, with alterations, Northrop Frye's archetypal structuralism relative to narrative, and in this endeavor, he asserts a "special complementarity" between written and filmed narrative:

> In written narrative, we begin with the consciousness of the hero and have to construct out of that consciousness the social and physical world the hero inhabits. But in film the situation is, essentially and

significantly, reversed. Film can show us *only* objects, *only* things, only indeed, people as things. Our activity in watching a filmed narrative is to infer, to construct the *selfhood* of the hero who might inhabit the objective world film so overwhelmingly gives us.[37]

For both Toliver and McConnell, narrative *qua* narrative is structurally equivalent in writing and film, but the method of presentation remains as an all important feature that cannot be equivalent. In their own terms, both see writing as more internal and mental, film as more external and physical—the marks of Bluestone. If the two media are complementary, they are also polar.

Another structuralist, William Luhr, makes a similar distinction and bluntly assesses its critical consequences. Regarding narrative structure, he asserts that "similar elements exist between film and novel, but their artistic configurations differ massively, so massively as to make ontological comparison aesthetically impossible."[38] Here Luhr returns us to Balázs's and Bluestone's view that a novel's subject matter is adaptable to film, but aesthetic "content" is not.

This separatist view has gained such predominance as to be accepted uncritically and taken as a given of popular film criticism. James Monaco agrees that a novel's story may be told in film, but the "difference between pictorial narration and linguistic narration" merits hardly more consideration than to describe it as "obvious and powerful." An influential reviewer such as Andrew Sarris approaches adaptations with "an automatic apartheid" in mind: "Whereas literature must strain laboriously to move form sensibility to sensuality, film floats almost effortlessly into sensuality and must then strain to achieve sensibility." Pauline Kael, in characteristically blunter terms, writes from the same premise: "Movies are good at action; they're not good at reflective thought or conceptual thinking." Richard Corliss praises Bernardo Bertolucci's adaptations, for "he knows that films observe and novels analyze. Films are outside; novels are inside. Films are about what people do; novels are about what people think." Small wonder then that popular reference books, such as Ira Konigsberg's *The Complete Film Dictionary*, should define "adaptation" as a mostly subliterary exercise: Konigsberg's entry begins with the straightforward point about "a work in one medium that derives its impulse as well as a varying number of its elements from a work in a different medium," but it inevitably reiterates the dictum that "Great novels have always been more resistant to adaptation because film cannot sufficiently depict their internalization of character or the richness and suggestiveness of their language."[39] Bluestone must have been right; you could look it up.

Some Contrary Views

I cannot argue with the obvious point that we read books and that we see and hear films. The question remains whether these foregoing theorists teach us about the aesthetic possibilities open to both arts or merely elaborate the obvious. I think that, however interesting the elaborations sometimes are, the conclusions about adaptations are obvious. If one assumes that art involves an inseparable relationship of form and content, and if one proceeds from such an assumption to define an art according to its medium, then the issue of film adaptations of novels becomes a very simple matter: the adaptation cannot be the same thing. From this conclusion, critics can develop many consequences. For instance, true filmmakers should not revert to older art forms to find subjects, but should write original screenplays that communicate cinematically[40]; and filmmakers who use literature as a source are usually trying to cash in on a best-selling novel or are trying to ennoble their venal industry by wrapping themselves in the pages of "classics." Richard Corliss, quoted above, refers to such books as "fodder," and Lester Asheim's study certainly shows the importance of commercial interests.

I know that producers do produce films to make money and that such money changers cannot be driven from the theaters. But, I also know that producers are not the only real filmmakers. More importantly, if a film involves more than a financial deal, it also entails more than its medium: more than a *thing* that is different from the thing that is a novel. On the contrary, the physics of light does not compose, the chemistry of emulsion does not speak, and the persistence of vision does not intend. To paraphrase Archibald MacLeish, these do not mean, they just are. Behind these things that are sit filmmakers who mean.[41] In order to discover what they mean, either in original screenplays or adaptations, we must use a manner of speaking that will account for their aesthetic choices and intentions.

Whatever insights all the foregoing theories have, on the question of adaptations, their conclusions follow obviously and inevitably given their assumptions. In a description of Rudolf Carnap's quoted by R. S. Crane, such frameworks raise external and abstractly practical "questions not about propositions within a framework but about the justification of the framework itself"; Crane pursues the question of whether one should, like the New Critics, treat poetry as a distinctive kind of language. He cites the problem that such frameworks focus attention on their presumed dialectic rather than on the elements within the work, "with the result, very often, that theoretical debates are set going which admit of no possible resolution since they define no concrete facts to which we may appeal."[42] By extension to film criticism, one could ask the parallel question of whether film ought to be defined as a particular kind of information, a percept, in contrast to a concept. If we answer in the affirmative, the issue of adaptations is easily resolved by deduction: the film cannot match the novel. A more matter-of-fact framework would begin without such abstract assumptions and would proceed inductively.

Morris Beja points out one immediate justification for an inductive approach that is too often overlooked: "When we place less emphasis on some abstract sense of theoretical properties and consider the real world, we cannot avoid the recognition that important filmmakers have in fact adapted novels into films which are themselves valuable and distinguished, and occasionally masterpieces."[43] Without completely overthrowing the foregoing theories, this point certainly qualifies the practicality of any film theory that absolutely denies the possibility of making worthwhile adaptations.

Two film critics, working almost concurrently and, I assume, quite independently, have called for an inductive criticism of film. F. E. Sparshott, attacking dogmatic definitions of cinema, responds:

> People use their languages to say what they wish to say, not what the language makes it easy to say. Most theorists of cinema insist that the outcome of this natural tendency is bound to be a bad film, but one hardly sees why. Whatever can be done with a medium is among its possibilities and hence "true to" it in a sense that has yet to be shown to be illegitimate. [44]

V. F. Perkins, also speaking in reaction to "the sins of the pioneers" who wrote early film theories, arrives at a similar call for less prescriptive judgments:

> Standards of judgement cannot be appropriate to a medium as such but only to particular ways of exploiting its opportunities. . . . The search for appropriate criteria leads us to observe limitations; it does not allow us to prescribe them. Anything possible is also permissible, but we still have to establish its value. We cannot assess worth without indicating function.[45]

Likewise, André Bazin, whose brand of phenomenology is perhaps not systematic enough to be too dogmatic, would allow the creators to create.

> Undoubtedly the novel has means of its own—language not the image is its material, its intimate effect on the isolated reader is not the same as that of a film on the crowd in a darkened cinema—but precisely for these reasons the differences in aesthetic structure make the search for equivalents an even more delicate matter, and thus they require all the more power of invention and imagination from the film-maker who is truly attempting a resemblance.[46]

Bazin realizes the material differences, but he does not make the mistake of turning those differences into evaluative criteria or prescriptive rules. Rather, he sees in the differences—matters that other critics view as insurmountable barriers to adaptations—a challenge to filmmakers that would likely bring about growth in the art. In this way, Bazin, writing well before Sparshott and Perkins, has already tried to set the particular issue of adaptations in relation to its proper variable: not the either-or, concept-percept variable of the medium, but the infinite variable of individual artists solving individual aesthetic problems.

In his latest book, *Coming to Terms*, Seymour Chatman echoes many of these thoughts. Following Bazin's lead, Chatman states that film's supposed difficulty with conveying thought may be a virtue: "It challenges the artist to rise above mere technical constraints." Like Sparshott and Perkins, Chatman correctly sees that the artist's capabilities count more than the medium:

> What a medium can "do" narratively depends very much on what its creator wants it to do, on the genre that he works in, on the kinds of conventions she can persuade her audience to accept, and so on. Any

insistence that the visual is king can be sustained only by excluding from the canon some of cinema's most brilliant works.

A logical corollary concerns the big question of fidelity, for critics too often blame weak adaptations on "inadequacies deriving from the medium" when they should examine "those deriving from the artistic infelicities of specific filmmakers."[47] That is to say, perhaps *The Sound and the Fury* can be made into a great film, but somebody other than Martin Ritt will have to do it.

If these critics present strong and convincing arguments, as I think they do, their ideas come in relatively brief articles or longer works not focused on the issue of adaptations. Since Bluestone, one of the few full-length treatments of the problem comes from Joy Gould Boyum, and she too disputes some of Bluestone's fundamental points. She uses a theoretical framework that emphasizes the audience's response in the construction of meaning. My own theoretical assumptions would not share such an emphasis, but Boyum's comments yet make some compelling points.

Early on, Boyum accuses Bluestone of a bias regarding the audience: literature, characterized by "complexity and quality," appeals to "an educated elite," whereas films, which "are mere entertainment," appeal to the masses; therefore, an adaptation must adjust the novel "not so much to its new medium as to its audience."[48] Whatever Bluestone's fears about bowing to the tastes of the masses, any critic still adhering to Bluestone's theory has not kept up with the times:

> For movies have done more than change their image: movies themselves have changed, and so have adaptations right along with them. The literary establishment seems not to have noticed, however, given that so many of the arguments it puts forth against adaptation . . . are really about film-as-it-was, rather than about film-as-it-is; about film when it was synonymous with Hollywood and had to submit to the taste of moguls, the strictures of the star system, and the censoring eye of the Hayes office; about film when it was more of a mass medium than it is today and, consequently, operated with very different notions as to the nature of its audience.[49]

Since the industry's and the audience's sophistication has grown, the critical assessments should show the same growth.

Such growth, Boyum states, does not occur as long as critics cannot get beyond the obvious distinction—"that visual imagery tends to the iconic, that words tend to the symbolic"—and realize that "both 'mean,' both involve perception and cognition, and both also involve what has recently come to be known as the process of 'decoding.'" Their common capabilities matter far more than any distinctions: novels and films are able

> to create . . . characters and actions, to situate them in time and place, and ultimately then to bring us into fictional worlds. The novel may indeed be, as Jean Mitry claims, "a narrative which organizes itself in a world; the film, a world that organizes itself in a narrative." Nevertheless, in both instances, narrative and world are created.[50]

Having done away with the problem of definitively distinct "languages," Boyum sees no necessary impediments to film's ability to adapt a novel's use of time, tenses, characterization, setting, description, or plot.

With such barriers removed, so are any barriers to "fidelity." For Boyum, a faithful adaptation depends on the filmmaker's interpretation of the original, "a reading which will either strike us as persuasive and apt or seem to us reductive, even false."[51] Quoting Martin C. Battestin, Boyum states that "analogy is the key" in achieving the former: "And here, whether it is transposition or commentary, whether it is literal rendition or free, we have what might be taken as the inescapable first principle of adaptation."[52] An interesting variation on the complaint of infidelity arises from her emphasis on the audience's response. Anyone who has read the original novel "will in some way already have made the movie"—in his or her own mind, that is. If the adapted film does not fulfill expectations, "a preference for the book" may actually be "an allegiance to our own imaginative re-creation": "ultimately we are not comparing book with film, but rather one resymbolization with another—inevitably expecting the movie projected on the screen to be a shadow reflection of the movie we ourselves have imagined."[53] Again, I do not favor a theory that emphasizes the audience's responsibility for making the work, but I do think Boyum touches on an important point. Many of the theorists with whom I disagree above misapprehend the presence of an artist's hand or the way that hand, in a novel or film, works on and in our imagination.

With so much exploration of the grounds outside or beneath the text, no one is taking calls inside. Nevertheless, Perkins, Sparshott, Bazin, Chatman, and Boyum have left messages: be open to the possibilities in the medium. Granted that material differences between novels and films exist, we need to be aware of the questions that focusing on such differences can answer. For instance, if we allow that viewing a film usually does not permit the full representation of a novel's events, we acknowledge a phenomenological difference as fact; such acknowledgment does not then force us to conclude that adaptations are also always simpler, for we cannot assume shorter is simpler. The actual difference in this instance leads to no deductive judgments for all adaptations. Individual adaptations may actually be simpler, but others may be as complex as the original novel or more complex.

Sparshott and Perkins warn that what to film and how to film it are not abstract questions. I know I sometimes think I could have done a better job than certain filmmakers have done, but these feelings cannot precede the film itself. If an abstract theory sets the parameters of judgment, though, it will constrain certain possibilities and the appreciation of certain achievements in advance. Conversely, the inductive approach Sparshott and Perkins call for has no *necessary* constraints on the filmmaker: "A theory of film is a theory of film *criticism* not of film *making*. We cannot lay down rules for the creators."[54]

Neo-Aristotelianism: A New Framework from an Old Method

A wider choice of variables has a significant bearing on my original question: Is it true that all or some novels cannot be translated into film? Again, if one assumes a distinction such as concept versus percept, then, since a percept is not a concept, a film adaptation cannot adequately match a novel; the answer must be true in all cases. However, if one does not admit such distinctions, or, more likely, if one admits certain obvious differences but does not make them essential qualities of either medium's aesthetic, then obvious deductions disappear. And if the criteria are as variable as individual artists' solutions to aesthetic problems, then no one can with confidence make broad generalizations about all novels, all films, or all adaptations. Such generalizations may follow from certain premises, but they hardly seem worth pursuing when the premises render the issue obvious. On adaptations, the critical pursuit flags for me when the contending sides debate whether seeing a film recreates the experience of reading a book, or whether one can film simple sentences such as "It is raining outside."

I would rather not view a novel as a verbal, psychological, or anonymously coded event; each would erect rather than overcome barriers to adaptations—or simply render adaptations irrelevant. Instead, I would view a novel as an aesthetic problem solved—or at least attempted—and communicated: an author has themes, moods, or effects to convey, for which he or she then invents an action to be portrayed with chosen techniques in words. The author makes choices more complex than finding a form adequate to the content. The material or medium does not signify much by comparison: the effects, actions, even some techniques may be communicated through the images and sounds of film, and communicated adequately to match the components of the novel.

Neo-Aristotelianism, or the so-called Chicago school of literary criticism, presents one theoretical framework that corresponds to my way of thinking and comprehends these broader questions. I find this framework to be especially adaptable because it proposes a method more than a rule or set of rules. Thus, what Aristotle has written does not set boundaries for this school of thought: the *Poetics* has nothing to say on novels or films; instead, Aristotle's method defines neo-Aristotelianism. Accordingly, neither I nor anybody else should hope to find some nugget in Aristotle's writing that, by deduction, could be refined into Aristotle's "statement" on adaptations. For instance, in the *Poetics*, Aristotle writes that tragic emotions may be aroused by spectacle, "but they may also result from the inner structure of the piece, which is the better way, and indicates a superior poet" since "even without the aid of the eye, he who hears the tale told will thrill with horror and melt to pity at what takes place."[55] One might naturally see a potential claim for the novel's superiority to film in this comparison, but later on, judging between epic and tragedy, Aristotle writes:

> And superior tragedy is, because it has all the epic elements . . . with music and scenic effects as important accessories; and these produce the most vivid pleasures. . . . Moreover, the art attains its end within narrower limits; for the concentrated effect is more pleasurable than one which is spread over a long time and so diluted.[56]

For the ambidextrous researcher, Aristotle "says" that film's resort to images shows weakness on the one hand and concentrated and flexible strength on the other. Therefore, and not to disparage anything Aristotle *does* say, "The *method*, not any one of Aristotle's conclusions, is what is decisive."[57]

In literary theory, the neo-Aristotelian method originally came about in response to deductive methods—especially those of New Criticism—similar to those I find at the root of the film theories I associate with Bluestone. Differing from "semantic" theories, so called for their definitions of a uniquely poetic language, R. S. Crane wants a critical language in which, among other goals,

> we can talk about the internal necessities and possibilities in poems and the problems these posed for their poets rather than merely about the necessities and problems defined for us by our special choice of dialectical premises; in which we can develop terms for distinguishing the formal causes of poems from their material constituents and technical mechanisms.[58]

Crane obviously wishes to overcome the limits of the common form-content dialectic, and he finds a useful framework in the language and method of Aristotle. The practical value of this method derives from Aristotle's making the object of his study "concrete wholes" and taking as his aim "the discovery and statement of the principles which govern poets when they make good poems" or concrete wholes.[59] Analysis of these wholes leads to examination of the four causes: final cause, effect, or end of imitation; formal cause or object of imitation (including plot, character, and thought); efficient cause, technique, or manner of imitation; and material cause, medium, or means of imitation. In this descending order of importance, these parts constitute the concrete whole according to the choices made by the artist. Notably different from Crane's main target, New Criticism, the method assigns a relatively minor role to the medium. A writer's diction and style, although important choices, are determined by larger choices. According to Elder Olson,

> In one sense, of course, the words are of the utmost importance; if they are not the right words or if we do not grasp them, we do not grasp the poem. In another sense, they are the least important element in the poem, for they do not determine the character of anything else in the poem; on the contrary, they are determined by everything else. . . . And when we are moved by poetry, we are not moved by the words, except in so far as sound and rhythm move us; we are moved by things that the words stand for.[60]

Words do not speak; rather, the writer uses them to speak. Thus, poetics is a productive science studying artificial objects rather than a theoretical science studying natural objects. This latter distinction should help us separate elements of artificial objects that occur as a matter of artistic choice and purpose from elements of natural objects that occur as a matter of organic necessity: the difference between a poem's having rhyme and a rose's having color.

In order to manipulate the subordinate causes successfully to achieve a final intention, the poet must direct them according to an end, an idea of a possible final effect before it is made actual. Crane calls this idea the "shaping cause": "An essential cause of poetic structure, the most decisive, indeed, of all the causes of structure in poetry because it controls in an immediate way the act of construction itself." Furthermore, since the shaping cause "is thus an indispensable first principle for writers, it would seem that it also might be taken, with fruitful results, as a first principle in the practical criticism of their works."[61] That is, if the shaping cause is a fact of the work's creation, critics may make the discovery of that fact the object of analysis: breaking down the causes, reconstructing the whole, and recovering and sharing the artist's intention. In contrast, an abstract theory begins with a general premise accepted as fact (for example, that poetry employs a uniquely ambiguous language) and proceeds deductively to examine works for their adherence to the premise, evaluatively ruling in or out the works accordingly; disagreement about the "factual" premise would render all such evaluation suspect. Crane's neo-Aristotelian method begins with the particular, factual elements of the work and inductively attempts to discover the factual cause shaping them—a fact revealed a posteriori rather than imposed a priori.

Regardless of however or whenever the writer grasps a shaping cause, it will always have more definition than any reader's understanding could have at the outset; a reader's first information from a work forecloses many possible ends, but opens up many others, leaving any single hypothesis impossible to maintain. Crane therefore proposes "to use systematically what has been called 'the method of multiple working hypotheses.'"[62] The reader thereby entertains whatever possible ends are likely and, led by the artist, revises and refines these hypotheses into one reconstruction of the shaping cause; that hypothesis would serve best that could most coherently account for the whole and most precisely account for the parts.[63]

Then, as for judgment, the critic would not vote up or down according to the work's consistency with a premise. Rather, the critic would judge the work relative not only to the necessities of the artist's formal intention but to its possibilities as well. Among our multiple working hypotheses may be those comparable to "what both the most and the least perfect artists have done when confronted with similar problems of invention, representation, and writing," as well as those that, in retrospect, may lead us to consider "theoretically the conditions under which any particular effect aimed at in a given work might be better or worse achieved."[64]

To summarize, then, the flexibility of the neo-Aristotelian method strengthens the reader/critic's views in several ways: by refusing to define a work of art as a simple joining of form and content (or medium and message, or signifier and signified); by insisting that the elements of the work are matters of factual artistic choices that are purposeful rather than matters of abstract definition that are necessary; and by making evaluative judgment a statement of comparison that views the work in relation to the realization of inherent possibilities in those factual choices rather than in relation to consistency with inherent necessities of those abstract definitions.

Among film theorists, Gerald Mast's ideas seemingly most resemble those I have outlined above and hope to adapt to film criticism. Mast breaks down the elements of the art into film (material), cinema (process), and movie (form)—all corresponding to Aristotle's three causes subordinate to the final cause (Mast's distinguishing terms have not caught on). The correspondence to Aristotelian methods stops here. He defines cinematic art as a "hybrid" of narrative and dramatic modes, of mimesis and kinesis; he sees problems in the abstract theories I have been discussing as coming from an emphasis on only the kinetic half of this hybrid, therefore rendering them as partial criticisms that "fall into the trap of worshiping machines and mechanical processes as ends in themselves."[65] Final effects, according to Mast, depend upon our "conviction" of the work's thematic unity as we experience it—at which sense of experience I think we part company. This conviction, for Mast, results largely from the phenomenology of the cinema's kinesis, the quality that makes the experience so "immediate, direct, and concrete," and whose succession cannot be stopped and dissected without losing the effect.[66] Thus he erects a phenomenological barrier between novel and film that emphasizes the mode of presentation—emphasizes, that is, the kinesis, just as he accused partial formalists of doing. Nevertheless, Mast notes that objections raised specifically regarding adaptations usually point to mimetic concerns slighted in favor of kinetic ones, and he answers that a balance must be maintained: "In cinema, if the kinesis does not serve and enrich our conviction in the mimesis of the narrative, it disrupts rather than aids the unity and density of that artistic microcosm."[67] I am unwilling to grant cinema a unique, definitive immediacy, but to the extent that this latter statement refuses to enforce a distinction between mimetic and kinetic media, I think Mast's theory avoids the traps I object to above. Nevertheless, I also think Aristotle's terms and methods could be put to better use.

The Important Distinction Affecting Fidelity

Among neo-Aristotelianism's many advantages over other frameworks, the approach does not allow for the out-of-hand dismissal of adaptations as an issue. A theory that analyzes and judges a work of art based upon organic necessities implied in a definition of the medium cannot allow that a work's qualities may be separated from its medium and reconstituted in another; so regarded, the issue of adaptations can easily be dismissed as an aberration of Hollywood commercialism. The problem engendered resembles that facing, say, a Sergei Eisenstein watching Renoir's long-take, deep-focus film, *La Règle du Jeu* or a Siegfried Kracauer watching Roeg's fragmented vision, *The Man Who Fell to Earth*: What does one do with the intelligent, affecting film that flouts all the prescribed definitions? Any critic whose method proceeded more inductively, as would a neo-Aristotelian critic's, can, instead of arguing that the good film is not really good, admit the film's achievement and go on to discover how it succeeded. Accordingly, just as a novel does not succeed solely because it is in words, so an adaptation does not fail solely because it is not in those same words. Both embody concrete wholes that are artificial imitations. The artist's use of a medium represents an aesthetic choice, not a necessity, in the making of an artifice.

An important distinction may be getting lost, one proposed by Coleridge in his argument with Wordsworth's theory of a naturally rustic diction in poetry and used again in his discussion of the suspension of disbelief: the difference between an imitation and a copy. Commenting on *The Tempest*, Coleridge states that, in an imitation, "a certain quantum of difference is essential . . . and an indispensable condition and cause of the pleasure we derive from it; while in a copy it is a defect, contravening its name and purpose."[68] That is, an imitation tries to capture some qualities of the object without perversely trying to capture them all. For instance, a still-life painting or a poem may pleasantly suggest the color and ripeness of an apple, but without tempting us to bite into the canvas or page; on the other hand, a copy such as a piece of wax fruit may tempt us to taste it, but if fooled, we are put off by the wax taste and disgusted with the apple as, perhaps, kitsch decoration. In the case of adaptations, the deductively abstract critics who emphasize the medium agree with Coleridge that the written work need not taste like an apple, but they insist that the film adaptation taste like ink. An inductive method encourages a more consistent critical attitude: an imitation, even if it adapts a prior imitation, should be judged by the choices it embodies and not forced to copy the prior choices.

Of course, in setting out to adapt a novel to the screen, a filmmaker usually makes many choices along the same lines as those of the novelist. For all the changes people can cite in a host of adaptations, a novel and its adaptation rarely share no more resemblance than the title—and one could argue such an "adaptation" exemplifies no more than a hastily purchased property. The average audience regards fidelity as a question of how much is left in: how much of the plot and how many of the characters survive the usual condensing of the novel's action. Even to critics thinking in terms of form and content, this question of quantity isolates content and, to that extent, illegitimately ignores form. The more particularly elemental analysis of the neo-Aristotelian would take us beyond this common notion of fidelity to more specific questions of technical and formal fidelity. Fidelity concerns the kinds of choices made, not the number of choices that match the author's.

Crossing the Language Barrier

Before going on to these questions, however, I think the question of material fidelity needs qualification. Obviously, the novelist and filmmaker use different means, and I have rehearsed at length what a significant stumbling block that difference presents for many critics' ideas on adaptations. Admitting this difference, I do not think we should forget that many of the novelist's words are spoken in dialogue, and film no longer has any problem portraying dialogue. Bruce Morrissette notes that even silent films could adapt language through subtitles; since the development of sound films, however, "The most ardent separationists would be hard put to argue that these verbal elements change their character completely in passing from the printed page . . . to the screen or sound track."[69] In addition to dialogue, the filmmaker may also take certain of the novel's passages verbatim and use them in voice-over narration. Critics can argue that such narration betrays a failure of the film's visual style (which may be a valid argument when the issue is better and worse choices for conveying an action or thought), but, as the corollary of a purist notion that film is definitively visual, not verbal, the argument starts to turn in circles and, of course, fails to account for those films that use narration successfully.

For instance, in dos Santos's *How Tasty Was My Little Frenchman*, a sixteenth century missionary writes a letter home, heard in voice-over, telling of altruistic and successful dealings with the cannibalistic Indians of Brazil; while we hear this narration, we see the Indians fight the Europeans and the oppressive "civilization" of their tribe. A more purely visual choice would have been to show the missionary writing, even letting us see what he writes, and then cutting to scenes of fighting. However, a point would be lost. This missionary is not a cynical hypocrite who writes one thing and then does or condones another thing; he is a blind idealist who writes one thing *while* we can see something else is the case. The purist who would reject such a verbal choice in filmmaking would have to reject sound in films altogether to remain consistent, would have film copy printing—have us see the letter (and even see the dialogue) so we could read it ourselves—rather than admit voice-over as a valid imitation of the letter. Few critics take such extreme positions, but any who would still emphasize the medium cannot deny that film dialogue and voice-over cross the material border between novel and film.

That is, assuming such a material border exists in the first place. Herbert Read has argued that some critics misunderstand the nature, not of film, but of literature: echoing Joseph Conrad's ideas of writing, Read states:

> If I were asked to give the most distinctive quality of good writing, I should express it in this one word: VISUAL. . . . To project onto that inner screen of the brain a moving picture of objects and events, events and objects moving towards a balance and reconciliation of a more than usual state of emotion with more than usual order. That is a definition of good literature. . . . It is also a definition of the ideal film.[70]

I agree with Read that the two media share more visual affinities than many would allow, although I would not go so far as to define both as essentially visual.

Leland Poague attacks the question of material differences on another front and takes the position that films and novels share the same medium, "neither language nor celluloid, but rather the stream of human consciousness, the human imagination which includes the artist's recollection (both conscious and unconscious) of all the literary works within the realm of his experience." Given this premise, he argues, "Only the physical mechanics differ, and those differences are, for critical purposes, relatively minor in their significance."[71] Again, I think Poague focuses on affinities that merit more attention than the "physical mechanics," but in regard to the issue of material, his argument discusses source material, not the physical matter. In terms of the productive science of these arts, Poague's ideas deal with form (where does the "material"— the characters, setting, and events—come from?) rather than medium (what is it made of?).

Critics may still raise the issue of linguistic qualities that would be impractical to read into the soundtrack of a film. What about metaphors, image motifs, assonance, alliteration, cadence, and tone? In analyzing a novel, we would have to account for these features, and in analyzing the adaptation, we might figure the filmmaker would have to do the same. A simple metaphor, "the herd of commuters," could be rendered on film by editing two shots together: a shot of rush-hour traffic spliced to a shot of cattle, or, as in Good Neighbor Sam, a shot in which the character "sees" sheep driving and riding in all the other cars. This example hardly taxes the artistic imaginations of novelists or filmmakers, but it does show the possibility of finding "equivalents." Even so, finding an equivalent for every trope would prove to be more of a problem. Filmmakers, therefore, may pick up and develop only selected motifs; Hitchcock, for instance, lights on the mention of Norman's hobby, taxidermy, and the heroine's name, Crane, and embellishes Robert Bloch's *Psycho* with images of stuffed and fallen birds. As for the other qualities, one might allow that editing rhythm can imitate an author's stylistic cadence, but such imitation cannot follow each word of every sentence, like the bouncing ball in a sing-along; and assonance and alliteration must be spoken.

In admitting these limitations, however, I cannot say they should stymie the filmmaker bent on adapting novels to film. Stylistic touches have more or less importance to the effect of the whole novel, but the material cause never suffices alone for that effect. Even the highly wrought diction of Henry James in *The Ambassadors*, writes James Phelan, cannot stand alone for that novel's achievement: "We may tentatively conclude, then, that language may become decisive for the success of the work, but that it never becomes the organizing principle of a work."[72] An adaptation of *The Ambassadors* (I have not seen the one made for television) would have great difficulty and probably no success in portraying its style,[73] and equally impossible would be matching the purely linguistic effects of self-conscious "anti-novels" (Phelan discusses Gass's *Willie Masters's Lonesome Wife* as an example). Even so, fiction rarely uses language as an end rather than a means; for those who experiment with or have mastered a style, diction usually remains subordinate to larger issues.

> Though created *out* of language, the worlds we experience in novels are more than worlds of words; they are, more accurately, worlds *from* words, worlds that contain the elements of character and action, which are essentially non-linguistic and which are more central to our experience of those worlds than the words which create them.[74]

Forced to imitate diction, films would fall short in some details, a few of them important to the work. Nonetheless, setting material questions in the proper perspective and allowing films to imitate those "worlds we experience," we can understand that the material difference between novels and films becomes a small limitation. I mentioned above the assertion that one cannot film the line, "It is raining outside." I would answer, so what? The line hardly tells an interesting story anyhow. Within a narrative context, however—say a plot in which the rain should evoke sadness, or cause comic complications—any filmmaker could arrive at that point in the plot and make it rain outside *appropriately*.

Over the Fence of Tense

Further material, technical, and formal questions of fidelity have commonly accepted answers that an inductive framework would call back into question. In particular, I am thinking of the truisms about tense, point of view, and thought. As mentioned before about tense, Bluestone announces that "The novel has three tenses; the film has only one. From this follows almost everything else one can say about time in both media."[75] Consequently, according to conventional wisdom, film always takes place in the present and has no past or future tense: flashbacks and flashforwards do not change the present tense either, for they too take place immediately before our eyes, "creating a strong *sense* of present tense, a 'here and now' experience."[76] This is no sense—it is a fact: as Sparshott recognizes, "because 'here' and 'now' are defined by one's presence," film's present tense is "true but trivial."[77] In this sense, as a matter of fact, the novel takes place in the present, for its action is "here and now" when we read. Bruce Morrissette's rhetorical questions make clear the obviousness of this point:

> Since Béla Balázs, it has been customary to state that "films have no tenses" and to claim, perhaps too hastily, that a filmed scene always takes place in an eternal present. . . . But cannot films also express, depict, or imply their own kind of past? After all, even a regular novel is always *read* in the present, and its "past," to which the film is accused of having no equivalent, is usually contained in a system involving the tenses of verbs. In reading a scene of the past, do we not mentally "see" it in the present?[78]

Hence the critical convention of discussing a work in the present tense: we do not say, "Huck narrated his own story"; rather, we say that, as Twain *wrote* it, "Huck narrates his own story." Verb tense is relative, and relative to our own reading and viewing, the experience of a novel or film takes place in the present.

However, relative to a certain action within a narrative, other actions take place in the past or future. Language marks these tenses with "-ed" or the auxiliary "will," whereas film has no set marks (wavy images or soft focus notwithstanding). The absence of marks, however, does not equal the absence of tense. Our ability to recognize shifts in the temporal frame amply proves that we recognize a past and future relative to a film's present.

Compare *Citizen Kane* to *L'Année dernière à Marienbad*. The former, although reportedly difficult for its original audience to follow, clearly uses past tense to portray the remembrances that the present tense Thompson is gathering for his story. The latter film remains difficult for audiences because Resnais deliberately frustrates our easy comprehension of temporal sequence; until we can decide when is present, we cannot know when is past (let alone whether it happened or is happening). In both, recognizing tenses prevents or clears up considerable confusion; and in the latter, the struggle to establish those tenses clearly suggests that film has a past and future tense since we notice when the filmmaker does not establish them clearly for us.[79]

The Point Missed Regarding Point of View

Bluestone's discussion of tenses extends to other temporal questions, and these lead him to conclusions about point of view—conclusions that still hold with later critics. He distinguishes chronological time from psychological. Film has "adequate equivalents" to match the novel's techniques for manipulating psychological time, generally variations in tempo and rhythm; neither the novel or film can render psychological time in the sense of Bergson's concept of *durée*, but Bluestone thinks film comes closer, mostly because its material, the strip of film, has more continuity than the novel's discrete words.[80] Chronological time is a different matter, though. Chronological time passes on three levels in the novel: the duration of the reader's time, the duration of the narrator's time, and the duration of the narrative events. These latter two may come into playful conflict, as when Sterne's Tristram Shandy learns that it takes him a year to record a day's action, thereby perpetually keeping his record from catching up to his present. In ever-present tense film, says Bluestone, no such conflict can occur: "Since the camera is always the narrator, we need concern ourselves only with the chronological duration of the viewing and the time-span of the narrative events." Significantly, Bluestone consequently eliminates a thinking narrator and assumes a mechanical one. In his example of Francis in *The Cabinet of Dr. Caligari*, Bluestone says the film does not really present Francis as the framing narrator of the flashback portrayed; instead, "the omniscient camera has included

Francis as part of the narrative from the beginning."[81] Poor Francis, under Caligari's ultimate control in the story, now falls under the control of the robot camera in his attempt to tell his story. As fitting as this idea may be for German silent films, I think it requires a hasty dismissal of a human point of view.

This virtual equation of the camera with the point of view recurs too easily in many critical frameworks. James Monaco writes that

> novels are told by the author. We see and hear only what he wants us to see and hear. Films are, in a sense, told by their authors too, but we see and hear a great deal more than a director necessarily intends. . . . More important, whatever the novelist describes is filtered through his language, his prejudices, and his point of view. With films we have a certain amount of freedom to choose, to select one detail rather than another.

Monaco states that film can thereby be "a much richer experience," but that the "persona of the narrator is so much weaker" for having been subsumed in the camera.[82]

This view of the camera receives "official" status in Ira Konigsberg's *Complete Film Dictionary*: "In film, the dominant perspective belongs to the neutral camera," and films that attempt first-person narration "are normally accompanied by a third-person camera"; occasionally the camera "acts as the character's eyes, but a constantly subjective camera technique has not been successful in film and has only been tried rarely."[83]

Part of the problem may result from simplifying the terms of choices available for points of view. The three common designations—omniscient, third-person, and first-person—fail to describe the variety of perspectives we encounter in fiction. Norman Friedman presents a much more detailed list of choices:

> (1) editorial omniscience, in which the narrator moves freely in the action's time and place, and not only enters the minds of the characters, but editorially expresses his or her own thoughts as well (for example, *Tom Jones*);
>
> (2) neutral omniscience, in which the narrator has the same freedom except that of expressing his or her own thoughts (for example, *Lord of the Flies*);
>
> (3) "I" as witness, in which a supporting character in the action acts as the narrator (for example, *The Great Gatsby*);

(4) "I" as protagonist, in which the central character in the action narrates his or her own story (for example, *Great Expectations*);

(5) multiple, selective omniscience, in which the apparently first- or third-person report comes directly through the minds of the characters (for example, *As I Lay Dying* and *The Waves*);

(6) selective omniscience, in which the apparently first- or third-person report comes directly through the mind of one character (for example, *La Jalousie* and *A Portrait of the Artist as a Young Man*); and

(7) dramatic, in which author, narrator and mental states virtually disappear and information comes almost totally through dialogue (for example, "Hills Like White Elephants").[84]

The scale shows a progressive diminishing of any subjectivity as an explicitly intrusive narrator gives way to the voice of a character, which in turn gives way to the mind of a character, which in turn gives way to nearly complete objectivity.[85] Along with this movement from subjectivity to objectivity, the scale goes from extremes of telling to extremes of showing, from extremes of condensation of action to extremes of expansion of action.

When we look at the two lists together, we can see the confusion brought on by the imprecision in terminology. Bluestone would designate *Caligari*'s point of view as omniscient, as opposed to first- or third-person, but he also would describe it as a mechanically objective point of view, as in the dramatic mode; the problem is that these designations lie on opposite ends of the scale—omniscience and objectivity do not go together. Furthermore, Bluestone would set films naturally closer to showing than telling (percept versus concept in his terms), and the expanded scale of showing would explain the usual inability of an adaptation to show all of a novel's action; but he would also have to admit the phenomenological point that film can greatly condense an action (as in the cliché "A picture is worth a thousand words"). So, is film omniscient or objective? Showing or telling?

I think Bluestone would get caught in this contradiction because he collapses material and technique: he equates the mechanical recording device with the point of view. The device of the camera is no more objective or omniscient than a pen—which is to say that point of view is not a question of means. If we see that the device may be used to imitate and portray a human point of view, the confusion fades. For instance, I think *Caligari* is best under-stood as portrayed through selective omniscience once the flash-back begins. The camera does not enter Francis' thoughts and por-tray the story of murder and paranoia for him; the camera could not invent the bizarre architecture and landscape. Instead, the di-rector allows Francis' thoughts to take over the film, and the cam-era, unable to comment, is used to portray those thoughts in all their horror. Insofar as expressionism often portrays mental states, selective omniscience best accounts for this filmmaker's intention.

The question may remain, however, whether film can imitate all these points of view or is technically more limited than the novel. At the objective, showing end of the scale, there seems to be no problem. *Caligari* and several other expressionist films clearly portray a character's mental view of the world rather than an omniscient narrator's view. Multiplying this effect of presenting mental states, a filmmaker could imitate multiple, selective omniscience; since the man's memories persuade the woman to create fantasies of rape, murder, and suicide that we see portrayed in *L'Année dernière à Marienbad*, this film is a suitable example. Of course, the character's or characters' mental states need not portray distorted or fantastic visions. Jake Gittes in *Chinatown* acts as our hero and narrative filter: we see southern Californian corruption through his realizations, much as we would follow a similar revelation through Strether in *The Ambassadors*.

As for the objective dramatic mode, film documentaries such as those by Frederick Wiseman might immediately come to mind, but fiction film also has such capabilities. Examples would fit Bluestone's notion of a mechanical recorder that can catch only the present events before it. Withdrawing any narrator's consciousness and presenting only scene and dialogue, Chantal Akerman's *Jeanne Dielman, 23 Quai du Commerce, 1080 Bruxelles* and Jim Jarmusch's *Stranger than Paradise* both rely on the audience to discover whatever meaning resides in their relatively unedited presentations.

At the omniscient, telling end of the scale, film also has the potential to imitate novels' points of view. In the novel, omniscience often involves authorial intrusion and manipulativeness: if authors—really implied authors—do not step forward to speak in their own voices and tell us what to think, they still tell of events and thoughts in such a way as to serve their purposes (which, of course, *actual* authors do). Thus, after Arabin's failed proposal to Eleanor in Trollope's *Barchester Towers*, the narrator speaks of Arabin's confused feelings and then suddenly scolds him directly: "That at forty years of age you should know so little of the workings of a woman's heart!" On the other hand, the narrator does not offer any comment directed to "you" the reader or character in *Jude the Obscure*. After the scene wherein Phillotson—a no more electrifying lover than Arabin— frightens Sue literally out of the window, Hardy's narrator describes the shocked husband as "a pitiable object . . . sighing a sigh which seemed to say that the business of his life must be carried on, whether he had a wife or no," and we know his character; the narrator does not tell us how to interpret the scene so much as we hear what it "seemed to say."

Neutral omniscience, as with novels, occurs more often than editorial omniscience in films. Many films move about in time and space (for example, *Casablanca* and *Nashville*); others read the thoughts of various characters (for example, *Psycho*), and partake of their fantasies (for example, *Nine to Five*) or dreams (for example, *Spellbound*) without being governed by those mental states. As for editorial omniscience in film, an infamous example occurs at the end of *Intolerance*, with D. W. Griffith's exasperating preaching. The final scenes of battle and prison form a coda to the four main stories in the film, a final plea directed to the audience: with the heavenly host superimposed over the armies and the prison walls dissolved to a flowery meadow, Griffith begs us to stop hatred. Films that have obvious lessons to teach or propaganda to disseminate would be further examples. Jules Dassin's *Naked City* opens with a voice-over narrator who says, "Ladies and gentlemen, the motion picture you are about to see"; this narrator introduces himself as Mark Hellinger, the producer, gives the other significant credits, makes claims for the film's authenticity, comments on the action throughout, and at the climax scolds a character, "Don't lose your head!"[86] More like an educational film shown in school—one with a man wearing a white coat and sitting behind a desk—Virgil Vogel's *The Mole People* eschews voice-over and brings out an actual person to introduce the film, a Dr. Frank C. Baxter, professor of English at the University of Southern California; Dr. Baxter discusses theories of worlds within worlds and concludes that the film presents "a fable with a meaning and a significance for you and for me in the twentieth century. Thank you, and goodbye."

Such intrusions occur in other than older films as well.[87] The non-fiction sequences in Dusan Makavejev's *WR: Mysteries of the*

Organism comment on the sexual repression portrayed in the story; the interspersed interviews with the actors in Ingmar Bergman's *The Passion of Anna* and the revelation of the film set in a final tracking-out shot in Federico Fellini's *And the Ship Sails On* both serve to comment on the artifice of the works.

The common notions of objectivity and omniscience, when clarified and sufficiently distinguished, hold somewhat true: films can easily assume objective or omniscient perspectives. But, are these the limits? Conventional wisdom asserts that films cannot adapt first-person point of view. Margaret Thorp relates this problem to verb tenses: "The first-person device in the movies will always be failure because the first-person narrator is obliged to speak in the perfect tense; he must tell you not what is happening but what has happened while the essence of the movie is immediate impression and experience. All time is time present." [88] Her assumptions anticipate Bluestone's: the point of view belongs to a mechanical recorder with no sense of recall, hence, no ability to consider past events or project future ones. Again, though, this notion misapprehends the illusion. We do not believe the events are actually happening "here and now" any more than we believe Huck Finn is writing (or dictating) "here and now." This intuitive understanding of the perfect tense allows us to distinguish a movie from a live, "mini-cam" report on the news.

The notion persists, nonetheless, that film's fluidity, which makes omniscience or objectivity so easy, is not only a possible choice, but a natural choice:

> Because film so rarely restricts its vision solely to what one person sees, an apparent total blend of narration and perspective is much more difficult to achieve in film than in the novel, say; the first person narration that often seems so straightforward in literature never seems so in film. [89]

In this last reference, the term "vision" is significant. We should remember that "point of view" is a "visual metaphor," [90] not a synonym for vision. Point of view is an artificial technique, a manner in which an author tells or shows an action selectively without the incidental or irrelevant details that can crowd actual perceptions. An "I" as witness or protagonist cannot report anything but what the "I" can know or see, but does not necessarily include all that is within the boundary. Put in other words, point of view imitates, rather than copies, a perspective.

Boyum, like other theorists, may think that "to present any action strictly and rigorously from the eyes of a first-person observer means excluding that observer from the scene—an effect which, if not totally unmanageable, can still seem very clumsy on screen,"[91] but I believe our experience of reading first-person narratives would deny this assertion. For instance, early in "A Scandal in Bohemia," Dr. Watson tells us of visiting Sherlock Holmes and being invited to examine a note that will introduce their next adventure; Watson says, "I carefully examined the writing, and the paper upon which it was written," and soon goes on, at Holmes's prodding, to describe what he observes—incorrectly, of course. Watson's point of view provides much fun in these adventures because his misperceptions match what our own would likely be, and together we are in awe of Holmes's acute senses. But, if we share Watson's point of view, we do not share his vision. That is to say, while we read Watson's narrative, we imagine we see Watson in it, if we picture the scene at all, rather than see the action as if we occupied Watson's place. Sidney Paget's illustrations, often showing Watson in the scene, tend to verify this point.[92]

Morrissette explains that critics forget a crucial distinction in such cases. Readers seldom identify with the "I," for they adopt "a *speaking* stance with respect to the words of the text" rather than "a *listening* stance": "Each of us is in fact surrounded in real life by a chorus of first-person narrators all addressing us with 'I,' 'me,' and so on, yet most often . . . we do *not* project ourselves fully . . . into the outlook of the narrator or speaker."[93] Therefore, in order to imitate a first-person point of view, the eye need not copy the vision of the narrator's eye (the attempt is usually not really made in the novel to begin with).

Robert Montgomery's perverse experiment, *The Lady in the Lake,* fails because he misses just this distinction. By shooting the film so as to put us in the hero's shoes, Montgomery creates a second-person narrative, not first-person.[94] So-called point-of-view shots, those that do portray what a character sees, certainly can strengthen the sense of a first-person point of view, but such shots are not the necessary choice for all shots, nor are they exclusive to first-person narratives.

To continue, then: just as we can distinguish the omniscient and objective points of view by determining what limits the filmmakers impose on their ability to select and portray events and thoughts, we ought to be able to recognize limits between those extremes when a film sticks to a character's conscious recall of plot. For example, Ranse Stoddard is an "I" as witness narrator of *The Man Who Shot Liberty Valance*. Examples of "I" as protagonist narration would be *Sunset Boulevard* and *Taxi Driver*. We know these narratives come out of the conscious recall of the characters because the characters deliberately address the story to an audience (and, again, objections to voice-over stem from a wrong-headed notion of film as a purely visual art). In sum, then, common or rare, fashionable or not, each of the fictional points of view outlined by Friedman remains a possible choice of imitation for the adapting filmmaker.[95]

Other Points of View

My conclusions notwithstanding, this question of point of view has, of late, been generating more critical work than any other issue regarding film and literature that one can examine. Unfortunately, the responses show little agreement on definition of terms.

Bruce Kawin's interesting notion of "mindscreen"—another approach to cinematic point of view that goes beyond the camera-as-recorder definitions—certainly anticipates much of my own thinking on this subject, but I do not follow Kawin all the way. Kawin sets straight one issue by noting that critics often mistakenly deny the existence of an implied filmmaker distinct from the actual—a distinction now commonly made in the novel between implied and actual author:

> While it seems reasonable to agree with one of the implications of this approach [i.e., camera-as-recorder]—that the organizer of the image must be offscreen—it does not seem necessary to deny the possibility that the organizer, as a persona of the artist or even just as a character, can be fictitious, and that he can include an image of himself (or an indicator of his offscreen presence) in the filmed field without compromising his status as narrator.[96]

This premise allows for first-person narratives, which he divides into three familiar categories: "What a character says (voice-over), sees (subjective focus, imitative angle of vision), or thinks. The term I propose for this final category is *mindscreen*, by which I mean simply the field of the mind's eye."[97] At first, this last idea sounds like a film equivalent for Friedman's selective omniscience.

So far, so good, but Kawin may elaborate on mindscreen too much, letting his comments on other points of view remain relatively imprecise. Besides first-person, other narrative voices include, in Kawin's terms, third person, point of view, and self-consciousness. The first two, versions of unlimited and limited omniscience respectively, invite confusion of subjectivity and objectivity (beyond the fact that the terms themselves do not seem adequate for their stipulated meanings). The last voice, self-consciousness, actually overlaps the other categories since it may "exist in combination with (or as an aspect of) any of these voices"; the difference is that "the film itself, or the fictitious narrator, is aware of the act of presentation," although such self-consciousness is most often expressed through mindscreen. In the context of Kawin's book, the imprecision of the other voices may not matter much, for he aims mostly to explore first-person film, particularly mindscreen, and more particularly yet, self-conscious mindscreen wherein the work seems "aware of itself, directs itself, conceives itself."[98] Even so, he muddles these classifications as well, and I think Friedman's divisions can lend some clarity to Kawin's insights and make them more useful.

Most centrally, we can see that mindscreen, as a rough equivalent to selective omniscience, moves a step away from first person and, to that extent, from the subjectivity of a narrator presenting someone else's story. Strictly speaking, in selective omniscience, no narrator exists since the story seemingly comes directly through a character's mind: no narrator, hence, no self-conscious narrator. Perhaps as a consequence Kawin would say the film is self-conscious: in lieu of a narrator, the work seems to fill the void. Actually, the self-consciousness belongs to the real filmmaker, who in turn could allow an implied filmmaker self-consciousness. This entrance of the filmmaker, though, pulls the point of view back toward subjectivity, and what Kawin calls self-conscious mindscreen might be a post-structuralist version of editorial omniscience. Whatever the case, I think that Kawin's discussion on point of view enlightens until he tries to make self-consciousness a kind of point of view. Self-consciousness requires a self; personal—as opposed to more objective—points of view can exhibit such reflectiveness, but the paradox of self-conscious objectivity resurrects and elaborates on Bluestone's camera-as-recorder and retains the consequential confusion of omniscience and objectivity.

Edward Branigan faults Kawin for collapsing terms as well: "It is not surprising that the effect of Kawin's approach . . . is to collapse cinema into mind. ... [E]very segment of a film is *someone's* mindscreen, potentially someone's mindscreen, or—when all else fails—the mindscreen of the text itself."[99] Branigan, however, sees Friedman's scale of telling and showing collapsing on itself also. In his *Point of View in the Cinema*, Branigan offers several interesting insights, but I think he dismisses so-called "orthodox" theories in terms incompatible with those theories.

Early on, Branigan takes care to distinguish terms: "point of view" does not, for him, refer to an audience's perception, attitude, or identification with any filmed object or action, nor to a linguistic code. Instead, "point of view is a feature of a text accessible to a logic of reading"; as such, it describes, not "consciousness," but "a symbolic process, ... a part of the generative capacity of a text and is one aspect of a reader's general competence."[100] More than a technical feature of the text, then, point of view also exists as a relationship constructed by the audience: narrators may be omniscient (that is, "assigned no origin by the text") or subjective (that is, "attributed to a particular origin," such as a character or "identifiable voice-over narrator"), and the audience may be "voyeuristic" (that is, an "unseen and unacknowledged spectator") or "personal" (that is, one who is directly addressed).[101]

In classical cinema, the construction of this relationship goes on at various levels. For instance, a film may be subjective (in ways different from those I discuss above) if it links "the framing of space at a given moment to a *character* as origin"; whether the link is direct, as in a point-of-view shot, or indirect, the audience understands that the character's subjectivity seemingly governs the narration.[102] I say "seemingly" because, according to Branigan, the constructed relationship between "telling and told" measures a "distance which need not be fixed but may be manipulated throughout the text." The manipulation of the audience's constructions makes narration "a series of levels each, in turn, embedded or framed by a higher authority. ... The levels are eventually cut off by the boundary of the artwork resulting in an overriding omniscience in the text—an effaced narrator, a frame which cannot disclose its own act of framing."[103] These levels bounded by the "effaced narrator" replace the "orthodox" narrators discussed by Wayne Booth and Friedman. Their theories focus on "consciousness" and the "reader's response to such mental expressions"; consequently, "Art is reduced to a special form of conversation ... where not only psychological states and intentions must be uncovered but also the norms and values of the participants."[104]

His argument, I think, does not engage these "orthodox" theorists' ideas of point of view, for the "levels" discussed are different, not contradictory. In summarizing his views, Branigan states:

> A given narration is a systematic restriction of meaning. . . . Thus point of view as a system of the text functions to control (expand, restrict, change) the viewer's access, not to a real object . . . nor to psychological states and attitudes, but to signification. Points of view are epistemological boundaries inscribed within the text.[105]

As should be clear above, my use of Friedman's scale of points of view fits this idea that a point of view sets an artificial limitation on information. For Branigan, however, within the levels of narration, "there is no consciousness of a narrator":

> The systematic restrictions perceived by the reader within a text are simply labeled as "narration" in order to be located when needed in the logical process of reading. . . . Just as meaning does not depend on intention so there is no need to construct a consciousness behind the fiction to explain the production of that meaning (narration). I reject Wayne Booth's assertion that "in fiction, as soon as we encounter an 'I' we are conscious of an experiencing mind." Instead, what is at stake is the manipulation of symbols by the reader.[106]

Another set of levels that is at work here, however, involves technical and formal functions. Technically, a point of view limits narrative information in a fiction, and at the level of technique, these limits bear no relation to a consciousness—for the technician would be the actual author, who is indeed effaced within the narrative. But, within the narrative, readers encounter point of view as more than technique. It has formal effects: point of view *imitates* a consciousness. Branigan says that the audience constructs point of view, yet the effaced narrator manipulates it. For the purposes of understanding our responses to a fiction, rather than having levels compete for control over point of view, we would more reasonably approach the issue on different levels to answer different questions: we can analyze point of view technically, but we first respond to it formally.

Another theorist, George M. Wilson, also finds little use for the literary theories on point of view that I employ above. Wilson's ideas share only some ground with Branigan's—"our conceptions of the central notion of 'point of view' overlap but do not coincide"[107]—so, as always, it seems, terms vary, and agreements and disagreements may depend on one's point of view—or definition of same.

In Wilson's definition,

> the concept of point of view should impose a categorization upon the domain of visual narration in actual films, a categorization that depends upon the structuring properties of the film's *overall* rhetorical organization, properties that determine the base from which an ideally perspicuous viewer assigns epistemic significance and value to the image track throughout its course.

Wilson thereby agrees that point of view involves the technical limitations imposed on a narrative, but whereas the narration may have a point of view, it has practically no narrator:

> In prose fiction, the "epistemic base" is identified in terms of the narrator, and many of the familiar classifications of literary point of view are concerned with the mediated or unmediated epistemic relations that the narrator bears to the narrated events. However, . . . it is dubious that fiction film generates any comparably general and central concept of a narrating figure.[108]

Later, in reference to theorists such as Booth, Wilson allows that "a network of substantial but limited analogies exists" between cinematic and literary concepts of point of view; nevertheless, "Since verbal telling and cinematic showing are such very different narrational procedures, the issues that get raised in each case are not at all identical."[109]

As does Branigan, Wilson, I think, treats point of view as only a technical question and neglects its formal qualities as an imitation. His discussion of first-person demonstrates the problem:

> As a form of restricted narrational authority this is to cover cases in which *every* shot of the film (or a lengthy segment of the film) represents the field of vision of the central character [or supporting character?] . . . . [B]ut the basic difficulty appears to be this. We do not and probably cannot see tracking or panning shots as corresponding to the continuous reorientation in space of the visual field of people such as ourselves. . . . [W]e do not see a straight cut, even within a scene, as representing the phenomenology of a shift in a perceiver's visual attention.[110]

Of course we don't. And the frame, at any aspect ratio, does not match our normal field of vision, but such discrepancies would matter only if we thought film should copy, not imitate, perspective.

The same problem applies in cases of less "subjective" narratives, the presumption being that the viewers must see what they hear: "In analogy with the literary case, it seems as though the very idea of filmic narration must presuppose the existence of visual narrators: if an *activity* of narration is conducted on screen, then there must be a filmic someone who is the *agent* of that activity." I cannot see why such a conclusion follows analogously from literature, for Wilson later notes that, in novels, "the narrating character may or may not be a character *in* the narrative that he or she tells."[111] In any case, literary practice supplies a more fitting notion of a cinematic narrator:

> Perhaps the narrator should be alternatively thought of as an agent, once more an invisible part of the total fictional construct, who now simply directs the audience's attention upon scenes of the narrative by setting a progression of movie views before them. . . . [I]ts correlate in literary theory is the concept, not of the narrator, but of the implied author of a work.[112]

Consequently, Wilson has films that essentially narrate themselves.

Among the films Wilson analyzes, *You Only Live Once* exemplifies this self-generating artifact. The film's narration is, he claims, "systematically unreliable." Distinct from the unreliable narrative of a novel, this film "does not present itself as the product of a narrator portrayed by the film"; instead, in "a sense that is not easy to explicate, the source of unreliability in this film seems to be the very mechanism of classical film narration itself."[113]

My own explication would encounter no such difficulties. Wilson discusses two scenes at length: in one, a tracking shot around Eddie Taylor's room at first seems to find Eddie in bed, but we soon realize that Eddie is elsewhere in the room and the man in the bed is Monk, a criminal acquaintance; in the second scene, a shot of a newspaper opens out to show a second and third version of the front page, each headlining increasingly worse news for Eddie. These scenes illustrate unreliability, according to Wilson, because the audience is led to believe something that proves not be the case, but I view the narration as reliably omniscient. Rather than an abstract metanarrator that deceives the viewers, I see an omniscient narrator who, for dramatic effect, withholds information. The effect of the withholding in the film's scenes resembles the brief uncertainty a reader feels when Mr. Pickwick meets an old antagonist in debtors' prison. Dickens tells how Mr. Pickwick's eyes fell "on the figure of a man who was brooding over the dusty fire": "Yes, in tattered garments, and without a coat; his common calico shirt yellow and in rags; his hair hanging over his face; his features changed with suffering, and pinched with famine,—there sat Mr. Alfred Jingle." This uncertainty lasts for only a line or two, but Dickens can stretch it out over a scene: early in *The Old Curiosity Shop*, a "mysterious individual" stands across from the shop, observing the coming and going of Quilp, patiently watching Nell's window, and at last reluctantly departing for home, where we finally hear the character identified as Kit, a friend to Nell and her grandfather. Wilson might reply that Dickens withholds these identities, but does not lead the reader to think the figures are anyone other than, in the respective scenes, Jingle or Kit. True enough, but Conan Doyle, in *The Hound of the Baskervilles*, briefly allows the reader—as well as Holmes and Watson—to think Sir Henry Baskerville has been killed, a conclusion caused by another man's wearing Sir Henry's "peculiar ruddy tweed suit." In literature, pronouns may conceal a character's identity, as Dickens does in briefly stretching out the shock of Pickwick's seeing a once proud adversary brought low, or in giving, for a bit longer, the reader some anxiety over whether Nell and her grandfather have others than Quilp about whom to worry; additionally, a narrator's inability to see everything clearly, as on a dark moor, may temporarily keep readers also in the dark. Such delays do not necessarily suggest unreliable narration, for we trust that we will get the correct information soon enough. The scene in Eddie's room, without pronouns, of course, accomplishes an essentially similar effect: the camera's angle withholds information, and only momentarily. Only in the world of the film must Eddie face a society that judges him on the basis of unreliable evidence.

In sum, Kawin, Branigan, and Wilson finally do not share my approach to point of view: that the work's point of view *imitates* the perspective of the person telling the story. The ideas of mindscreen, effaced narrators, and implied authors, as employed by these theorists, lead to narrations without narrators, films that seem to invent themselves or present themselves in spite of a putative narrator. Certain technical questions raised by these approaches have interest regarding the director's making of a film narrative, but these are mechanical matters and do not fully account for an audience's understanding during the narrator's telling and showing of the film's narrative.

Seymour Chatman likewise insists upon such a cinematic narrator: "If 'to narrate' is too fraught with vocal overtones, we might adopt 'to present' as a useful superordinate. Thus we can say that the implied author presents the story through a tell-er or a show-er or some combination of both." He adds that this presentation "entails an agent even when the agent bears no signs of human personality"[114]—for example, when no voice speaks to the audience in a film.

Chatman's line of reasoning in regard to point of view, and the related issue of description, has shown some evolution. In earlier writings, he defined narrative as a "deep structure quite independent of its medium"; as such, it could be manifest in any medium (including written words, drama, film, comic strips, dance, and programmatic music) capable of "double time structuring," combining the story time of the plot with the discourse time of the presentation.[115] Chatman therefore saw no barrier to the adaptation of a novel's narrative to film, and he elsewhere asserted, "There is no privileged manifestation."[116]

Despite this accommodating attitude, Chatman still concluded that material differences between written and filmed narration brought about differences in respective capabilities for description and perspective. Regarding description, he stated that "in its essential visual mode, film does not describe at all but merely presents; or better it *depicts*, in the original etymological sense of that word: renders in pictorial form." Such depiction in discourse time is not separate from story time, as description would be in a novel when a narrator halts the story to set a scene or describe a character. Thereby follows a contingency regarding point of view:

> The fact that most novels and short stories come to us through the voice of a narrator gives authors a greater range and flexibility than filmmakers. For one thing, the visual point of view in a film is always *there*: it is fixed and determinate precisely because the camera always needs to be placed *somewhere*. But in verbal fiction, the narrator may or may not give us a visual bearing. He may let us peer over a character's shoulder, or he may represent something from a generalized

perspective, commenting indifferently on the front, sides, and back of the object, disregarding how it is possible to see all these parts in the same glance.[117]

This point practically returns to Bluestone's dichotomy: writing is conceptual whereas film is perceptual.

In the later *Coming to Terms*, Chatman reconsiders some of these views. Dividing texts into Narratives, Descriptions, and Arguments, he now allows that film may be descriptive, even "predominantly descriptive" in the case of documentaries. Nevertheless, because typical narrative films "are more visually specific than novels, and filmmakers traditionally prefer visual representations to verbal ones . . . the medium privileges tacit Description."[118] This qualification does not simply resurrect his earlier views, for Chatman notes that filmmakers need not adhere to traditional and privileged practices: thus he discusses how the opening shot of *Rear Window* shows explicit description, and how the early freeze frame in *All About Eve* lets De Witt carry on a description of Eve while the story time pauses—just as in a novel.[119] Chatman can discuss these explicit descriptions now that he accounts for an implied author who "empowers others 'to speak,'" the others being narrators he previously regarded as "optional" or "absent."[120] Before, with no narrator there to offer the description, theoretically, the description could not occur.

Thereafter, Chatman goes on to distinguish among points of view—not only a variety of technical choices as Friedman lists, but several uses of the same term that should mean different ideas. The new definitions, unlike his new thinking on narrators, add terms without always clarifying terms. For instance, he separates "slant" and "filter": the former describes "the psychological, sociological, and ideological ramifications of the narrator's attitudes," whereas the latter refers to "the mediating function of a character's consciousness . . . as events are experienced from a space within the story world." Both can fit into Friedman's list (an editorially omniscient narrator betrays a certain "slant," and "filter" clearly resembles, as Chatman notes, the selective omniscience of a Jamesian narrator), but "slant" may also refer to the "bourgeois" concerns or seamlessly real "style" of the "classical Hollywood film."[121] The term thereby includes issues of cultural history, not only technical choice, so Chatman, trying to clarify confusing uses of "point of view," has not reduced the confusion by much.[122]

The distinction between "slant" and "filter" also affects the issue of reliability. When a narrator's "slant" is unreliable, the audience should see through the narrator's untrue or inaccurate story. In other works, the narrator may reliably relate a story about a flawed protagonist, one who acts out of "misguided thoughts," innocently or not; such a case involves "fallible filtration."[123] Again, however, new confusion replaces old. "Fallible filtration" deals with questions of characterization, not point of view, which of course may explain the distinction Chatman wishes to emphasize, but not the need for new terms to describe the distinction. Unreliable narrators stand out in contrast to reliable ones. Just so, one might ask if a "fallible filter" stands in contrast to any that are infallible (putting aside for now the Gospels of the New Testament); even Sherlock Holmes, who solves every mystery he confronts, cannot always discover the solution in time to prevent his client's death, as in "The Adventure of the Dancing Men." Chatman's distinction clarifies little about unreliable narration because "filters" must be fallible at least a little.

In any case, these distinctions notwithstanding, Chatman has come to agree that the material differences do not necessarily raise a significant barrier to a filmmaker's adapting a novelist's technical choice regarding point of view. As should be clear from the foregoing, not all linguistic styles are adaptable to the screen, but film's visual and aural spectacle does not preclude presenting the narrative with any of the self-imposed limitations to information that choices in point of view entail. These limitations involve selection: the less omniscient a point of view, the narrower the selection of information available to the narrator and, hence, the reader or viewer. In film adaptations, technical choices of scaling and ordering of the action should pose no problem, except insofar as selection becomes a practical problem beyond the choice of perspective.

Thought

The same critics who emphasize material differences often treat the issue of thought in a corollary manner: just as film cannot, they think, imitate first-person narration, so it cannot enter the minds of any characters, portray their thinking, or expand upon the abstract ideas they may entertain. According to Bruce Morrissette, such a view runs contrary to some very early critical assessments of cinematic processes:

> Almost in the same fashion as automatic writing, the film was considered to be the cinematography of thought, even of the unconscious. Poetry is metaphoric; the film is, or can be, metaphoric; therefore film was poetry, and the aesthetic response to it was substantially the same as that evoked by verbal poetry, though perhaps more immediate or intense, since the verbal path was short-circuited, as in the pure poetic state recognized by the surrealists in dreams.[124]

These views did not long prevail among most critics.

The work's formal structure, corresponding to Aristotle's object of imitation, comprises three parts: plot (in the narrower sense of fortune), character, and thought. Bluestone and his critical descendants would allow that plot, as a causal, unified sequence of circumstances and actions, adapts well enough to externalized portrayal. Moreover, to the extent that such outward actions inform us about characters and their rising or falling fortunes, they would agree that film adapts that aspect of characterization well enough also. But, is character always something we see acted? What about characterization conveyed through thoughts and feelings?

In regard to thought as a character's mental activity (and not as a part of the formal structure), Bluestone states the case:

> The film, by arranging external signs for our visual perception, or by presenting us with dialogue, can lead us to *infer* thought. But it cannot show us thought directly. It can show us characters thinking, feeling, and speaking, but it cannot show us their thoughts and feelings. A film is not thought; it is perceived.[125]

I think he mistakenly implies that a book can transcribe or copy thought, presuming that both are verbal. "But it could be countered that written literature itself has only words on pages to work with, and that putting them there is also an act of externalization—and that, in any case, thought is less exclusively 'verbal' than Bluestone's distinction seems to imply."[126]

Furthermore, inasmuch as we cannot gain access by any means at all to anyone's mind or stream of thoughts—let alone through words—Bluestone's point about inferring thought would suggest the limitations of all media. Nevertheless, even imitated implicitly, as long as we get it, the thought is part of our information. In *Sabotage*, when Sylvia Sidney looks at the knife—highlighted for us by its bright gleam and the clatter it makes on the plate—we can infer from her expression the thought of murder, and more deeply, her shock at herself for having the thought even as she must control that emotion in front of her husband. Conrad's *The Secret Agent*, although presenting a different sort of action, goes on at some length telling us about Mrs. Verloc's inspiration to murder her husband, her fear, and her cool execution of that idea. Significantly, the thoughts in her mind, whether told to or inferred by us, come through clearly, and our understanding of her character in the novel matches our understanding of her in the film.

Even if thought were verbal, written versions of thought would necessarily be imitations. As much as Molly Bloom's soliloquy, with its associative transitions and lack of grammatical marks, "looks" like unmediated thinking, Joyce yet selects and composes it with aesthetic and dramatic purposes in mind. Thought is not only verbal, though; we can all bring to mind sensations of sight, sound, touch, taste and smell, not to mention abstract concepts beyond words and senses. Words can imitate those thoughts that can be put into words, but so can film—and film can imitate visual and aural thinking too. For instance, the "noise" on the soundtrack of Lodge Kerrigan's *Clean, Shaven* portrays the protagonist's disordered, schizophrenic mind even as we view his actions in the external world.

Nevertheless, many critics persist in maintaining that "certain kinds of novels are seemingly more adaptable to film than others"; such adaptability is

> a function of the extent to which the novel presents the interior world of its characters. . . . Film has difficulty approximating these interiors for at best it can show the external manifestations of consciousness through dialogue, expression, action, or the generally awkward device of voice-over narration.[127]

However, if these "external manifestations" serve quite as well as written language in conveying thoughts, I see little point in arguing which method serves best.

Voice-over allows us to hear what Marion imagines the discovery of her embezzlement will be like in *Psycho*. Is the omniscient narrator's report of her thoughts actually more direct or more effective in the novel? As for non-verbal thoughts, in so early a film as *The Life of an American Fireman* (1902), the circular dream balloon superimposed over the shot of the sleeping fire chief shows a dream of his wife and child; less bluntly but more effectively, the flash-cuts of Hiroshima and Nevers show us the depressing memories and feelings preoccupying the character of the French actress in *Hiroshima Mon Amour*. Would the fireman's dream or the actress's memory seem more real to the audience if, in print, some narrator described these thoughts?

> A particular element of thought is not tied to a particular linguistic expression (synonymy is possible); more importantly, a particular thought can be expressed very clearly through means other than its direct articulation.... A glance at another art form, the movies, also indicates that thought has a nonlinguistic essence.[128]

In fact, the failure to understand the fuller spectrum of thought may explain the consequent "failure" of an adaptation of a novel that is supposed to be unadaptable. As Bruce Kawin explains in *Faulkner and Film*, the screenwriters who adapted *The Sound and the Fury* assumed that the action conveyed through Benjy's consciousness would be impossible to recreate faithfully. Their assumption caused them to miss an opportunity.

> [Benjy] shifts among times and places too abruptly for them, and has no words with which to express his feelings. Clearly their method of putting the whole story into what they call "the present," and of telling it in the third person, mandates against any imitation of Faulkner's experiment here.... What makes Benjy's narrative so difficult to read, however, is not its montage but the fact that it is *words* about wordless experience.

Kawin goes on to show how the sense of time and place would be easier to keep straight in a film because of what the audience could see, and how the subjectivity of Benjy's feelings would be comprehensible because of what the editing would necessarily suggest.

> It is even arguable that the inherent difficulty of the Benjy section stems from the possibility that *it* is a kind of adaptation: that it was conceived as a visual montage and recast into language. So although it would be difficult and challenging to film this sequence as Faulkner

wrote it, it would hardly be impossible, and the result would—*without* oversimplification—be more accessible than the novel.[129]

When we can disabuse ourselves of the notion that words can reproduce thinking, we can understand how artificial imitation suffices to convey thought in works of art—and because they are artificial, imitations can be neither natural nor privileged.

"Thought" may have two other interpretations related to the formal structure, Aristotle's object of imitation. Friedman says Aristotle means "the conception of things entertained by the protagonist," including attitudes, reasonings, and emotions.[130] Thought then refers to the quality of a character's mind, and character refers to behavior motivated by that quality of thought. Northrop Frye, on the other hand, translates Aristotle's meaning as "theme," as in "What's the *point* of this story?"[131] Either way, critics in Bluestone's camp would say the whole of a character's mind or the abstractions of an artist's themes and beliefs lie outside the reach of film portrayal. Therefore, since film must stick to action and behavior, film's thought or theme can never be very profound.

The charge that film cannot deal in abstract ideas or themes logically develops from the premise that film cannot portray thinking:

> Many people believe that a corollary is that while literature is a more "intellectual" medium, film is the more emotional. . . . Sometimes a similar but actually quite different generalization says that film is a simple rather than a complex medium (in content, not execution). . . . Perhaps the most important if obvious source of this difference is in length.[132]

Of course, the premise of literature's exalted intellectuality leads to question begging, but the reference to length may offer a clue to the persistence of the notion. Feature films run a certain length by conventional practice, not by necessity or definition; granted, however, the convention may not disappear soon. Intellectually superficial films—like many in Asheim's sample—and most films today—like most novels—amuse more than they challenge. Questionable theorizing arises from using the common Hollywood product (of an essentially thirty-year-old art, in the case of the films Bluestone analyzes) as representative of the art's potential achievements. I daresay that a survey of best sellers would cause despair over the aesthetic life of literature. The conventional practice is not, by deduction, the measure. If *Wuthering Heights* as a film cannot match the intellectual vigor of Brontë's novel, so what? Do such examples mitigate the themes or other films? The mechanization of man in *Metropolis*, the vanity of nationalism in *La Grande Illusion*, the elusiveness of truth in *Rashomon*, the summation of a life in *Wild Strawberries*, the destructiveness of love in *Jules et Jim*, the alienation of a culture in *Blow-Up*, the politics of sex in *WR—Mysteries of the Organism*, the paralysis of materialism in *The Discreet Charm of the Bourgeoisie*, and the cultural emptiness of *Nashville*—all these may stand next to much literature as intellectual equals. To the charge that films have no profound ideas, we can find some that do.

Faithful to What?

For the common filmgoer's notion of fidelity, the main objection usually refers not to ideas but to the practical inability of most films to include *all* the events novels present. If quantity is the issue, we might recall that, until about 1915, film producers believed audiences would not sit for what we call feature length films. Today, after Granada's twelve-hour production of *Brideshead Revisited*, filmmakers willing to use television may be no more selective than novelists. As for theatrical releases, the problem of conventional length may be giving way just a little: audiences do not like to sit for more than four hours—the outside limit for the most accommodating film buff—nor return to theaters for further installments, but the relative success of Rainer Werner Fassbinder's *Berlin Alexanderplatz* (presented over consecutive nights or weeks) and Claude Berri's *Jean de Florette* and *Manon of the Spring* (presented months apart) indicates some change in this attitude.[133]

As with style, though, the real issue remains quality, not quantity. If a film lacks certain events or characters, it becomes a more or less serious problem relative to intended effects; it is not a problem by definition.

I think we can see the relative significance or insignificance of certain changes by contrasting two adaptations of *The Big Sleep*. Howard Hawks's version in 1946 could not explicitly portray Carmen's drug habit and nymphomania; it could not include the nude photographs or her attempted seduction of Marlowe. As the sources of blackmail and the motivation for Carmen's ugly proclivity for murder—the facts that begin and end Marlowe's involvement in the case—these details might be seriously missed. Michael Winner's version thirty years later explicitly presents these details and renders events and dialogue much more "faithfully." So, why does the latter fail in comparison to the former? I do not think the absence of Humphrey Bogart causes the failure; Robert Mitchum plays a fine Marlowe and cannot, in all fairness, be faulted for not having as cultivated a cult. Instead, I think Hawks's version exploits the book's best qualities: the sense of mystery, danger, and decadence that so envelop depression-era Los Angeles that only a weary, hardened, but romantically noble detective like Marlowe can confront and emerge from it with honor intact. Winner's version preserves the details as if the mention or presence of dead bodies and the blackmail of a young woman were not ugly enough; he does not consider that not showing the ugly details might even enhance the imagined decadence. But, in Winner's contemporary, suburban British setting, the details embarrass more than shock: drugs permeate society too much to be a rare decadence, and the nude pictures of Candy Clark look no more pornographic than an old *Playboy* centerfold. Rather than a hardened, but romantic hero, any good cop could handle this job. Furthermore, in the novel, Mrs. Regan can talk to Marlowe about her sister's photos and say, "She has a beautiful little body, hasn't she? . . . You ought to see mine," and readers of 1939 would see her as scandalously brazen. In Winner's film, the line makes her sound like a hackneyed tease. For Hawks's film, however, the Production Code would not allow such an obvious proposition, so he substituted the banter about horse racing and "who's in the saddle." The unspoken and the unseen do not confuse us as much as they cause us to infer a morality loose enough for the drama. The movie, like the book, then, needs to go beyond the Holmesian unraveling of the crime; it needs to feel sordid so that we can feel more relieved at Marlowe's persistent honor than at his clever detective work. In emphasizing atmosphere over details, Hawks departs from the original to be more faithful to its effects than Winner seems to realize.

These questions of material and technical correspondences and differences lead—indeed, have already led—to questions of form and final effect. Films, as artificial objects, embody an intention (or unifying principle, or shaping cause); that embodiment or structure, imposed to bring about that intention for the audience, is the work's form. We read the relationship between cause and effect both ways: an intention causes an artist to impose a certain form that will cause a certain effect on the audience; perception of that form will cause the audience to reconstruct the intention.[134] A choice about form or structure leads to choices, already discussed, about technique and material. Even with the admitted limitations facing the film adapter in these latter two areas, "the same governing conception could conceivably be embodied in different ways and is therefore neutral in relation to that choice. A novel may be transformed successfully into a film *without changing its original effect*, for example, or into a play, and vice versa."[135]

Although not in the majority, some writers on film have seen the possibility of this formal convergence. Bruce Morrissette acknowledges that the critical trend lately favors a "philosophy of textuality," whose semiotic and post-structural concerns would push the novel and film farther apart. Morrissette points out that, this philosophy notwithstanding, artists and audiences "continue to hold, consciously or unconsciously, to the idea that there exists, beyond the words on the page and beyond the images on the screen as well, a common field of the imagination in which the work of art—visual, auditory, or verbal—takes on its effective aesthetic form and meaning."[136]

Evaluating the Result

Throughout my argument so far, I have been trying to show that adaptations can do many of the things they are too commonly thought to be incapable of doing—that is, imitate, in a fashion equal to the achievement of the original novel, various narrative techniques, forms, and effects. The theorists with whom I disagree can point to a great deal of conventional practice to support their claims, claims that become the premises of later theories. Convention does not define necessity, however, and the deductive application of these claims renders such criticism invalid. Still, by showing what I think is possible—that film can reproduce a novel's effects through its own techniques—I cannot say what is now necessary. Adaptations involve artistic choices that can imitate the novelist's choices, but they need not and often do not.

When the more deductive theorists state that adaptations cannot make the same choices, they often logically conclude from their premises that the adaptations always somehow simplify the novel, resulting in a superficial and generally inferior work. With assumptions about technique and form called into question, however, so are the consequent judgments.

The answers cannot be definitive. If a film can imitate a novel technically and formally, doing so will not necessarily yield a good film, let alone an adaptation that surpasses the original. No prescriptions govern all novels and film adaptations. At best, particular cases may serve as models.

Crane writes that Aristotle's aim in the *Poetics* "is the discovery and statement of the principles which govern poets when they made good poems," and which can then be the principles critics use to judge poems.[137] By the same token, I think we can examine adaptations in order to determine what choices a filmmaker makes when bringing a novel to the screen and to discover how he or she may or may not succeed relative to the novel. Such an evaluative judgment grows more complicated than the evaluation of a single work, for now we must judge two works of art and compare them.

Any value judgment draws a conclusion about a relationship between the object judged and the criteria of judgment or the value: "The value is not a discernible property of the thing itself; it is a certain relation between the thing—indeed in terms of real or supposed properties of the thing—and something further. It exists as a relationship exists, and the term 'value' is a relative term."[138] The materialist theorists would determine such relationships on the basis of some kind of verbal or cinematic trait presumed to be a necessary part of the art's definition. Judgment then becomes a matter of definitive necessity rather than of value: the work fits the definition or it does not. Obviously, too, the translating of a "verbal" quality, if a necessity of a work's value, into a supposedly "non-verbal" medium must eliminate that basis and, hence, its value. Claims of this sort appeal to the "authority" of an allegedly objective perception of properties inherent in the medium.[139] If, as I argue, such properties are neither natural nor necessary, the judgment only completes a circular argument.

Out of the multiplicity of theoretical and critical questions, we can get as many evaluative criteria. Nevertheless, the relative standard of judgment should "be determined in adjustment to the particular necessities and possibilities of the form the artist is trying to achieve."[140] For example, we could not fairly fault the verisimilitude of the special effects in *The Wizard of Oz* by contemporary standards set by *Twister*, nor complain that the film does not, as a growing-up story should, show us the mature result of Dorothy's fantastic education (for starters, what does she do when Miss Gulch returns for the at-large Toto?). The former complaint misrepresents the filmmaker's choice of technical devices, which cannot be found wanting relative to an impossible choice of using unavailable devices. The latter complaint misunderstands the film's form: whereas it has an education plot, it is not a *bildungsroman* and is complete when Dorothy attains more mature attitudes; to go on would be unnecessary—as would the demand to do so.

At the same time, criteria that do take into account a film's necessities and possibilities will not necessarily produce agreement. Measured by the technical standards of the day, *The Birth of a Nation* may have astounded audiences, but as a narrative, it told a sentimental and embarrassingly racist story; the youth of the art does not excuse its thematic infelicities as it would its technical ones. In another case, one might view *The Deer Hunter* as a very moving narrative of men in war and, from a different angle, a very misleading representation of men in Vietnam. With both opinions open to argument, even if the mimetic and the historical issues could be settled individually, neither judgment would have priority over the other, for the judgments remain relative to the applied standard.

For the purposes of my original question, the judgment of an adaptation's adequacy depends on the same categories that guide analysis: according to the material, technical, and formal choices the artist has made, what effects are necessary and what peculiar powers are possible? Accounting for the necessities of an artist's achievement "is only half of the problem, for it is true of the most mediocre writers that they usually do, in some fashion, a great part or all of the things their particular forms require, but do little more besides. The crucial question, therefore, concerns not so much the necessities of the assumed form as its possibilities."[141] This standard of hypothetical possibilities cannot unfairly impose on artists because the possibly pleasurable or moving effects of a work depend upon their better or worse choices; the relative standard depends, not on what they cannot or have not attempted, but on what they *do* attempt, what they ask of themselves.

For instance, among the popular series of comic book films, few disappoint at the box office, but many disappoint on the screen. *Superman*, for one, fulfills the necessities of its plot: the extraordinary hero develops morally, has a love interest, fights a worthy and devious (albeit comical) opponent, and winds up vanquishing the evil he opposes and saving the woman he loves— all while continuously exhibiting his wonderful powers. Early on, however, the film seems to emphasize Superman's alien, mythic, and therefore lonely, nature. As his parents prepare to send him to Earth, his father speaks of his unique powers and the moral mission he will face; his mother qualifies each remark, noting how he will be different and unaccommodated. The capsule's rising to the ceiling and breaking through the skylight recalls the birth of Frankenstein. His early life with foster parents, his summons to a wasteland to build a fortress of solitude, the asking of questions and seeking of answers with his father—all correspond to some details of the life of Moses or Jesus. But, when we first see him fly, this Superman, part monster and part prophet, flies to the funny-page world of Metropolis to become all cartoon. The hero who confronts his separation from society resolves his problem simply by keeping busy: catching helicopters, seeing through dresses, and rebuilding dams. Such activity, for us as well as for him, takes our minds off the existential issue introduced earlier. The comic-book treatment, unobjectionable in and of itself, fits only a comic-book beginning. The possible drama of an existential Superman gets lost.

I arrive at this judgment of *Superman*'s failure "by considering theoretically the conditions under which any particular effect aimed at in a given work might be better or worse achieved"; the problem stems from an inability to decide between an existential or comic-book hero (or between disputing writers) and then to pursue that characterization consistently.

Another way to measure a work's achievement according to its possibilities would involve "having our minds stored with memories of what both the most and the least perfect artists have done when confronted with similar problems of invention, representation, and writing"[142]—and filmmaking. With some adjustment, this standard would apply to adaptations. We may not have resort to a most and least perfect artist, but we always have a prior artist. As in the case of *The Big Sleep*, the novelist's achievement is always there for comparison. If we accept the fulfillment of a plot's possibilities for uniqueness and emotional power as a standard of judgment for individual novels and films, then the assessment of an adaptation could be in comparison to that of the original novel. In such a case, an artist chooses a different medium, but otherwise may imitate many of another artist's technical and formal choices. Without rendering final judgment of either, we can state whether they produce equally affecting works or that one surpasses the other in developing the possibilities their comparable choices offer.

Final judgment is a compound judgment. Obviously, filmmakers adapt many bad or mediocre novels, and if a filmmaker imitates the novelist's choices—if, that is, the adaptation remains faithful—then the film will be the novel's equal in emotional power or pleasure: equally bad, however. A happier circumstance results from an adaptation of a good novel that faithfully imitates the aesthetic choices that make the novel a success, and thereby the film also. Clearly, fidelity entails fidelity to effects rather than details. The filmmaker can omit or alter some details, as did Howard Hawks in *The Big Sleep*, and still maintain the final effect of the novel.

The choice to be faithful to a novel's effects implies a choice to be unfaithful. The supposedly common infidelity arises when a filmmaker omits or alters some detail necessary to a good novel's power. Although this charge comes too easily from some critics, it holds true on occasion. Aside from commercial concerns that may cause these alterations, simple misinterpretation may lead to some problems. Dudley Andrew states, "The broader notion of the process of adaptation has much in common with interpretation theory, for in a strong sense adaptation is the appropriation of a meaning from a prior text.[143] To prove such a case, a critic would need to show where the filmmaker mistakes the novelist's intention—where the filmmaker wants to make a choice similar to the novelist's, but mistakes what that choice should be; or wants to improve upon the novelist's choice, but misapprehends the original reasoning. For instance, unless one understands Henry James's *The Turn of the Screw* as a tale of a sexually neurotic governess, one will view Jack Clayton's *The Innocents* as an adaptation of a misinterpretation. Divergence from any novel, while not necessarily deliberate, would be damaging all the same if the change dilutes or destroys a necessary or valuable effect.

When filmmakers do make deliberate changes, they presumably are trying to improve upon the original or take it in a different direction. The important point yet remains: if fidelity does not insure quality, as in the faithful adaptation of a bad novel, infidelity does not insure lack of quality. A bad novel may have something the right filmmaker can develop into a powerful theme. Even a good novel, adapted by a perceptive and imaginative filmmaker, may yield further or different pleasures the novelist did not consider.

The following discussions exhibit practical examples of this theoretical argument, and I think the application of my inductive framework to the analysis, judgment, and comparison of the works will prove valid and fruitful. The standard of judgment derived from the potential pleasures and powers in the work—as opposed to an abstract standard—leads to fairer and sounder evaluations. For instance, accidents of production will matter less. When I say the vagueness of some crimes and sex in Hawks's *The Big Sleep* does not make the adaptation simpler or "cleaner" than the later version, I am implicitly asserting that changes made in adherence to the Production Code are more accidental than essential; omitting all the crimes would be an essential fault. Of course, my standard also will not give undue priority to the means of imitation; critics who emphasize the medium isolate a single element rather than place it in relation to all other elements of the work—in this case, elements more important than material. Such emphasis posits the choice of a certain medium as a value in itself for certain subjects—a highly arbitrary presumption—and renders judgment of those other elements a function of the one element, the medium. Lastly, my standard allows for the alteration or omission of certain details: the dropping of a character or scene may be acceptable to the extent that the function of those details contribute in minor and, therefore, not absolutely necessary ways to the whole.

Olson reminds us that "we shall never know all about art or the values of art until all art is at an end; meanwhile, artists will continue to instruct us."[144] Balázs, Bluestone, and other theorists have looked at adaptations, made many important observations, and, unfortunately, rendered some conclusions obvious and necessary by definition; the discussion of the art has come to an end for them, and, therefore, so has the art. But filmmaking and adapting novels to film continue. Production practices have changed since Balázs's and Bluestone's times, and critical fashions have as well; yet, little progress has been made in the criticism of adaptations. As Dudley Andrew suggests, I see nothing to be gained by arguing "over the essence of the media or the inviolability of individual art works," nor by allowing "theorists [to] settle things with a priori arguments."[145] My framework, inspired by neo-Aristotelianism, may seem to have an ancient basis, but its inductive questioning cannot be summarily discounted as out of date. As long as film artists continue to adapt novels to the screen, these questions keep the discussion going and keep the criticism even with what is going on.

Say It Ain't So: *The Natural*

And I say it is not against reason (to perform the promise). For
the manifestation whereof, we are to consider: first, that when
a man doth a thing which . . . tendeth to his own destruction,
howsoever some accident which he could not expect arriving
may turn it to his benefit; yet such events do not make it
reasonably or wisely done. Secondly . . . there is no man can
hope by his own strength or wit to defend himself from
destruction without the help of confederates. . . . And therefore
he which declares he thinks it reason to deceive those that help
him can in reason expect no other means of safety than what
can be had from his own single power.

—Thomas Hobbes, *Leviathan*

. . . his aim
How not to hit the mark he seems to aim at,

His passion how to avoid the obvious. . . .

—Robert Francis, "Pitcher"

I say that film production methods have changed since the days of
George Bluestone's samples, but not all productions necessarily
show these changes. Bluestone's assertions, based upon and
supported by Lester Asheim's methods and statistics, would seem
to retain a great deal of explanatory power in the case of some
recent films. For instance, among Asheim's thirty-nine
conclusions, the following kinds of alterations might yet aid a
producer in making a novel into a "property": the novel is "almost
invariably condensed," which requires the loss of material "the
novelist apparently considered essential" and the "rearrangement
of material that is retained"; since the presumed audience's
"comprehension is generally lower for the film than for the

novel," most details become "more explicit" than implicit or metaphorical; for the same reason, the "romantic love story is stressed," and unhappy endings or any "tone of negation" never remain completely; excessive violence, sex, and obscenity are not adapted "even where they are integral parts of the plot or characterization"; instead, the use of stars, which enhances the importance of any previously minor character, adds "an air of glamour which often exceeds that conveyed by the original novel."[1] These conclusions, which variously apply to adaptations such as *Wuthering Heights* or *The Grapes of Wrath*, clearly apply as well to the adaptation of Bernard Malamud's *The Natural*—and the Hays Office and the studio system had nothing to do with it.

For whatever reasons, *The Natural* represents the kind of film adaptation characteristic of the era Bluestone studied: in those days, acquiring and adapting a novel was more like making a "vehicle" or cashing in on a "property" than endeavoring to meet an aesthetic challenge, much less produce a work faithful to the original. Pauline Kael, in fact, suggests that this vehicle has been washed and shined up for its principal passenger, Robert Redford:

> There may be a rule of thumb for gauging when a star has become so concerned with the politics of his image as a hero that he's afraid of acting; it's when he'll only play roles in which he's more sinned against than sinning. And the way that this picture has been designed, the myth of Robert Redford transcends the myths of baseball heroes.[2]

Redford himself offers the old excuse that movies are different from books: the novel is "so richly allegorical. . . . It's difficult to combine all of these elements into a picture, so, yes, we dared alter Malamud. Film is just not a literary medium, I'm afraid."[3] These comments echo Bluestone's assertions that literary tropes represent a "packed symbolic thinking which is peculiar to imaginative rather than to visual activity." To translate a metaphor into a "literal image" would render it "absurd."[4]

Of course, as I say above, such broad assertions about the relative capabilities of films and novels have no necessary theoretical truth, but they may influence a filmmaker convinced in advance of their conventional wisdom. Barry Levinson, the film's director, said in a radio interview that the ending was too depressing to keep. This assertion speaks to concerns other than aesthetic ones. Bluestone says much about commercial and social forces that can compromise an artistic idea in films, and he notes that, after years of practice, "The unconscious or conscious adherence to convention has an enduring influence on film content."[5] Again, though, these practices and conventions have no theoretical necessity, so they cannot explain why any one adaptation *had* to turn out as it did.

In the event, this adaptation fails. Critics who attack the film usually complain about the complete reversal of the novel's ending, but this version starts in a direction that leads inevitably to such a conclusion. In a way, this circumstance resembles what Bluestone says about *Wuthering Heights*. First, the change in the ending (that is, dropping the second half of the novel) causes changes elsewhere: "From this central deletion in the film follows almost every other deviation from Emily Brontë's text." Then, in regard to the novel's richness, the filmmakers must consider the audience:

> This combination of local mythology and mystical insight endows the book with an extremely complex set of values. But given this complexity, we are more prone to understand the changes which occur in the film version of the book. It is too much to expect that a mass audience will be able to accept conventions which time and distance have made remote, let alone the peculiar intricacies of Emily Brontë's private world.[6]

All these kinds of concerns—commercial and social, but not theoretically aesthetic—lead to the changes in adapting *The Natural*. Yet if the adaptation reflects, probably unconsciously, Bluestone's ideas, those ideas still do not excuse the adaptation. Unfortunately for the filmmakers, no theoretically necessary alteration in translating a novel to the screen causes their version, which they "dared alter" from the original, to follow a plot that lacks any real drama to an ending that offers, if I may call it so, a spectacularly empty satisfaction.

What the filmmakers misunderstand or ignore, I think, is Malamud's characterization of his "hero." Roy Hobbs comes to the game of baseball with the potential to join its greatest heroes, and Malamud, through imagery and allusion, compares him, not only to those stars, but also to the heroes of several classical and medieval legends. This potential, however, is not enough. As Tony Tanner notes, "All [Malamud's] novels are fables or parables of the painful process [of moving] from immaturity to maturity— maturity of attitudes, not of years."[7] Roy possesses physical prowess, and he knows it too well. What he does not know encompasses almost everything else an adult—let alone a hero—should know. In the novel, then, Roy's progress must take him beyond his "heroism"—that is, beyond the athletic records and fame that his skills win for him. *The Natural* portrays a maturing plot of character in which Roy suffers as a hero so that he may win another chance to become a good man.

Roy's character comes with a rich set of associations. A "natural" refers to that rare player who excels with seemingly divine grace, but also to the "innocent fool" of medieval literature.[8] In regard to the former, many critics have noted the clear allusions to players and events of baseball lore: Roy recalls Babe Ruth in his practical orphanhood, his switch from pitcher to slugging outfielder, his home run to cheer a sick boy, and his bellyache heard round the country; his shooting would also recall the attack by a crazed woman on Eddie Waitkus in 1949, after which the recovered Waitkus led the Phillies to their first pennant since 1915; other details allude to lore both daffy—such as Rabbit Maranville's love of crawling on hotel ledges, or the St. Louis Browns' hiring of a therapist to cure their "losers' syndrome"[9]—and sad—most notably the "black sox" scandal.[10] Roy's participation in the scandal comes at the completion of a cycle that is natural to the game in another way: its season. James M. Mellard notes that Roy makes his big debut on 21 June and fails after the autumnal equinox when the team clinches a tie for first place.[11] Indeed, this "natural" leads his team almost all the way to the Fall Classic; instead, he takes a classic fall.

This boy of summer gets himself more and more lost the further he moves from his natural origins into these cycles. Early in the novel, still on the train taking him to a try-out with the Cubs, Roy looks out and sees

> within the woodland the only place he had been truly intimate with in his wanderings, a green world . . . that made the privacy so complete his inmost self had no shame of anything he thought there, and it eased the body-shaking beat of his ambitions.[12]

This Arcadian world must be lost to anyone other than a child or a childish dreamer. In Roy's case, his ambitions remove him from this Arcadian dream to the city of Chicago and alternative dreams of fame and fortune; there, he keeps an assignation with Harriet Bird—a woman who has called herself "a twisted tree" (35)—and is shot by her, falling "as the forest flew upward" (41). Much later, reliving some of his mistakes, he is riding along once more, looking out the window, being driven by Memo Paris down a dark, tree-lined road with the headlights off:

> He found himself wishing he could go back somewhere, go home, wherever that was. As he was thinking this, he looked up and saw in the moonlight a boy coming out of the woods . . . . After fifteen seconds he was still there. (122–23)

Roy switches on the lights, but too late, for he thinks they hit whoever or whatever was in the road:

> "I heard somebody groan."
> "That was yourself." (123)

So far and so long away from his home—that fifteen seconds is, in miniature, the fifteen years separating these deadly encounters with women—Roy cannot recover that idealized childhood and is in danger of never growing out of his actual childhood.

Nevertheless, if nature suffuses the refuge Roy has lost, it also endows him with the force he can muster to save the devastated park of the Knights. When Roy joins the team, Pop Fisher, the manager, sums up the their situation well: "It's been a blasted dry season. No rains at all. The grass is worn scabby in the outfield and the infield is cracking. My heart feels as dry as dirt for the little I have to show for all my years in the game" (45). The team is playing poorly, the stands are nearly empty, even the dugout's water fountain offers only rusty water, and Pop laments, "I shoulda been a farmer" (45). Pop is skeptical of Roy's advanced age for a rookie, and he scoffs at Wonderboy, Roy's bat fashioned from a tree struck by lightning. When Roy first gets into a game, though, he triumphs over the ball and nature: "Wonderboy flashed in the sun. . . . There was a straining, ripping sound and a few drops of rain spattered to the ground" (80). Roy literally knocks the cover off the ball and brings rain that lasts for three days. Thereafter, the grass is green in the field, the team plays harder and better, the fans return to the stands, and Pop feels healed and contented.

This miraculous ability to restore the Knights shows Roy as comparable to more than Babe Ruth. Many critics, most notably Earl R. Wasserman, have catalogued the correspondences to classical myths: Roy is a king ("Roi") like Arthur with his Excalibur; or a knight like Perceval, whose search for the Grail will restore the Fisher King and the Waste Land. Malamud obviously underlines these references with names like Pop *Fisher* and Memo *Paris* (whose name recalls one man's choice among women that led to disaster, a problem that Roy shares to some extent); and Malamud adds details such as opposing pitchers' warily "probing his armor" (74) when Roy comes to bat, or Roy's stopping before Memo's box in a car given to him on "Roy Hobbs Day" to ask her out—much as a knight in a tournament would ask to wear his lady's colors. These allusions to myths, along with those to baseball lore, are not the key to Roy's story so much as they are the challenge to his character; explaining the references does not explain Roy's conflict and resolution. "Myths are 'endless stories' for Malamud, and the 'endless story' of his novels has been the conflict between myths and the outer world . . . and it has been the task of the heroes of his novels to see beyond myths without at the same time losing sight of them."[13] Roy cannot maintain this vision because he remains a "natural" in the second sense.

As I note above, a "natural" can also be an "innocent fool." At the outset, Roy certainly acts like a boy. On the train, he needs to be led to the bathroom, and he cannot figure out how to order in the dining car. This boyishness includes childish enthusiasm for succeeding in the game. After he strikes out the Whammer, Harriet Bird suddenly shows interest in Roy, and she quizzes him on his aspirations. Once she gets over the surprise that Roy has yet to make the majors despite his mastery over the Whammer, she asks him what he hopes to do in his career. He boasts that he will "break every record in the book" and that people will recognize him as "the best there ever was in the game" (32–33),[14] but she wonders if something else is not in his dreams. Roy struggles to see what she is getting at and then concludes that she must be referring to money, which he assures her he will accumulate. Only with more prodding does he think of the sheer enjoyment of athletic endeavor, but he feels as though "he had just flunked a test" (34). So he should. Harriet has tried to make him say he understands his position as a hero: she has compared his triumph to "David jawboning the Goliath-Whammer, or was it Sir Percy lancing Sir Maldemer" (31–32), and now she too cannot quite articulate the values by which he might inspire people.

So, Roy is a fool, but here he may be an innocent too. Harriet, of course, turns out to be insane. She lures Roy to her room and shoots him because, as we are given to understand she has done before, she wants to slay any top athlete who fails to uphold heroic values. (In fact, Harriet must have been on the train to meet the Whammer, and Roy's pitching ironically saves the Whammer's life as it ends his career.) Furthermore, one must admit, Roy is just a kid. His boastfulness may be excused somewhat by the fact that any teenager with the prospect of a major league tryout and the exhilaration of striking out baseball's best hitter can be allowed a little pride.

But, "pride goeth before destruction, and an haughty spirit before a fall" (Prov. 16:18), and well after Roy has suffered a fall or more, he still thinks like a kid. Following another triumph, a game-winning home run, Roy meets Iris Lemon, another woman who was there to witness his victory. Unlike Harriet, though, Iris has no trouble putting into words the inspirational value of a hero: "Without heroes we're all plain people and don't know how far we can go. . . . [I]t's their function to be the best and for the rest of us to understand what they represent and guide ourselves accordingly" (154). Roy, however, can only regret his years out of the game: "If I had started out fifteen years ago like I tried to, I'da been the king of them all by now. . . . I'da broke most every record there was" (156). His words recall his responses to Harriet, and this failure cannot be excused by his youth. Most obviously, his experience includes his nearly fatal encounter with Harriet, and at this time, despite his phenomenal play, he ought to remember his slumps as much as his victories. In short, Roy is no kid and no mythic king, and he refuses to admit as much.

Roy's childishness is evident in several other parallel actions. In a good and natural sense, Roy is a son who wants to do well for a father. He has no actual father who figures in the plot, but at the outset, he has Sam Simpson, the scout who is taking him for his tryout with the Cubs; such a find will enable Sam to return to full-time scouting, and Roy, he says, wants him to succeed because his Roy feels "more devoted to me than a son" (21). Having taken a couple of insults from the Whammer and Max Mercy, a nationally syndicated sports writer, Sam initiates the challenge leading to Roy's striking out the Whammer. As Roy later tells Harriet, he was thinking only of defeating the Whammer because they could not afford to lose the money Sam had bet. Years later, Pop becomes his pop, another father with a jinxed past in the game, a susceptibility to insults, and the possibility of losing his job. Pop sits up waiting for Roy, advises him about women, and once offers to help him out with money—just as a father would for any son. Roy, touched by emotion, still puts him off this time: "Wait till I get you the pennant" (127). Much later, Roy learns that just the pennant—not necessarily a World Series win also—would satisfy Pop. Roy's ambitions had never had such a limit, exalted as the pennant is, but this admission suffices to make Roy promise to get out of the hospital and play for Pop.

Roy's most admirable deed comes as a result of satisfying a father, and Roy gets to be fatherly himself in the deal. A fan, Mike Barney, tells Roy that his son may be dying in the hospital, but that he has promised the boy Roy would hit a home run for him; he explains that the boy will get to listen to the game on the radio, and "I know if you hit one it will save him" (142). Unfortunately, Roy is having a tremendous slump at the plate, and Pop has benched him because Roy refuses to try another bat besides Wonderboy. In the ninth, with the game on the line and Mike Barney in despair, Roy and Pop give in to each other simultaneously; Roy sets Wonderboy aside, and Pop tells him to pinch hit with Wonderboy if he wants. This moment is when Iris stands up to show confidence in Roy, and he hits a home run for Barney, for Pop, and for the son he has never had. He triumphs miraculously—the ball sails between the pitcher's legs and then climbs—but more important is that Roy offers to sacrifice something of himself for this victory and thereby shows that he could, at least this once and after much stubborn delay, see beyond his king-sized delusion of individual heroism to the king-sized heroism of social duty. Unfortunately, Roy's ego responds more to the home run: saving the little boy also revivifies the little boy in Roy.

These fathers have some good influence on Roy, but their adoption of him has a price: Roy's elimination of any competing "son." When Sam sees the Whammer's frustration, Sam feels ambivalent at best, for along with pride in his "son," he also has pity and respect for the passing hero. With the Knights, Roy's "older brother" is Bump Bailey, the self-absorbed star of the team who never helps the team. The first time Roy hears Bump, he thinks he is hearing the Whammer's voice, and he learns that Bump too attracts Max Mercy's attention. Pressured by Roy's outstanding performance, mostly in practice, Bump finally puts out a real effort—too much effort, in fact, for he chases a ball he cannot catch and dies hitting the outfield wall.

In supplanting these "brothers," Roy takes their place off the field as well as on. His fateful relationship with Harriet does not last long, but in that short time, Roy takes on more of the Whammer's qualities than athletic prowess. The Whammer had been flirting with Harriet, so he strikes out in two senses. Roy shows no more seriousness in his attraction to her. Having sat through her little test, Roy tries another kind of pitch: he puts his arm around her shoulder and, as the train rocks, lets his hand slip onto her breast. It is the kind of thing one might expect from a teenager in the backseat of a car—expect, but not excuse.

As with the test of heroic values, Roy also later fails the test of sexual responsibility. One image neatly sums up his problem. A girl, who earlier promised Roy a kiss for every time he knocked down the pins at a carnival booth, surprises him when she comes to award him kisses for knocking down the Whammer; he tries to avoid her, but she pays her debt enthusiastically while he looks past her to see Harriet staring at him. With Memo and Iris, Roy again will find himself kissing one woman while looking at another.

Memo, like Harriet before her, is part of what the defeated "brother" leaves to the conquering Roy. He has an ironically insatiable desire for her: having had her one night, owing to one of Bump's pranks, he vainly pursues her thereafter even up to the brink of ruin. Also like Harriet, Memo represents temptations Roy should resist. The lure of sex without love overpowers him even though she tells him quite plainly, "I'm strictly a dead man's girl" (94). Roy, however, thinks that he can make her forget Bump just as he has made the fans forget him.

Instead, he forgets himself. Memo's life sounds much like Roy's in many respects. When he manages to get her away for a nighttime ride to the beach—but settles for a talk beside a polluted stream—he learns that she too was deserted by her father when she was young; that she went to Hollywood as a teenager to pursue the dream of stardom; that the dream failed; and that she wound up with a substitute father in Gus Sands, the bookie—"Oh, he's just like a daddy to me" (119). Her failure as an actress, she explains, came about because "I knew what I was supposed to do but I couldn't make myself, in my thoughts, into somebody else" (120). Roy wants to tell her his sad story, but does not. More important, he does not see how her situation resembles his, especially in his vain effort to be someone he is not. At this moment, for instance, he tries to replace Bump. He kisses her and, as with Harriet, grabs her breast, only to be told that it hurts because it is "sick" (122).

Sick or not, it is the breast Roy wants, and Memo lures him further from himself with her body as the prize. When the Knights are within one game of winning the pennant, Memo throws an early celebration, promises to sleep with Roy, and then makes sure the team eats and drinks too much—all presumably at the behest of Gus, who wants to insure his bet against the team. Roy could lead the team away from this feast, but he "couldn't walk out on Memo" (183). She puts him off, though, by arousing his other appetite, that for food, and a bellyache lands him in a hospital bed rather than Memo's. Thus weakened, the renewed temptation of possessing Memo can yet make him forget his biggest dreams of triumph: he accepts a bribe not to hit in the playoff game because he wants enough money to win Memo as much as he wants to be a pennant-winning hero.

Roy has quite an inner conflict here. As mentioned before, he wants to replace Bump on the team and lead them to a pennant— for Pop, in part, but more for his own glory. He also wants to replace Bump and lead Memo to some wistful return to home:

> Sometimes seeing her in a house they had bought, with a redheaded baby on her lap, and himself going fishing in a way that made it satisfying to fish, knowing that everything was all right behind him, and the home-cooked meal would be hot and plentiful, and the kid would carry the name of Roy Hobbs into generations his old man would never know. (179)

On Memo's side are the blandishments of Gus and Judge Goodwill Banner, the team owner who will take over Pop's share of the team unless the Knights win the pennant.

With Gus, Roy has engaged in big and little gambles—the guessing games at the nightclub and the crap shoot at Memo's apartment—and learned the ebb and flow of luck that resembles the coming and going of batting slumps. Gus even tells him, "Once in a Series game I bet a hundred grand on three pitched balls," which, except for the amount, is the same bet Roy won for Sam; Gus lost that bet, but adds, "The next week I ruined the guy in a different deal" (108). With the judge, Roy also receives lessons for life. Although the cheap owner wants only to avoid raising his new star's salary—he even convinces Roy that the team has money due for expenses on Roy's behalf—the judge counsels him wisely: "What I am saying is that emphasis upon money will pervert your values. . . . Avoid gambling like a plague. . . . And stay away from loose ladies" (99, 101). All these lessons seem especially apt when Roy finds himself in the hospital with the judge's offer of a bribe to fail at the plate. The doctor has told him that his old bullet wound will prevent his playing any more: like Gus's opponent, Roy won a bet on three pitches, but now one of the consequences from a loose lady-cannon may ruin his hopes. Playing the odds, Roy cuts his losses: he can abandon the dream of selfish glory, and yet have the money to win another loose lady if he will only sell out his team.

To ward off this temptation of winning Memo by losing the game, Roy has tangibly little help. Sam comes to him in a dream and advises, "Don't do it" (196). Neither his teammates nor Pop comes to see him in the hospital. From Iris, Roy has a letter he has delayed reading. He was about to read it when he received Memo's invitation to the party; in the hospital, he is again about to read it when Memo comes in to make plain her needs and the possible way Roy may fulfill them. Only after he has accepted the judge's deal does Roy read the letter and learn in detail of Iris's early motherhood and years of self-denial, the consequences of her own unfortunate relationship with a stranger. Her life, like Memo's, parallels Roy's. The lesson Memo draws from her life— her mother's hard life and her own hard luck in her profession—is the need for financial independence: "I made up my mind to have certain things" (200). But Iris draws a different lesson, as she tells Roy beside the lake: "We have two lives, Roy, the life we learn with and the life we live after that. Suffering is what brings us toward happiness" (158). The letter recounts her own journey toward happiness through suffering, but Roy has already accepted Memo's lesson "to have certain things."

Fortunately for Roy, his decision is not final; unfortunately, his change of heart is too late to win him everything he wants. Surrounded, as Roy is, by people with pasts as haunted as his own, he must learn to measure his own life against the lives of these others. Most point him in the direction of accepting less in life, but he always ducks the responsibility. After his shooting, the fact that he has Sam's wallet providentially keeps his name out of the papers. Despite Pop's humbler goals, Roy tosses them aside to show off, chase Memo, and regret it all later. And even after Iris's trusting display of vulnerability, he practically forces himself on her, recalling the event as "banging her" (187); she even tries to ask first whether he is wearing protection, but he carelessly pushes her down and continues his notion of making love. They conceive a child that night, and it becomes a responsibility Roy must accept, but he cannot have this family and this loving woman along with the glorious heroism he has dreamed of for so long.

Roy learns from the past when the past forces itself upon him. With so much that he wants to hide, Roy often has the feeling of being followed, and his biggest follower in this sense is Max Mercy. Max thinks that he should remember Roy, and he feels insulted at not being privy to Roy's life. He offers Roy money for an exclusive and warns, "You're a public figure. You got to give the fans something once in a while to keep up their good will to you" (103–4). The advice is self-serving, but it is correct as well. Only briefly, for the Barney boy, does Roy give something of himself. The rest of the time, Roy hides from himself—the man of slumps and lost potential. In his last time at bat, when he wants to win, not for himself, but for Pop and Iris and the baby, he cannot be someone other than that man. He has hit some fouls at Otto P. Zipp, the one fan who cannot forgive Roy's part in Bump's death, and accidentally hits Iris; all he has left then is a massive shot that goes foul and splinters Wonderboy. A young farmboy, Herman Youngberry, comes out of the bullpen and strikes out the game's best slugger. Youngberry should follow Roy in history, but Mercy's following Roy's story results in scandal and the banishment of Roy from that history.

In baseball and the novel, however, Roy has two strikes; there are three. Failing to hit a home run allows Roy a chance to succeed at something more important. With Harriet and Memo, he has swung and missed twice when his lust made him chase bad pitches. He may turn to Iris to avoid striking out forever, and we can rest assured that he has learned her lesson: he has lived his life of learning and suffering, so now he may live the rest of life after that. First, he returns Wonderboy to the earth by burying it in the stadium. Then, he returns the bribe money to the judge, and he gets out of a slump of sorts by hitting him and Gus; Memo tries to shoot him, but this time he is only grazed. He can leave them, knowing "I never did learn anything out of my past life, now I have to suffer again" (236). We last see him weeping "many bitter tears" (237), but he will no longer be followed, he will no longer be tempted by selfish success, and he will no longer have anyone between him and Iris. He is "wild with love for her and the child" (225), rather than wild with the immature self-absorption of record-breaking achievements. Roy has to be expelled from the mythic world of baseball glory, but now he can live without that glory. The boy at the end pleads, "Say it ain't true, Roy" (237), and about heroism detached from social responsibility, Roy could say exactly that.

In the movie, Roy could say the same thing, but why would anybody ask? Putting aside Malamud's examination of heroism that distinguishes false from worthy myths, "The filmmakers simply bought the myths ... and threw the flag, mother and the old farm, literally, into the deal."[15] Even some of the film's admirers must admit its over-the-top sunniness. *Newsweek*'s David Ansen, in a review accompanying a glowing cover story on Robert Redford's career, excuses the film's departure from the novel's ending: "One can safely say that if the filmmakers had presented 1984 audiences with Malamud's downbeat ending, a lot of popcorn would have been hurled at the screen"; he adds, however, that the writers "might have made Hobbs a touch less pure and more susceptible to money: heroic figures are even more heroic when they overcome temptation."[16] The problem with this mild assessment is that—aside from the condescension to the audience—the novel's ending is not so downbeat: Roy has, after all, overcome temptation and become a better man. Without that temptation, the plot lacks serious conflict. Rather than an education plot of character, the film portrays a simple action plot of fortune: we wonder whether the good but occasionally naive Roy will make the team and then lead them to the pennant. Any outcome other than resounding success would strike us as pathetic. Under the circumstances, no one would hurl popcorn at the screen because too much of it is already up there.

As in the novel, Roy acts naively, even somewhat clumsily, as a young man who has a chance to play for the Cubs. His conversation with Harriet, after striking out the Whammer, contains much of the same immature boastfulness. She again makes mythic allusions, comparing his victory to "Sir Lancelot jousting Sir Turquoin—or was it Maldemer," and he again sits uncomfortably, wondering what she is talking about. When he brags, "I'm gonna break every record in the book. . . . When I walk down the street, people'll look at me and say, 'There goes Roy Hobbs, the best there ever was,'" she asks whether he wants something more, and he again fails to comprehend what else he could want. Of course, he may want her; at this point in their conversation, he leans close to her as if to kiss her, but this Roy would never grab her breast. Harriet asks, "Do you have a girl?" and he looks down shyly. She then gets up to go, and rather than pursue her—let alone molest her—Roy asks, "Would you come watch me play sometime?" Roy's immaturity recalls a little boy's more than an adolescent's.

Years later, after sitting out of baseball following his shooting at the hands of Harriet (who must be even nastier and crazier to pick on such a lad), Roy retains his boyish charm, but not the childish attitude. Called in to meet the judge, Roy does not enter with demands for more pay, nor leave with more debts. With no embarrassment, Roy asks the judge to explain what he means by "canard" and "prevarication." To the offer of more money, Roy responds, "You wanna pay me more money, that's up to you," and then, striding in to a close shot, asserts, "Well, let me put it to you this way: there's no way I'm gonna let you steal this club from Pop." As he leaves, Roy mischievously switches on the lights.

Roy is innocent, not only in the sense of "naive," but of "guiltless" as well. He may feel a little shame over the incident with Harriet: late in the film, he tells Iris he should have been able to "see it comin'," but he seems to accept her reasoning, "You were so young." More important, though, is that Roy feels no need to hide from himself or to run from whatever is following him. Although Max Mercy does not recognize him at first, with no mix-up about Sam Simpson's wallet, Max soon recalls Roy and his feat. Thereafter, Max's desire to dig up some dirt on Roy has little to do with Roy's character and much to do with the question of whether bad men will thwart Roy's heroism. Given Roy's character of goodness, that question cannot trouble us long.

Notwithstanding Harriet's remark about jousting, Roy's strengths belong to him; they are not on loan from the gods. His powers are mythic, but the myth is not Homeric or Arthurian. Levinson uses no steeds or shining armor. Roy's story is, more simply, the myth of good over evil, here with a smattering of baseball lore. What Levinson does have at his disposal includes plenty of backlight, lightning, slow motion, and swelling music to underline Roy's heroic achievements. Even before Roy gets on the train, we see him in the "best light." On the night he learns he will get a tryout with the Cubs, he runs to call Iris outside (for here she is a childhood sweetheart). Silhouetted against the soft night sky in an open field, he promises her that he will give his very best. They run into a barn, and in a shaft of moonlight he promises to send for her and kisses her; she leads him by the hand out of that light, telling him, "It's all right," and the screen fades to black as they go to make love. The strength of Roy's figure against the sky and the blessing of light from on high reinforce his inbred values associated with home, the farm, and the good woman left behind.

Then, in the film's best sequence when Roy strikes out the Whammer, the cast of light tells us all we need to know of Roy's power. As the contenders take their places, the sun is setting behind the Whammer, just as it is setting on his career. Roy peers in, the evening light on him full and golden. He throws the third strike, in slow motion, into that light, but just prior to the pitch, shot from a low angle slightly behind Roy, we see Roy lean in and block that red sun out. Thus, Roy eclipses the Whammer.

His victory is short-lived again, for when he answers Harriet's summons to her room, he sees her dark figure against the harsh backlight of the hotel window, but this contest does not involve his talents; now he is the one brought down in slow motion. Nevertheless, such darkness cannot keep Roy. When the story moves ahead to his joining the Knights, Roy walks out of a dark tunnel into the light of Knights Field; in the locker room, as the equipment manager suits him up, Roy has a light behind him that gives him a halo. Later, as noted above, Roy will bring light into the judge's office, and when Roy slumps at the plate, an angel of light visits him in the form of Iris: with a broad-brimmed, white hat that catches a shaft of light in a halo about her head, Iris rises in the stands and inspires Roy to smash a pitch right through the clock in Wrigley Field. Chicago had been the place where Harriet brought time to a stop for him, and now it is where a celestial light returns him his strength and his childhood sweetheart—in a sense, returns his past, that time lost. His conflict with the judge, Gus, and Memo continues, but with Iris back, Roy never really gives us cause to worry. The final triumph, then, comes when he bats in the last inning in the last game with the pennant on the line. Both Roy and the pitcher, shot in low angles, have the stadium lights over their shoulders. With no sun to eclipse, Roy hits a tremendous home run into the lights, shorting them out and causing a rain of sparks: that is, facing the Pirates and the "pirates" who would steal the team, he puts their lights out.

A bolt of lightning heralds this hyperbolic moment, just as it had his first home run. Levinson toys with the supernatural only a bit, though: Roy's bat, Wonderboy, comes from a tree struck by lightning, and that lightning stays in Roy's bat. Rather than supernatural myth, Levinson develops the sports-celebrity myth. Thus, after Roy's first miraculous home run, Levinson takes us from the field to the tunnel beneath the stands, cutting on the flash of a photographer's flashbulb: reporters are mobbing Pop and Roy, asking about the new star. Newspaper and radio reports catch Iris's attention and bring her out to see Roy in Chicago when he hits the clock; there again, after crossing the plate, he goes toward the stands to see her, but several flashbulbs, seen in extreme close-up, punctuate the scene and blind him. These flash photographs can bring him down as well as build him up, however. At the nightclub where Roy meets Gus, his move to the dance floor with Memo is accomplished with another cut on a photographer's flashbulb. Soon, Roy's relationship with Memo develops in a montage of flashbulbs and society page pictures; a sports page headline calls him a "Flash in Pan," and the montage ends with a fading, burnt bulb. The slump that comes with Memo does not last, of course, for the road trip to Chicago will bring Roy to Iris; the flashbulbs will be on the field, not off; and Roy will eventually smash all the lights and retire triumphantly.

Supporting these miniature lightning bolts from photographers are other media to build Roy's sports legend. In homage to older sports films—but also to move the story along—Levinson employs many inserts of headlines telling us the Knights are slumping or Hobbs is leading them toward first place. A few times he includes black and white newsreels marking important points in Roy's ascent. The most notable medium, however, is the radio. Kevin Thomas Curtin argues that the frequent voice-over of the radio announcer "clearly acknowledges the added power that infuses mythic presentation from an oral commentary." The Homeric parallels that Curtin develops seem unconvincing to me, but the association between great moments in sports and the sound of their reporting strikes me as a perceptive insight. As Curtin points out, when Iris overhears two men arguing whether Roy's sudden emergence is for real, the believer does not care for any skeptical analysis, for he knows what he *heard* on the radio.[17] Such broadcasts, if we cannot believe our eyes, confirm Roy's heroic feats, and each viewer shelves them in an audio library of similar moments.

Of course, the radio also refers us to an era before television and fat contracts, a simpler time of supposedly stronger values. This story is set in that time, and these values guide Roy throughout the film, not just at the end, as in the novel. Thus, if the novel's Roy struggles to be a worthy son to various "stepfathers," the film's Roy has a good father and remains true to him and to later spiritual fathers. In the early flashback, we see Roy learning the game from his father: slow-motion catches in golden fields as a cute, red-haired girl looks on (she turns out to be Iris). His father tells him, "Ya got a gift, Roy, but it's not enough. Ya gotta develop yourself. Rely too much on your own gift, and you'll fail." Death takes this wise counsel away when Roy's father collapses and dies beneath a tree, but something of its wisdom remains: the night of his father's death, lightning strikes the same tree while Roy watches; he sees the glowing wood and fashions Wonderboy from it. Roy must remember his father's lesson when he gets the call from the Cubs, for he cautions Iris, "They're lookin' at a lotta guys." Later, with Harriet, he will show a little more cockiness, but we see that he begins with his values firmly rooted in home and family.

Roy's relationship to Sam remains much as it was in the novel. In regard to Roy's place among the Knights, Pop shares some spiritual fatherhood with Red, whose role grows to accommodate Richard Farnsworth's casting. (And, to provide some of the film's better lines, as when two hapless Knights bungle a double steal by both showing up at second base: Red allows it was "kind of a bad play there.") Roy's efforts to please Pop, though, remain free of much distraction by other desires. In his hospital bed near the end, Roy fears that he has let people down rather than considers how best to sell them out. Talking with Iris, he says, "I wish Dad coulda—. God, I love baseball." He needs no more reminding, and instead of Pop's almost pleading for his return, Roy goes to him. Pop is reminiscing in the locker room with Red, about how his mother wanted him to be a farmer, when Roy comes in and says, "My Dad wanted me to be a baseball player." Pop answers, "Well, you're better 'n anyone I ever had," and Roy is ready to suit up and win.

If Roy acts like a good son, he also stands as a good father. Unlike the novel's Roy, who feared the responsibility of adulthood, the film's Roy shows a natural, if you will, affection for kids. In this version, after striking out the Whammer, we see no kissing one woman while looking at another. On the contrary, we see Roy running to get back on the train and being chased by a boy who has been holding his jacket and wants to know his name; Roy tells him his name and then tosses him the ball as a souvenir. Throughout, Roy's triumphs and slumps take place mostly in the eyes of young boys, whose faces we see in several inserts. To underline the point, Levinson includes a newsreel called "Roy Hobbs: Baseball's Oldest Rookie Hero to Young." Therein, he tells the gathered youngsters that, to play the game, "you have to have a lot of little boy in ya"; despite the era—or in a nod to our own sensibilities—he also tousles the hair of a little girl as if to encourage her to play as well.

With such a noble stature, Roy would not agonize over hitting a home run for a sick boy, so the film deletes that episode. Doing good for kids would be an everyday feat for this Roy, and his treatment of Bobby Savoy, the batboy, shows as much. Bobby is not sick, but he certainly is shy and overweight. When he admires Roy's bat, Roy tells him to get a piece of wood and they will make him a bat too. In the final contest, after Roy splinters Wonderboy, Bobby brings him his bat, the "Savoy Special," and with it Roy hits the winning shot. Roy hits all his home runs for all the kids.

This fatherly attitude affects the other players as well. Although in the novel the team plays better with Roy, they are merely hanging on to his talent, suspicious of his selfishness; here the team plays better because he brings out the best in them—that is, the little boy in them. After witnessing Roy's first big hit, Olsen admires the engraved lightning bolt on Wonderboy and remembers, "When I was a kid, my father gave me his collection of squadron insignias, the kind flying aces used to wear. It reminds me of that." The next day, Olsen is wearing a lightning patch on his uniform sleeve, and his bat comes to life—much to the surprise of everyone watching. This entire team comes to see Roy in the hospital because he has made them an extended family: the players are all brothers, sons of Pop and fathers of Bobby.

Roy would never let this family down, so the judge's only leverage with him is to threaten Roy's "sons." The judge confronts Roy in the hospital with photos Max has unearthed from the incident with Harriet. This "nasty business" at first seems only a potential embarrassment to Roy, but when the judge adds, "Oh, ho, Mr. Hobbs, if kids should see this—" Roy reacts with shock. Roy makes no explicit deal with the judge, but the threat adds to the despair of learning that the same wound will prevent his playing anymore. Iris brings him out of it by reminding him, "Think of all those, all those young boys you've influenced. There's so many of them." Here is where Roy thinks of his own father and decides to go on. If he needs more encouragement, Iris has a trump card: a note she sends to Roy in the dugout tells him her son is his son from that night years ago. With a home and family already secured, Roy cannot be tempted by money or Memo. The only question is how far the winning shot will fly.

Further lessening the drama, aside from Roy's golden goodness, is the relative weakness of his adversaries and temptations. Bump, for instance, remains a selfish character, but otherwise more ridiculous than cruel. He does not trick Roy into bed with Memo nor make other crude, sexual jokes. The exploding cigarette he gives Roy in the novel becomes, in the film, a cigar in his back pocket, which, as he explains to Max, is why he neglected to slide into base on a particularly crucial play. His demise is as clownish as his character: rather than running into the outfield wall, he runs through it, more in the fashion of Daffy Duck than Pete Rieser.

Max Mercy, as I have stated above, acts more as an irritant than as a nemesis. When he first meets the mature Roy, Max fails to recognize him. Later, although he boasts to Roy, "I got a terrific memory," he cannot recall the contest with the Whammer until he sees Roy, in practice, blow a pitch by a hitter. Even then, having retrieved his own material on that feat, he, incredibly, cannot put together Roy's past—and without Sam's wallet to cause Roy's misidentification, Max could hardly have failed to hear of the shooting so soon after their first meeting. In terms of the drama, this lapse may not matter much: if the past does not haunt Roy, its discovery cannot cause any real harm. Max hangs on to look for embarrassing information, but he cannot threaten Roy with anything Roy fears in himself.

Likewise, Gus and the judge have little to offer that would seriously tempt Roy. The scene in the judge's office shows Roy's confident honesty, and Gus, having spied on the encounter, says, "He's not as greedy as Bump. He'll be hard to work with, but we'll get him." However, he immediately fails to get any other reaction from Roy. At the nightclub, although the conversation and betting tricks are similar (if less mean on Roy's part), Roy does feel foolish in this version. Thus, when Gus waves off Roy's debt saying, "Someday you'll maybe do me a favor," Roy forthrightly answers, "Don't bet on it," much to Gus's evident surprise. He fails again at the premature celebration in Memo's apartment; unable to tempt Roy with money or Memo or any other appetite, he resorts to having Memo slip Roy something to make him sick. When the judge cannot take advantage of Roy's apparent weakness in the hospital, they can only sit back and watch Roy triumph over his injury, not struggle with his conscience. In fact, Roy visits them *before* the game in order to reaffirm his honesty. Gus, trying to intimidate him, says, "You're yesterday's news, kid. You had a great gift, a talent, but it's not enough." Of course, Gus only reminds Roy of his father's wisdom, and, rejoined with his team, Roy will have enough.

All of Roy's problems in the novel involve the wrong women, towards whom he gravitates, and in keeping with the dilution of Roy's adversaries, these women pose less of a threat to the film's Roy. Obviously, Harriet still shoots him, thereby making herself a substantial foe. As discussed above, however, she represents less of a sexual temptation to him than she does in the novel. On the train, he wants to kiss her, not paw her. When he goes to her room, rather than finding her, as in the novel, naked but for some transparent lingerie, he sees her dressed in a gown with a prim, black veil (Roy holds family values, and this is a family film). Also, as we learn later, she eventually has the decency to throw herself out the hotel window, apparently finished with her crazy rampage against sports heroes.

Memo, on the other hand, becomes quite sympathetic: unlucky, perhaps too friendly with the wrong crowd, and even worthy to be second choice behind Iris for Roy's woman. She remains attractive to Roy, but he is not sexually obsessive about her. In the novel, his first sight of her is an inadvertent view of her in her underwear through an open door; soon thereafter, Bump tricks them into the same bed for a night. Their first meeting in the film is more a "cute meet" on an elevator that is not moving. Once Bump is gone, she shows real interest in Roy; in fact, he becomes more a worthy goal for her than she becomes an impossible appetite for him.

Even before Bump's death, Memo shows a little desire to get beyond the bad men who keep her. She always sits in the stands with Gus where he can monitor Bump and his bets. From her demeanor, we see she is bored—until Pop replaces Bump in the batting order with Roy. At the nightclub, she roots against Gus as he makes small bets with Roy over how much Roy has in his pockets; she shows anxiety over the outcome, relieved to tell Gus, "You lose," but clearly crestfallen when her quick assumption proves hasty. After she gets Roy alone at the beach (no polluted streams here), she explains the trap she lives in. Her background is unchanged. Her attitude is what seems softer, less cynically materialistic. She tells Roy, "I'm not waiting for true love to come along, Roy. I never have. . . . Bump was swell, real swell, but typical. You're not like him, or anyone else. Gus gives me things, things I've never had in my life. Anything wrong with that?" Unlike her character in the novel, Memo here shows more self-awareness in her defensive confession; her last question indicates that she has yet to fool herself into thinking such acquisitiveness is her only way out.

Noteworthy as well is her perception that Roy has qualities to admire. This Roy certainly is more admirable than the novel's Roy, but Memo's rejection of him in the book shows more cynical manipulation than good judgment. Here, her falling for Roy contributes to our pity for her. The next night, she comes to Roy's room. She says Gus "thought somethin' happened to me last night. It did." She must mean she has fallen in love with Roy, and now, naked underneath, she drops her mink (but the shot is from the waist up and behind—this is a family film) and gives herself to him. The night at the beach and this visit to his room bracket the beginning of Roy's slump, out of which the encounter with Iris brings him. Memo calls Roy, at Gus's behest, to check on him, but she has interests of her own in learning of this other woman. After their unemotional conversation, with Gus listening at her end, she pauses after Roy has hung up and adds, "And I love you too." Gus asks whether she is in control, and, although she answers, "Sure, Gus," she is holding back tears. She shows the same sadness when she watches Roy being carried out of the party. Memo is the character torn between doing the right thing for one she loves or selling out for money, but the film is not about her.

She still brings Roy the offer of a bribe to stay out of the big game. In this case, however, she also feels genuine concern for Roy's well-being. She has heard that he could die if he plays again (the silver bullet has been festering in his stomach all these years, and now his stomach "could easily just blow apart," according to his doctor—a fate that could look even sillier than Bump's). Aside from the money, she pleads that he walk away for her and for his health. Roy cannot accept the terms, of course, and when he comes to the judge's office before the game, she is there also. She picks up a gun from the desk and fires a shot into the floor. Whether she could not bring herself to shoot Roy or herself is unclear. As Roy takes the gun from her, she cries and says, "I hate you." Her tears belie her words, though, and what she hates is herself as Roy has made her come to know herself: a woman who is, in the end, unworthy of Roy.

She must remain unworthy, if pitiful, because Roy already has a woman who is worthy of him. Iris is the woman who has always been near Roy to boost his confidence—not at all like the woman in the novel who makes him question his own cockiness. We see her in the opening scenes watching Roy develop his talent, and when he has doubts that he can make the Cubs, she tells him, "You're gonna make it." Not only does she boost his confidence, but she helps him overcome any genuine shortcoming in his character. He promises to send for her, and, when they meet later in Chicago, Roy must feel some shame for not keeping his word. In the confectionery, over lemonades, they both express surprise that the other has yet to marry, and when she asks, "What happened to you, Roy?" he fidgets and answers, "My life didn't turn out the way I expected." The situation has changed greatly from the novel: there, Roy complains that his "goddamn life" did not turn out as he expected, but the complaint merely earns Iris's curt "Whose does?" (156); and then he coaxes her into going skinny-dipping before making love on the beach. Here, we get no swearing, no sex—and no deservedly curt reply: Iris lets him off the hook by saying she must go.

The next day, his confidence and talent fully restored (he hits four homers in one game), the time is better, and he can tell Iris what happened with Harriet. When their long conversation brings them to her apartment, Iris offers hints of the life he can still have with her, but she does not push him. He learns that she has kept the farm and says, "Good. It's home." He learns that she has a son (no daughter, let alone a grandchild), and she gently lets Roy avoid learning too much: "His father lives in New York. . . . But I've been thinking that he needs his father now." They embrace briefly, and she encourages him to catch his train. He, of course, is the father, but Iris will not impose such a distraction on Roy.

She continues to protect him in the hospital. Fully aware of the event and the material in Max's hands, Iris brings Roy excuses: "How could you possibly know she'd hurt you, or how could anyone? . . . You were so young." When Roy changes to bemoaning his lost potential for records and fame, she offers comfort: "You know, I believe we have two lives. . . . The life we learn with and the life we live with after that. With or without the records, they'll remember you. Think of all those, all those young boys you've influenced." The proverbial lesson is the same one Iris delivered in the novel. Here, though, Roy already knows the truth of her words, for he has been living by them. He does not need to hear them in order to see how he has been selfish with his talents; this Roy needs to hear them only to overcome the brief despair that he may be unable to use his talents in a good cause.

Roy learns of his son, wins that good cause, and returns to his home. We see the ball he hit continue its flight into the stars and, in a match cut, seemingly come down in the glove of his son. He and Roy are playing catch in the golden wheat fields of the farm— just as Roy and his father played in the film's early flashback— and nearby, in a cotton dress, stands Iris, watching and looking satisfied—just as she had done as a girl. This character must strike some as impossibly saintly. Even Glenn Close says of her character, "I like my role in *The Natural* . . . but in a way I'm just a fantasy figure for the Redford character"; further into the interview, she becomes more blunt in her assessment of Levinson's use of her character, stating, "I've felt very insecure throughout the entire filming, insecure and manipulated."[18] Roy's character, however, is almost as saintly, so this plot has no need of an Iris who will challenge him to be better; she merely must be there when he needs a little boost.

In the end, although the climactic home run may feel wonderful to the audience, they too are manipulated. The scene is spectacular and the outcome of the game is satisfying, but nothing important has been accomplished. Roy's triumph comes over weak, even silly adversaries. His character is too good to be seriously tempted by the venal blandishments they offer, or seriously intimidated by the slight threats they hold. Relative to Roy's character, what is the significance of the Whammer? or Harriet? or Bump? or Memo? In the novel, each holds up a mirror to Roy, and Roy always refuses to see himself until too late; his failure, at the end, to hit the game-winning home run fortunately allows him to face himself and turn out better. In the film, each represents only an occasion to do well or to be briefly frustrated; his final home run means only that he finally does well. Good for him. But Roy can hardly be said to be saved by this triumph, and even the game does not matter that much, in the grand scheme of things (Levinson conveniently forgets that, having won the pennant, the Knights must play the World Series).

Moreover, no one can say that these changes have anything to do with the translation from page to screen. The heroic imagery would have required a properly measured tone, but many of the metaphors in the novel do not require our acceptance of their literal truth—the problem that Bluestone thinks renders such tropes "absurd."[19] Thus, one could easily imagine point-of-view shots that would have conveyed supernatural images; for instance, such shots could show the Whammer's view of Roy's pitch as "a meteor" (30), Vogelman's fearful perception of Roy as a knight "in full armor, mounted on a black charger" (231), and Roy's haunted sight of Youngberry on the mound in a fog "full of old ghosts and snowy scenes" (233). These and a few other special effects could work, for if the filmmakers adopted such a concept of the story, the film would not have to translate every image in order to preserve the function of that imagery—to refer us to other heroic characters and feats for comparison, not to be accepted literally.

Obviously, the nastier language, the sexual activity, and the anti-heroic hero all comprise narrative elements, not style. The move to clean up these elements puts these filmmakers in the company of many who went before, but the move reflects no necessary alteration in bringing a novel to the screen. Bluestone states that the contrary forces of art and commerce lead to compromises in filmmaking where, "more than in any of the other arts, the signature of social forces is evident in the final work."[20] These forces, however, have no theoretical necessity—especially now that controversial subjects and characters have become commonplace.

Some could argue that the film is simply another work that should not be held accountable to the original novel. This argument, however, would allow the filmmakers to get away with condescending to the audience. The two works share several plot details, but the filmmakers clearly make deliberate changes. We can look at the same source, the novel, that they began with, and we can fairly judge whether the deliberate alterations result in a more or less powerful effect or whether the versions can be seen as equally powerful in different ways. On the one hand, we have a story of a talented boy finally learning to live as a man, after several strong temptations to sell out, for the sake of values that are superior to those that obsession with his talent can bring him; on the other hand, we have a good, talented man recovering from one serious setback to use his talents to defeat bad people. The dramatic diminution of the latter strikes me as obvious. Any challenging plot and characterization must go the way of the mythic allusions: onto the cutting room floor with everything else thought to be "too much" for a "mass audience."

The diminution of the drama in this adaptation may be summed up in the different image patterns that occur in the novel and film. The former uses trains often, not just as a location of action or means of transportation, but as an image of Roy's inner conflict: train imagery describes both the fears he runs from—

"Then he felt he was heading into a place he did not want to go . . . and it went on, a roaring locomotive now" (64)—and the ambitions he vainly runs after—"in his dreams he still sped over endless miles of monotonous rail toward something he desperately wanted" (91). Roy is a driven man until he can face those fears and let go of those selfish ambitions. At the end, another train is starting up in his insides, but we can be satisfied that Roy will be able to get off rather than hang on.

The film, on the other hand, uses elevators as a recurring means of movement. A couple of assignations begin with the opening of elevator doors, and Roy meets Memo on an elevator. There, his unease at being stuck in it with a pretty lady must have something to do with his memory of Harriet: as he tells Red, he is "just not used to hotels." More appropriately, though, the image fits the movement of the plot: we see Roy through his ups and downs. Instead of power and drive, we get the call, "Going up." As for the dramatic possibilities in the novel, they are "going, going, gone!"

Why? The Case of *Looking for Mr. Goodbar*

> Among those whose reputation is exhausted in a short time by its own luxuriance, are the writers who take advantage of present incidents or characters which strongly interest the passions, and engage universal attention. It is not difficult to obtain readers, when we discuss a question which every one is desirous to understand.... To the quick circulation of such productions all the motives of interest and vanity concur, the disputant enlarges his knowledge, the zealot animates his passion, and every man is desirous to inform himself concerning affairs so vehemently agitated and variously represented.
>
> —Samuel Johnson, *The Rambler*, No. 106

> It would be easy enough to say any one of a lot of things about Gloria, and many things were said. It could be said that she was a person who in various ways—some of them peculiar—had the ability to help other people, but lacked the ability to help herself. Someone could write a novel about Gloria without ever going very far from this thesis. It was, of course, the work of a few minutes for the 1931 editorial writers ... to find in Gloria a symbol of modern youth.... There can be no symbol of modern youth any more than there can be symbol of modern middle age, and anyway symbol is a misnomer.
>
> —John O'Hara, *Butterfield 8*

On 5 January 1973, three days after the fact, New York city newspapers reported the murder of Roseann Quinn, twenty-eight, a dedicated and well-loved teacher at St. Joseph's School for the Deaf. The article in the *Times* included the conventionally fuzzy photograph of the victim, but as the story developed, a picture of Roseann Quinn's sad life became sharper. From an Irish-Catholic family, she had had polio as a child, which in turn led to scoliosis

101

and, finally, a slight limp that lasted all her life. When found, she had been stabbed eighteen times, sexually mutilated, and left with the sculptured bust of a woman perched on her face. The reportedly casual nature of her relationships with men and the supposedly attendant dangers of such a "lifestyle" quickly became the focus of much sordid interest in the crime. Luckily for the police, who had few clues, an informant led them to the murderer, a homosexual she picked up in a bar.[1]

Judith Rossner attempts to answer some of the questions raised by such a case in her novel *Looking for Mr. Goodbar*. The novel became a bestseller, and several reviews added critical praise to the book's popularity, but this success notwithstanding, I do not think the novel rewards our attention. *Looking for Mr. Goodbar* narrates several years in its heroine's life, and one need not be aware of Roseann Quinn, let alone be curious about her life and death, to feel that we learn too little about Rossner's fictional heroine to understand that life. We get characters who are too schematically drawn and actions that are too cursorily motivated. Aside from the sad pattern of events leading to the murder, the book attempts to tell us what such a crime says about our society. The answer, that women are victims, should not seem so unconvincing, even uninteresting: the issue suffers in its simplified and reductive portrayal in the novel.[2]

The question then becomes why anybody would wish to base a film on such a trite work. (Some might answer money: it is a truth universally acknowledged that a fiction writer in possession of a popular novel must be in want of a film deal.) In this instance, Richard Brooks must have seen more in the novel than I do, for he adapted it for the screen and directed it.[3] The novel's innocent heroine does encounter various revolutionary ideas, but Rossner uses these causes mostly for markers to date the book, concentrating instead on a rather incredible drama of the sexual revolution. Brooks exploits the same topics without discovering any more of value than Rossner has. That is to say, Brooks has made a faithful adaptation of Rossner's novel, and his fidelity has been wasted on a weak novel. In this instance, unless the bottom line is the bottom line, Brooks simply must see a veritable conflagration of social issues where I see a flame that is hardly worth the candle.

To give Rossner her due, her story of the pathetic Theresa Dunn (the name given to her heroine/victim) contains some naturalistic touches that can arrest the reader with a depressing recognition of something squalid or hateful beneath the surface of everyday actions or conversations. The murderer's confession, which precedes the novel's action, captures the rage of a killer in his own words, and it sets the stylistic tone for much else said by or to Theresa. Caroline Blackwood, on the astringency of such talk, comments that Rossner "has a very good ear for 'awful' conversation, for indicating how throwaway, breezy, slangy remarks can have a much crueler, more lethal effect, and show up much more of the speaker's personality, than the speaker ever intended."[4]

In this confession, Gary Cooper White (a movie star's name echoing that of John Wayne Wilson, the actual killer) recounts an affront at the hands of Theresa; she has put him on the defensive by picking on his southern accent and questioning his sexuality, yet, even after he has been, in his crude terms, "balling her," she is throwing him out. He thinks he has done something wrong until she explains, "Because you ain't sleeping here."[5] White, rather dull witted, obviously feels insecure around Theresa, and when she is not very direct with him, he gets confused. Defensive, rude, confused—these terms sum up his state of mind during and after the crime. In a preface to the confession, the narrator remarks that White clearly thought of himself "as the victim of the woman he had murdered."

Rossner's style lets us hear such desperation in several other "awful" conversations. Verbal barbs make for figurative victims. Martin Engle, Theresa's English teacher, flays her with small talk when she goes to work for him, small talk calculated to enlarge himself. Because Theresa has an obvious crush on him, his exploitation of her discomfort shows simple meanness, especially when he insensitively inquires about her limp. Rossner brings out Theresa's "overwhelmed" state of mind in the rush of clauses asserting the unreality and impossibility of the scene: "'I don't limp,' she finally said, except that her voice came out in a whisper" (48–49). Moreover, this style recalls the confession: both "victims" feel uneasy, confused, and so shocked they nearly cannot find words to recover themselves. Theresa does not lash out at Engle in rage, as White does at her, but in both instances words prove to be as destructive, in their way, as any weapon that may come to hand.

If Theresa does not kill Engle, she does learn the martial arts that pass for conversation in this novel. Theresa's first date with James Morrisey contrasts with her first day of work, for now she is the one who comes armed. Once again, small talk has the purpose of belittling another, but James is not a stationary target; he deflects her thrusts and even tries to lighten the mood with a joke. Theresa will not relent, however, and has one blow strike her on the rebound when she petulantly asks if she needs to change clothes before going to a restaurant and he replies:

> "Why would the way *you* dress embarrass *me*?"
> She was embarrassed herself now, of course. (167)

Such language makes Theresa a victim in two ways. Obviously, her own attacks ricochet and hit her just as painfully as anything inflicted by Engle. More subtle and terrible, her character comes to relish the combat: Engle hurts her, and she learns to hurt others by imitation. James will not join the fight, but Theresa will later push another antagonist, White, too hard. White therefore can claim to be the victim, and Theresa thereby brings about her own death: the ultimate victim who is cut figuratively and then literally. Rossner's language in these conversations truly cuts both ways, but the unkindest cut is for the woman.

Congruent with this verbal warfare is the sexual battle. Engle takes advantage of Theresa's infatuation sexually as well as verbally, joining the two prongs of his attack in his avowal that "he always disliked women after fucking them" (70). As for James, he avoids contact sporting, but when he does make love with Theresa, he puts on a prophylactic shield. For Theresa, the abuse has virtually the same results: psychological or physical pain. Otherwise, she has her sparring partners in one-night stands, weekend flings, and, her favorite, the furious affair with Tony Lopanto.

This thematic congruency does not, unfortunately, extend to the style. One reviewer has written that the novel "lets you read some pretty hot descriptions of sex with a good conscience and for the sake of the psychological insights."[6] But clichés intrude: "loosely entwined" bodies at an orgy (87), or Tony's frenetic sexuality completed when he "moaned with pleasure" (158). Such entwining and moaning offer little heat and less insight. Furthermore (and not to be too prudish), not every detail of every act Theresa performs matters to our understanding of her mind.[7]

In the prefatory "About the Confession," Rossner uses an editorially omniscient narrator, who addresses the reader directly to explain why this story needs to be told: "[Gary White] seemed to think that almost anyone in the same situation would have committed the same murder" (1). Placement of this preface and the confession before Theresa's story immediately erases suspense about its outcome and thereby focuses our attention on those circumstances leading to the crime. The circumstances, however, involve much more than White's background and the way Theresa treated him. The rest of the preface takes care of the former—his unsettled life, his pregnant wife, his brush with the law in Florida, and his degrading relationship with a homosexual, George Prince—and his confession takes care of the latter. The narrator, by presenting these two sections, shows how White is made a "victim" (although certainly not to the extent that we would excuse the murder). These sections comprise only a few pages. The rest of the novel delves into the victimization of Theresa: the circumstances that, if understood, would lead us to think that almost anyone in the same situation would have *suffered* the same murder.[8]

If the style suffers from some strained imagery, the form fails as a whole because of its central image: the scar of sex. Rossner writes of the ultimate victimization of women, particularly poor Theresa, and the action of the plot depicts Theresa's pathetic movement through suffering to death. The suffering matters more, for we know about the death early on, and it merely completes the unfortunate pattern of her victimization. "The meeting of murderer and prospective murderee is totally haphazard. Theresa Dunn drifts to her death as joylessly and pointlessly as she has drifted through her life."[9] Theresa's life certainly follows a haphazard and pointless line, but these terms do not explain much by themselves. Norman Friedman writes that a pathetic plot's ability to move us depends on the protagonist's indirectly self-defeating tendencies as well as the degree to which these tendencies are caused by nature or by society: "If it is society, then we are not left with the melancholy satisfaction of that's-the-way-things-are, but rather with a disturbing sense of what's-to-be-done."[10] Accidents of nature and society both cause Theresa's suffering. To find the novel moving, we must believe in these causes. I do not think we believe.

Rossner obviously exploits the fact that the actual Roseann Quinn had polio as a child; in the novel, this accident of nature supposedly explains Theresa's character by the way it changes her personality. We are told that she does not remember having polio, although nature leaves her a cruel reminder: weakened by the disease, her spine slowly becomes curved. Her parents, overwrought at the death of a son, do not notice the curvature when it could easily be treated with a brace, so Theresa must undergo spinal surgery and remain in a cast for over a year. When her parents look at her with guilt, she feels ashamed and confused. Before the surgery, she would not tell anyone of her pain because she thought that the pain was a punishment. Thus, she transforms an accidental physical defect into a reason for her own guilt.

The death of a child causing a parent to ignore another child's disease, the guilt of the parent over that ignorance, and the guilt of the immature child over somehow being responsible for everything—all these are credible human actions. Rossner strains such credibility by making this briefly described guilt the only foundation of Theresa's character. Thus, the night before she starts college, Theresa examines her scar in a mirror: "Now she remembered how for a long time she'd had a sense of it not as a seam in her skin but as a basic part of her. As though the scar itself were her spine, the thing that held her together" (30). A few pages of trauma and resentment of her sisters—Brigid is too athletically active, Katherine too sexually active—establish the basis of Theresa's behavior, but, as one reviewer remarks, "It is not enough. We really know nothing of her."[11]

In the event, Theresa continues to think of herself as a scarred woman and relates to others through pain. When Engle tries to apologize for the remark about her limp, Theresa tells him she would "rather be seduced than comforted" (50). Engle laughs at her here, but later, when he learns of the pain she tries to hide and of her polio and scoliosis, his shock "stirred up something buried way down inside her, that sense of her illness as a badge of shame" (55). He asks to see her scar, for which she must undress, and the seduction is complete. Her backaches go away, but she knows that his interest in her illness is "the way it had begun" (60).

When the affair ends with her graduation, she regards the scar as "just a neat seam where someone had opened her up to get her straightened out" (82). Much later, when Tony sees the scar, she tells him, "I was a hand puppet and that's where they stuck their hands in to make me work" (163). The scar thereby signifies, not only an accident of nature, her disease, but also her sexuality. Theresa feels pain until Engle makes love to her (from behind so that her scar is visible). When she loses Engle, she thinks that he "opened her up" and that his sexual surgery left "her straightened out." As with her disease, Engle's rejection brings shame, and Theresa compensates by seeking out further pain at the hands of unloving men.

Theresa picks at love like a scab, making a healthy relationship impossible. In her own family, Theresa simply resents Brigid's physical vigor. She has sisterly talks with Katherine only when Katherine has had an abortion or when one of them has broken up with a lover, so in a way, they share the same scars: through Katherine, Theresa meets her first one-night stand, visits her first singles bar, and makes her first pick-up; and, tragically, when Katherine has no time for her, Theresa goes out and makes her last pick-up. With her parents, disease becomes the only bond. When her father is operated on for cancer, she makes a rare visit, as he notes. Since disease or pain is required for love, Theresa cannot enjoy the love of her family.

Of course, Theresa could accept James' love, thereby following Brigid's lead more than Katherine's, but she will not allow it. When he proposes, she rejects marriage as something good only for having children, adding that she "can't stand children" (199). However, she loves her nieces and nephews, and as James reminds her, she loves her students. She responds, "Not when they're sick, I don't," and immediately feels she has said "something very important about herself" (199) that she wishes they both had not heard. Theresa puts a quick end to the conversation, however, and the therapeutic self-analysis ends also.

Such an examination of herself cannot get in the way of the plot. Theresa later tries a "consciousness-raising group" and is impressed by one woman's feeling that her appendectomy scar marked her as severely as Theresa's scar marked her. Then she dreams of being strapped to a psychiatrist's couch and hearing a machine tell her, "We're going to straighten you out, Theresa" (259). Her keen sense of the obvious makes her understand that the dream recalls her surgery, and she perhaps sees how she has been trying to escape from the operating table in bed with her lovers. She decides to seek counseling, to get a new apartment, to start a new life for the new year. Then she does not do it. Instead, on New Year's Day, she picks up Gary White, he asks about her limp, they make love, they argue, and he kills her—and "cures" her. On one level, Theresa can come to see that the disease is not her fault, that it is cured, and, therefore, that she put the scar behind her. On another level, to the extent that the scar is her sex, she cannot be healed. Rossner enforces the equation that to be a woman is to bear the scar through which men enter and manipulate her body. One reviewer resents Rossner's theme: "Rossner is no Hawthorne and this is no 'Birthmark.' Rossner seems to imply that Terry is Everywoman, doomed to the singles bar, the one-night stands and the final violence of murder."[12] Rossner strains the disease metaphor, and because of it, the novel limps to its inevitable conclusion.

The equation of Theresa's scar with female sexuality renders the "disease" more a fact of society than an accident of nature. The scar represents oppression, and in Rossner's social scheme, religion represents a chief oppressor. Theresa connects her disease with sin when she tells Engle that she believes the former to be God's punishment for the latter. She goes on to say that she abandoned her faith when she saw other sinners go unpunished, but the connection remains: with Tony, "It was one thing to sin and another to enjoy it so thoroughly" (156).

In fact, Theresa cannot feel pleasures that have no guilt attached. For instance, the sense of goodness she sees in James makes him unattractive to her. Theresa wants a decent and honest lover, but cannot have one because she would foul him with her own sinfulness. One time, she refuses James' help in cleaning up a kitchen mess because, "You look as if you've never gotten dirty or messy or wrinkled or . . . laid" (195). At first, James avers that one could be called worse names than "virgin," but he goes on to confess an affair with a priest in college. Their relationship has no chance now: Theresa is so perverted by her Catholicism as to need guilt to enjoy a lover, but James can never be such a lover because a priest has perverted his masculinity. In sum, religion smothers or perverts innocence; in Theresa's case, religion compounds the shame of her disease since she confounds the scar with her sexuality.[13]

Rossner would have us believe that Theresa has lost her faith and become somewhat cynical, even masochistic, after this loss. But is Theresa all that world-weary? Early on Engle calls her "innocent" (44), and that remark stuns her because she thinks that she is anything but. In fact, the evidence is to the contrary: she does not understand that Engle's "home-rolled" smokes are marijuana; she does not recognize the word "orgasm" and must look it up in a dictionary; and her horrified reaction when Tony introduces her to oral sex shows she had never imagined such acts. Even late in the novel, we have Theresa and Evelyn discussing a women's group that would delve into problems that women may think are personal and emotional—having children, in this instance—but that are really cultural; despite her initial denial, and despite all her experience since, she remains so innocent of the issue's implications that she misses the point.

The issue is not whether to have lovers, husbands, or children, but whether these relationships should define a woman's identity. This confrontation of an innocent with the various revolutions could be interesting. Rossner often refers to a person or idea in relation to "the second half of the twentieth century," and the action of the novel pointedly begins in 1960 and ends on 1 January 1970. However, of all the causes of the 1960s, Rossner focuses on the sexual revolution. As with the issue of religion, the subjects of drugs, politics, consciousness-raising, underground papers, vegetarian diets, and so on all serve as props or simple street signs to mark the way.[14] And the most prominent sign indicates that the sexual revolution is a one-way street.

Innocent Theresa cannot drive down that street, so Rossner has a spare Theresa: a function of the scar that is also a "seam" holding together her two halves. This theme of doubling, not trite in itself, describes the sexual revolution in a schematic and simple fashion. Theresa breaks down into "a Miss Dunn who taught a bunch of children who adored her" and "someone named Terry who whored around in bars when she couldn't sleep at night." She thinks neither would miss the other, but "she herself, Theresa, the person who thought and felt but had no life, would miss either one" (136). Rossner wants us to believe in an overstanding self— the Theresa who combines Miss Dunn and Terry into a character with feelings about whom we will care—but the simple dichotomy holds little interest.

Aside from the naiveté discussed above, Theresa's innocence manifests itself in childish, romantic fantasies. Early dreams develop naturally out of her scoliosis, allowing her to imagine herself "a princess getting tortured in a dungeon" rather than "a crooked little girl being tortured by doctors" (20). No longer a little girl, she fantasizes about being a ballerina, with Engle as the sole and enthusiastic audience. Even after Engle discards her, Theresa pretends that he misses her and is vainly trying to find her. Otherwise, her fantasies again relieve loneliness: "An imaginary lover lay beside her; they seldom spoke, they just made love or were together" (91).

Reading also amused her as a child, and this enjoyment leads to her occupation as Miss Dunn. The very few scenes set in her classroom feel cloying: the children are too open and sweet, and Miss Dunn is too wise and sensitive. Even when a hangover from her other life makes her miss school, Miss Dunn uses the children's resentment and fear to start a discussion that results in a healthy airing of emotions that would make psychiatry an anachronism if it went on. Miss Dunn, therefore, never heard the word "orgasm," still needed an imaginary friend, yet could guide children through any educational or emotional difficulty. What becomes of these qualities in Terry? The simple answer is that the naive, dreamy teacher learns quickly on the real streets.

Her first teacher is, of course, Engle. When Engle tells her that "he always disliked women after fucking them," Theresa is shaken by such a crude reduction of their affair. She remembers this lesson, however, for with Tony, she will not talk to him after sex because "talking was so much more complicated than making love. . . fucking, she should call it, since it was hard to see how anything she did with him could be about love" (162). Now we know where Terry gets her cynicism.

A second "learning experience" comes when Katherine and Brooks introduce her to Carter. Theresa tries drugs for the first time, takes Carter to her apartment, and he becomes her first lover after Engle; however, she never sees him after that evening. Now we know where Terry learned the rules of the one-night stand. Eli offers a supplementary lesson. In this instance, accompanied by Katherine, Terry learns to be a pick-up in a bar. After his long story, Eli takes her to his place and to his bed, but when she is asleep, Eli wakes up the incredulous Terry to take her home. She never sees Eli again either, and now we know how she learned to cruise bars and eject lovers.

Soon after, she takes her final exam: she gets picked up in a bar; lets the man buy her drinks; talks to him sarcastically; takes him back to her apartment; has sex with him; wakes up realizing that "she had to get him out" (134); and sends him packing. She passes the test well—even forgets to get his name—and graduates to James and Tony (with an occasional refresher course over certain nights or weekends).

James and Tony, the source of conflict in the second half of the novel, reflect the simple dichotomies that make up Theresa's life. For her, James—"Every Irish mother's favorite son. Pink, smooth-faced, well shaved. Hairless. Neat as a pin" (142)—is likable enough, but she cannot imagine him as a sexual partner. When she later does have sex with him, he dismays her by wearing a condom. Tony, on the other hand, is a "punk": "Very Italian, with dark hair and dark eyes" (147). With him she enjoys immediate, hyper-active, and vaguely dangerous sex. So, she has a choice between the pale, asexual James and the dark, priapic Tony— between black and white, just like the other good-bad divisions. Even Theresa perceives the starkness of her life's compartments: with James "her whole self had been engaged... except for her sexuality.... While with Tony there was no boundary except around her mind, which was not susceptible to invasion by him" (214). Theresa straddles the life of the mind and the life of the body, joining them only in the seam, the scar that marks women.[15]

Theresa cannot escape the binding dichotomies of sexual oppression—neither in herself or her choice of men—because Rossner makes the dichotomies, no matter how extreme or false, absolute. Even as Theresa finally starts to see herself and her problems clearly, even as she starts to think of changing, her New Year's resolution dissolves in the need "to get laid" (269). Then she rehearses her entire victim's education: she picks up Gary White, talks to him sarcastically, takes him home for sex, tries to evict him, and, lastly, true to the heritage of the scar, goes under the knife once more.

Even as she gets into her deathbed, Theresa is thinking, "I can't believe I'm doing this.... [I]t's someone else" (276). If Theresa's character credibly develops any sense, this death arbitrarily betrays that development. She tells herself, "You couldn't control which men you met, or which ones liked you.... If you drove a car you could make fairly sure that you wouldn't smash into something else, but you could never control whether someone smashed into you" (255–56). Thus, Theresa should not feel impelled to go to the bar and "get laid," should not deliberately "smash into something else." On the other hand, to the extent that she merely represents the false dichotomies of Rossner's sexual theme, the murder works as well as any other ending—and makes as much sense as having her run over by a car.

Rossner has taken the qualities that most provoked curiosity in the Quinn murder case—Irish-Catholic background, childhood disease, beloved schoolteacher, but also swinging single—and given us a morality play of black and white choices: women may choose body or mind, but those who choose body are going to suffer. Since women suffer such oppression by their nature, we are left to think that such is the way things are; and since society, here, so rigidly enforces this oppression, we are further left to think that nothing can be done. But, since the portrayal seems so false, we are left to think that *Looking for Mr. Goodbar* does not really touch on, let alone explain, the life of someone like Roseann Quinn.

At first glance, Brooks's adaptation of *Mr. Goodbar* would seem to confirm several of Lester Asheim's conclusions—conclusions that became the statistical bases of George Bluestone's work. Accordingly, the film version stars an actress, Diane Keaton, who does not look as plain as the novel's descriptions would suggest, compresses the action, eliminates scenes and characters, and straightens the chronology but retains the broad outlines of the plot and characterization.[16] Even so, despite notions that adaptations must be unfaithful to the original novel, Brooks's film, numerous changes and all, finally remains faithful to its source— and therein lies the source of the film's failure.

The infidelities do not significantly alter the effect of Rossner's novel in the adaptation. For instance, most critics remark on the absence of Gary White's confession. One calls Brooks's construction of the plot "meretricious," and another accuses him of "extraordinary shallowness" for turning the story into a "thriller."[17] They imply that the suspense about who kills Theresa cheapens the sad determinism of Rossner's story and distracts us from Theresa's development.

I agree that Brooks exploits the suspense, but I disagree about the result.[18] For suspense, Brooks changes James's character, but we hardly think differently of him. In the film, James secretly watches Theresa; also, after a fight with her, he confesses that a story of his sad childhood[19] was all a fabrication, and he leaves laughing and crying almost at once, as if deranged. These incidents certainly make James seem potentially psychotic, not merely neurotic, as in the novel. In fact, James does get violent in one scene in which he lashes out at her bed before she runs away. Even so, these incidents lead to few new inferences: Theresa still cannot accept James as a lover, for he is hardly a plausible sexual being in the first place.

Brooks's film may allow viewers to wonder who will do it, but like the novel, it keeps most attention on how Theresa gets herself into the occasions of such sin. In the scene in which Theresa first notices Tony's luminescent switchblade—a scene that remains essentially faithful to the novel—she feels threatened, and the viewer can obviously add Tony to the list of suspects. Here, however, Tony enjoys her fear and laughs about how her heart and breath race with no escape, "waiting for it to happen, right?"

Brooks may play with viewers' suspicions, but he arouses them in a manner faithful to Rossner's Theresa: the end will come out of nowhere, so we can only watch her and wait for it to happen.

The same conclusion applies to other characters too. In the film, Theresa's sexual education does not include lessons from Carter or Eli; instead, Brooks collapses her sexual progress in such a way that Theresa completes it under her first teacher, Engle. Nevertheless, even without Carter and Eli, Theresa's lessons in victimization are faithfully sufficient at the hands of Engle: Theresa still feels oppression and guilt, and these feelings still motivate her actions.

Likewise, if the characterization of her father tends toward extremes, that characterization yet finds its basis in Rossner's novel. Brooks's version of Mr. Dunn embodies the same guilt in a fanatic: his Irish-Catholic fears and prejudices suppress his guilt, and, as it develops in the film, the genetic basis of Theresa's disease is the objective correlative of that guilt. Rossner deploys religious stereotypes to establish the background to Theresa's character; Brooks merely turns up the congenital volume on that stereo.

Other changes leave Rossner's themes intact. The film includes several more scenes of Theresa in her classroom as a teacher (a teacher of deaf children, like the actual Roseann Quinn). These scenes again feel as incredibly warm and fulfilling as those in Rossner's book, but more important, they emphasize the split between Theresa's daytime and nighttime personalities, even if they do not explain that split more.

Some critics also note changes in the period. Just as Rossner deliberately brackets her story in the 1960s, Brooks deliberately establishes his version's relation to that rebellious decade. Very early in the film, Theresa, alone on New Year's Eve (the nephew for whom she is babysitting clearly does not count as company), listens to a television announcer proclaim: "1975 has just become history. It was only five years ago that ten thousand women marched for liberation. . . . This was to be the decade of the dames." Rossner wants to show the oppression of women in an age that should have known better, and Brooks wants to show the continuation of the oppression from the time of Rossner's novel to the year of our bicentennial—another age that should know better. The vulgarity of the phrase "decade of the dames," especially in the mouth of a television journalist, and the notion that such film clips would be aired at the stroke of midnight on New Year's Eve, both show a singular lack of subtlety on the part of Brooks. Still, neither does the novel traffic in much subtlety. In bringing Rossner's story up to date, or in making any other changes, Brooks does not alter the schematic morality play about women as victims.

Brooks's cinematic style, like Rossner's literary style, works to support this theme with mixed results. First of all, Brooks retains the verbal aggression evident in so much of Rossner's dialogue, and if one wants to insist that dialogue does not matter to cinematic style, Brooks sometimes adds to the effect with a telling use of reverse angles and reaction shots. When Theresa goes to Engle's office, he enters wearing a thigh-length robe and picks on Theresa, asking her why she works for him despite the low pay. She answers that "practically every girl in class" would do the work for free just to be with him, but he interrupts: "But I chose you. Know why? Because you're the only girl in class who knows syntax and grammar and can spell. And that's the only reason." As he makes this pronouncement, we see Theresa in a close shot; her face registers the pain and embarrassment, and she sets down her pencil and glasses with resignation. In his robe, Engle must be aware of her infatuation, and he even taunts Theresa into acknowledging the fact. When she makes her admission, he cruelly abuses her vulnerability by denying any real attractiveness in her. The pain he inflicts, clearly seen on her face, becomes all the more literal when she gets up, goes to her coat, and fumbles with her pill bottle. The scene contains different dialogue, but otherwise, the situation and the abusive conversation recall the scene in which Theresa first goes to work for Engle in the novel. Later, Engle again joins the sexual and the verbal as two sides of the same blade: when, after a "quickie" in his car, Theresa complains to Engle that "we never talk, or touch, or anything" after sex, he replies, "I just can't stand a woman's company right after I've fucked her."

Furthermore, despite some changed dialogue, the film follows the book in displaying how Theresa learns to use that verbal sword on others, but not so well that she escapes unhurt. In the novel, she belittles James for his punctilious dress and behavior. In the film, James is a social worker with whom Theresa must plead for help on behalf of a student, so she belittles his punctilious observation of the rules. Later, when James has met her family and become her father's favorite, she lashes out at him all the more to maintain some distance. Seeing her apartment for the first time, he notices some obscene wind chimes she has inherited from Katherine's broken marriage: "This place isn't like you at all." She replies, "It's exactly like me—especially this," and she slaps the chimes; then she leans back on her bed and challenges him: "You ever had a woman that way? . . . Or maybe you don't like women. Maybe you go. . . ." He interrupts her before she can finish the insult: first he yells, "Shut up!" but he recovers himself, gently strokes her chin, and says, "You don't like to hurt people, so why do you do it?" We can see that these insults glance off him and strike her. After he leaves, we see her still seated on the bed in a medium shot; she looks up to the ceiling, sighs in distress, and half-heartedly makes a fist to pound on the bed. No narrator tells us how she has hurt herself, but the self-inflicted wound is evident enough.

As in the case of the novel, the film tries to make up with supposed explicitness what it lacks in sound stylistic purpose in its depiction of sex. Brooks sometimes succeeds, as in the scene when Theresa reduces Engle to mumbles by standing over him, and slowly raising her skirt to the level of her naked hips before settling down on him. This scene shows Theresa using her sexual favors as Engle taught her to use them: to put an end to conversation. Appropriately, Brooks's camera angle has us, like Engle, looking up to her straightforward eroticism. Moreover, in several of the lovemaking scenes, Brooks shows Theresa's face in close-up, usually from one side, thereby leaving her detached from and uninvolved with her lover.

More often, however, Brooks uses worn-out conventions for depicting sex.[20] Usually, he dissects the act in very subdued lighting, as in Engle's initial seduction of Theresa, by editing brief shots together: close-up of his hands unsnapping her bra, close-up of hands on skin, close-up of her face, close-up of her panties coming down past her knees, close-ups of faces, limbs, backs, and stomachs. Brooks also adheres to the silly ban on male nudity. When Tony jumps out of bed to bounce around in time with the music on the radio, he is still wearing a shirt—albeit unbuttoned—and a jockstrap! He may believe that sex is some kind of athletic workout, but here he seems to have forgotten what he wants to exercise. In the last analysis then, the depiction of sex stumps both Rossner and Brooks; they can do it, but they cannot make us very interested in reading about or viewing it.

A couple of other details of Brooks's aural and visual style bear mentioning. On the soundtrack, Brooks emphasizes the oppression and despair of Theresa's life by using noise and volume, such as in the scene during which we first see Theresa's family. Following Engle's seduction of her, a scene that is intimately quiet, this scene erupts, suddenly and harshly noisy.

In a couple of other scenes, Brooks uses an off-camera sound to suggest rather bluntly Theresa's inevitable fate. After she argues with her father and leaves home, the shift to Theresa's new apartment occurs with a cut on the sound of the toilet flushing in the bathroom, blatantly suggesting that Theresa's life is being flushed away. Like some of Rossner's metaphors, it is weak and, therefore, unfortunate as an attempt at a clever style.

On the other hand, Brooks's cutting on sound works more effectively elsewhere. From the very first scene after the titles, where the noise of a subway train assaults our ears, Brooks keeps up the assault. Throughout the film, Brooks uses dozens of sound cuts: the sudden clanging of a school bell to signal her first day on the job; the jarring ring of a phone call that will bring bad news; the blaring of a disco tune to move the scene into a singles bar; the popping of a wine bottle's plastic cork to show the move from the bar to the more intimate apartment; the ringing of an alarm clock to announce the end of that tryst; and the tooting of a party horn in a bar on New Year's Eve—a cheap toy that is an ersatz trumpet of Gabriel, summoning Theresa to her last date. Cumulatively, the noise effectively oppresses us as well as Theresa. Her world is loud, abrasive, and threatening, and regardless of her attempts, such a world, like noise, cannot be completely tuned out. In this accumulation of noise, Brooks succeeds at conveying this oppression, and I think he succeeds precisely because the effect accumulates rather than peals off the soundtrack in sudden bursts.

Unfortunately, a visual motif of Brooks's style fails because it is so schematically obvious. Like Rossner, Brooks portrays Theresa as a woman with two contrary personalities, and he chooses to emphasize the extremes of these two personalities through lighting and setting. Scenes at the school take place in high-key light, and scenes of Theresa's sexual life take place in low-key light or darkness. Even Theresa divides her life into light and dark when she explains to Tony, after their first night of sex, that she sets an alarm clock "so you'd leave before morning. . . . Comes daylight—work." The bars, of course, should be dim, but her apartment seems dark even when the lights are on; we also never see her on the street in her neighborhood except after dark. Naturally, the vamp would shun the light of day. James gives her a strobe light (a prop introduced by Brooks) because it reminds him of her: "Light and dark. On and off. Now I see ya, now I don't." When her vampiric existence ends with the stake through the heart, Brooks's lighting motif is literally flashing on the screen so it will not be missed: we see a sideways close-up of her face, lit on one side and dark on the other, receding in stroboscopic blinks from the screen. She dies as she lived: in light and dark, pierced by knives and phalluses.

Brooks's style has merits and flaws, then, but, finally, the latter predominate. Nevertheless, like the novel, the film does not fail because of its flawed style. Rather, the style seems correctly pitched to the plainly singular note Brooks wants to trumpet—and he is interpreting Rossner's sheet music correctly.

Some critics think that the film simplifies the novel. Joyce Sunila charges that Brooks "loses the entire texture of the book—the depressions, the thoughts of self-loathing, the intricate rationalizations for self-hate that dissect with surgical precision how masochism is programmed and operates in the female psyche."[21] In other words, Brooks simplifies the point of view to the extent that Theresa's mind is not opened for our reading.

Actually, he does not shift the point of view so radically. As Sunila states, the narrator, privy to Theresa's thoughts, allows us to hear her two selves in argument. The neutrally omniscient point of view in the film stays mostly with Theresa, portraying her memories in flashbacks and dramatizing some of her fantasies, but also briefly leaving her in order to show another character. What then is lost? Without the preface, the film audience loses the give-away of the ending. However, we do not need the precise information of who did what to Theresa in order to feel foreboding, nor do we need to hear Gary claim to be a victim for us to see how, in a perverse way, he is. Brooks decides against voice-over for Theresa's thoughts, but he does not thereby abandon her mental states. Scenes of Theresa alone—curling up in bed with a pillow between her legs, talking to herself in the mirror, gesticulating and mumbling arguments with an absent but imagined James or Tony—serve well to show her loneliness, despair, anger, and fear. Other lines, usually spoken in discussions with James, even suggest the rationalizations of her way of life. For instance, James remarks on the sadness of people who are looking for something in singles bars, but Theresa responds that she frequents bars because they make her "feel good": "It's better that way, you know. I mean, you drink and you dance. None of that awful small talk. Makes for a hell of a time." Later, when James says she is lonely, she shouts back: "Alone! I'm alone, not lonely." This distinction offers ample evidence of how much she thinks about the problem and how hard she must fight to maintain her claim to independence. In the last analysis, then, despite Sunila's argument that some of Theresa's anguished mind is not played back on the screen, the same anguish remains evident in the end.

Even so, that anguish does not matter much, for Brooks's real fidelity to Rossner's novel shows in his formal choices. Once again, the pathetic plot of Theresa's ultimate victimization fails to be as compelling as it should be because the schematic motivations and accidents of her existence strain credibility.

To begin with, Theresa's character radiates from her central, definitive quality of having the scar: her shame, her drive for abusive sex, the guilt shared with her parents, and, ultimately, the sign of her gender. In the scene in which Engle haughtily takes advantage of her vulnerable infatuation for him, he relents when he sees her fumbling for her aspirin bottle. He asks about her back, and as Theresa explains, we see in flashback the brief, painful account of her polio and scoliosis. Now Engle wants to be tender, and Theresa states, "I'd rather be seduced than comforted." At first Engle laughs at this line and acts as if he would never take advantage of her innocent offer; but he then helps her off with her dress, turns her over to touch the scar, kisses it to stop her protests—"Don't. Don't, it's ugly"—and finally completes her comforting seduction. In these two early scenes, Brooks establishes the centrality of the scar: her aching need to be seduced; her shame for not being attractive; and her vulnerable attractiveness to men.

These motifs persist. The first time she brings Tony to her apartment, her backside prominently faces the camera in one scene when he notices the scar. She stiffens and asks if it bothers him, but he caresses it and renews their lovemaking with his favorite refrain, "You like that." Even on her last date, Theresa becomes a little more exciting for Gary when he notices her scar before beginning a passionate embrace he will not be able to finish without multiplying her scars. Theresa knows that her ache and the remedy—pills and men—are not healthy. Before meeting Gary, she throws away all her pills, and, by association, the ache they soothe. But she cannot stop the pain and its need. The ache cannot be tossed away any more than the scar can be removed.

Herein lies the guilt that bonds her to her parents, especially her father. In the novel, her parents' guilt comes from their failure to notice Theresa's scoliosis in time to treat her without surgery and its disfiguring scar. The flashback mentioned above conveys as much, but, as we learn later, Mr. Dunn also feels guilty for something he could not change and will not discuss. When Brigid announces she is pregnant with her second child, Mr. Dunn brags, "My mother had four: all boys, all perfect." Theresa responds, "Five, papa. You always forget Aunt Maurine." Mrs. Dunn adds a quick orison, "God rest her soul and forgive her," but Mr. Dunn angrily storms out before more is said. The mystery breaks out into the open when Theresa and her father argue about her not having children: "You know why. . . . Scoliosis, papa. . . . The kind you get from rickets, and rheumatism, and my kind—congenital. The kind you're born with. . . . In the blood. . . . Your blood, papa." He weakly tries to fend her off with his line about the four perfect boys, but he breaks down and recalls the exception, his sister, Maurine, who suffered in her "poor, twisted little body" before she took her own life. The argument ends when he asks Theresa, "Tell me, girl, how do you get free of the terrible truth?" The answer, in both novel and film, is that you cannot. Theresa's scar is genetic, and her guilt and her father's guilt are, therefore, baseless even if understandable.

Nevertheless, his guilt implicates Mr. Dunn in the other genetic inevitability of the scar: Theresa's oppressed gender. Men and nature conspire here to make women feel pain, need the temporary sexual pain killer, and pass on their pain. Some critics have objected to the genetic device as a cheap, unnecessary trick, but the real trick comes from the novel and its identification of women with the scar. Unless the scar be kept open for babies (as, for example, in Brigid's case), the pain persists under the "healed" wound. Theresa has an actual scar, but the tortured Maurine and the man-haunted Katherine must feel the same mark. The film gives the knife an additional twist in that now Mr. Dunn cannot change his blood any more than women can change their sex: he joins Gary as an oppressor who feels as trapped as his victim.

Like Rossner, Brooks adds religion as a secondary oppressor. For Theresa, everything that feels good pricks her conscience as it picks at her scar, the stigma of her sinful life. In the opening scene, Brooks establishes the ambivalence Theresa feels toward her Catholicism. The paper Engle reads aloud tells of her last confession: her sins were envy of Katherine's beauty and lust for

Katherine's boyfriends, but, feeling no contrition, she is afraid to confess as well as not to confess. Confused, Theresa remains haunted by religion. On Easter, Theresa leaves a family celebration to enjoy the spur-of-the-moment dalliance with Engle after which he says he cannot stand a woman "right after I've fucked her." Hurt and angry, she gets out of Engle's car and runs to a subway platform. When the train stops, Theresa cannot get on, startled into immobility by the doors' opening on an expressionless nun. Turning her into a pillar of salt would have been only slightly less subtle. Furthermore, Theresa cannot love anyone who might lead her from Sodom to the Church. James would accept this lot in life, but she will not allow it. When James tries to overcome her disparaging attitude, he tells her over the phone, "You know, whenever I have a problem, I go to church." Looking bored, she simply hangs up the phone and goes out to the bars. These "hang-ups" haunt her, though, as when a huge, black cross rears up to confront her in a dream of her father's death. Following Rossner's broad strokes, Brooks's use of religion oppresses us as much as it does Theresa.

Social and religious culture may show many doors wide open, but the oppression of women in this film slams the doors shut—another visual and aural motif in Brooks's style. Thus, as in the novel, the women's liberation movement may move, but it does not necessarily advance; the few thresholds that women cross do not compare with the several new ones that men alone may cross, because in the sexual revolution, women still suffer the casualties, albeit on a new front. In the film, Theresa can get an education, find a job, live in her own place, and seemingly do what she wants with whom she wants; however, she must live and act in a setting that is degrading. The very first scene shows Theresa on the subway where she is bumped by a man studying a *Hustler* magazine. After she moves into her own apartment, a brief montage shows Theresa buying things for her place, and the shopping trip takes her past lurid pornography shops and garish strip-joints (a milieu that, along with shots of the bar scene, is anticipated in the opening titles sequence). The only question for Theresa concerns how she wants her oppression—old-fashioned or sexy?

Theresa has observed the results of this limited choice in her two sisters. Brigid, who represents the father-James choice, is an unattractive model because she has a dull husband and, too often, another baby on the way. Katherine, who represents the Engle-Tony-et-al choice, is unattractive for exactly the opposite reason:

she has a nice or exciting husband (twice and still counting), but the volatile mixture of pills, booze, sex, and therapy causes her to abort as many pregnancies as Brigid carries to term. Theresa follows Katherine, but, as discussed above, genes determine her refusal of Brigid's choice to marry and have children.

Theresa acts as if she enjoys her life, but the acting personality stands separate from the off-stage personality: the woman whose scar is attractive to men as distinct from the woman who feels the scar's pain, the same double personality in the novel. Brooks wastes no time establishing the theme. In that same confession read aloud by Engle in the early scene, Theresa concludes by questioning the lust she felt: "Was it in my mind or body?"[22] The terms sum up, once again, the impossible choice we are to believe women face—impossible because Rossner and Brooks present the choices as such uncompromising extremes.

Theresa's life also splits between fantasy and reality. She daydreams that Engle will hold her after class in a passionate embrace, and that she is a graceful ice skater with Engle as her enthusiastic audience—and that she will step in front of his car after he drops her. Later fantasies still show her insecurities, but involve uglier scenes. Seeing two prostitutes approaching a car, she imagines herself, whorishly decked out, leaning against the car and looking back at her real self on the sidewalk: the two selves smile at each other. Lastly, afraid that Tony may betray her nighttime self to her daytime employer, she fantasizes the police kicking in the door and arresting her for drug possession—a sordid story that her parents would see on the television news. All these fantasies betray an innocence beneath her cynical surface.

Brooks develops this childish quality by expanding on Theresa's teaching. The addition of one character, the withdrawn Amy, is important because Brooks identifies Theresa with Amy. Theresa must draw Amy out of her solitude (she does not have a hearing aid as the other children have), and when Theresa first gets Amy to speak, Amy repeats after her, "My name is Miss Dunn." The sweetness of this identification renders Theresa's other life all the more shocking. As Tony says when he learns her occupation, "Teacher of little kids cruising crummy bars—Jesus Christ! no wonder this country's all screwed up." Theresa laughs when she should be startled into recognition.

In any case, Theresa does arrive at some recognition of herself, but too late, because, as in the novel, beneath her affected cynicism, she lacks experience of the world. Even in 1975, she is ignorant of cocaine, and her sex life begins ridiculously. With Engle, she tries to initiate her own seduction by unzipping her dress, but she awkwardly snags the zipper. Then, although she obviously feels pleasure, she also feels doubt and embarrassment when he is done quickly, leaving her fumbling with her own clothes, trying to put her bra on over her dress.

For all her adventures, Theresa remains tentative or uneasy. At Katherine's, when her sister, brother-in-law, and another couple watch sex films and invite her to "watch the kiddies play," Theresa exhibits obvious curiosity. She is the kiddie, though, for she is the one to fall asleep and later get up and look in on the adults together in one bed; invited now to join in the play, she shakes her head and quietly backs out of the primal group scene. Later, in her first tryst with Tony, she mistakes his priapic stamina for her own inability, her voice betraying the same nervous insecurity as it did before with Engle. Even with Gary, when his sexual ambiguity reins in his ardor, Theresa blames herself: "Maybe it's me. Whatever, it's not your fault." In her innocence, Theresa denigrates herself. Too innocent or scared to stand up for herself, Theresa usually takes it lying down.

I say usually because, as in the novel, Theresa learns from the abuse she takes. Theresa the victim can sometimes play at being the victimizer, and Engle is her main teacher. He cuts their first lovemaking short, promising "fireworks" the next time, because he is late for class. Theresa enacts the same denouement with Tony by setting an alarm clock so that he will leave before morning—so she too will get to class on time.

Theresa's meanest practice of Engle's lessons occurs with James. When she becomes upset because James and her father get along so well, James asks, "What is it—me? Something I said? Something I did?" She laughs and says: "I know someone else who said the same thing once. I just realized how funny it was." Much later, when she confronts James for following her, he asks, "Weren't you ever in love?" Without turning to look at him, she says, "I was even more unbearable than you." In both instances, James's anxiety and vulnerability remind her of the emotional trauma Engle put her through. However, rather than remembering the pain well enough to prevent or soothe it, she remembers its cruel infliction and tries her own hand at the lash. Therefore, Engle remains Theresa's mentor, if not her lover.

If Engle provides her basic education, Katherine is a sort of finishing school. Katherine helps her get settled after she leaves home and advises, "Now, what you need, first and most, is a bed—a bed big enough for everything." Theresa obviously recalls what "everything" entails. She never tries group sex, but the bed does become a party invitation. When she first brings Tony home, he looks around the empty flat and asks: "You said there was a party. So where's the party?" Theresa throws back the covers and answers, "Right here." Later, she offers the same invitation to James, but it is clearly a taunting challenge calculated to embarrass him.

Theresa, however, does not learn from Katherine's mistakes. When they are discussing the collapse of Katherine's second marriage, Katherine slaps the wind chimes and with a sweeping gesture says, "Here lies love and lies and lies and lies." She tells Theresa to take anything she wants and leaves. A matching sound-cut, as Theresa sets the chimes jangling again in her own apartment, shows that she takes nothing from Katherine's experience that will help her avoid repeating it. She ignores the consequences of others' behavior as she mimics it; at least she ignores the consequences until too late.

In the meantime, Brooks makes quitting such a self-destructive education impossible because Theresa has not much to choose from among men. Theresa tries general promiscuity when James or Tony do not satisfy her. The manner in which these tawdry affairs appear, strung together in a montage of funny episodes that Theresa collects and adds to as she repeats them, points up her inability to escape worthless lovers; they are the only kind available.

Of course, aside from promiscuity, James and Tony, as in the novel, provide little to choose between. William Atherton plays James with curly top, wide eyes, and baby face; Richard Gere, as Tony, uses bedroom eyes, open shirt, and athletic hips and legs. Neither requires a great performance so much as a physical type. Theresa's father glowingly lists James's qualities: Catholic, former seminarian, and faithful provider for "his sickly mother"— practically eligible for sainthood, as Theresa jokes. Tony has no religion (no certain job, for that matter) and no family background other than a bitter memory of his mother's throwing him out. As a saintly son, James insinuates himself into Theresa's life through her family. He gets to her father's hospital bed before Theresa knows he is ill and drives Mrs. Dunn home, stopping at church on the way. As the rootless cast-off, Tony insinuates himself into Theresa's life through her door: several times, he picks the lock and lets himself in. The same contrast holds true at work. James visits Theresa at school, but when she signs an introduction to her students, he stops her because he has practiced four days, learning to do it himself. Conversely, Tony shows up unannounced one day on the playground to threaten her with exposure unless she pays him to keep quiet. Amy's brother, heretofore a fairly extraneous character, comes out and puts Tony away with some well-placed punches (clearly a substitute scene for one in the novel where Tony takes a beating at the hands of his mother's boyfriend). James comes openly, whereas Tony sneaks in to press blackmail.

Surely, James seems safer, but he lacks sexuality. Around Christmas he gives her a ring, yet insists, "I didn't say anything about marriage." He goes on about being all she has that is worthwhile, but he also states that she must quit her other activities to keep him. In anger, when she rejects him, James pulls down the wind chimes and then flails her bed, yelling, "Stupid, stupid." He demands sexual fidelity in exchange for asexual companionship. Hence, the ring without marriage.

Tony, conversely, wants sex without marriage. Therefore, when he chases another man out of Theresa's bed, he has none of James's anger: "Before ya start, I forgive ya, so relax, okay?" Theresa has enjoyed the sexual bouts with Tony, but she is not willing to have him breaking in on her whenever he pleases. She throws him out, telling him, "I am my own girl," and that finally makes him angry. Whereas James becomes a maniac over jealousy of her sex life, Tony becomes one after denial of her sexual favors. Theresa may choose between sexless possession or violently free sex.

Theresa eventually refuses to be possessed, but her determination does not avail, for if neither James nor Tony can claim her, they drive her to the man and the setting necessary for her final victimization. Following Tony's threats and her jailhouse fantasy, Theresa tells herself, "I'm through," immediately collects all her drugs and flushes them down the toilet; a couple of days later, on New Year's Eve, when Katherine and her boyfriend surprise her, they find her cleaning the apartment. Definitely trying to reform, she never escapes. On New Year's Eve, she tells the bartender, "This is it, my last night cruising bars." He understands her resolution, but he refuses to share one last drink for luck: "Confidentially, with me, one's too many and a million's not enough." Theresa replies, "I got the same problem with men."

A singles bar, however, is the wrong place to get away from booze and men.

In fact, Theresa practically sets her own trap. James comes to the bar, they have words, she breaks away from him, and she goes to a stranger, Gary, and asks him to be with her because some other man is bothering her. Brooks has not introduced Gary at the beginning, so viewers will not be anticipating this inevitability, but he follows Rossner in making the meeting no less accidental, no less unfortunate in its timing, no less meaningless in its consequences—and no less necessary: in this fictional world, Theresa is a victim, and victims die.

In the novel, despite the preface, Theresa's destiny yet seems arbitrary and meaningless. Brooks's method of introducing Gary emphasizes this thematic problem. One of Theresa's casual dates takes her to a gay bar, and we see Gary for the first time: a sophisticated, bearded man holds a beer out to him, and Gary, clad in denim and neck scarf, kisses him after drinking. Theresa next sees them on New Year's Eve among a group of homosexual revelers attacked by a gang. Not having done so earlier, Brooks must call an awkward halt to the proceedings in order to follow Gary and his rescued friend. In a parking lot, Gary rips off a drag costume while yelling at his companion, the formerly sophisticated man who now wears a clown suit with a big red nose, and is whining pitifully—about as cruel a caricature of homosexuality imaginable. Leaving him, Gary gets out his real shame, shouting, "You're the nellie, not me. I'm a pitcher, not a catcher!" From this conversation, plus the Joe Buck accent and wardrobe, we gather that Gary, new in town, has been living as a homosexual's kept man. To get away, he goes to the bar Theresa frequents, violently rebuffs a homosexual proposition, and meets Theresa. Running from lovers, being bothered by men in the bar, turning to each other—Gary and Theresa are now in sync and the story can continue.

Theresa's evening with Gary then briefly recapitulates the sad story that brought her to him. She lets him take her to her apartment, but, trying to be true to her resolution, she does not want him to stay; however, this door has, figuratively, been open too long to close now—she has no real choice again. First, his talk recalls her problem with James: "I got the same problem. . . . All the time cryin' and spyin', hangin' on. . . . Day and night—love me, love me." Although she has seen him before, her innocence resurfaces when she asks, "How long ya married?" Gary thinks she may be insulting him, but he goes on to explain how he came to town alone and broke, somewhat like Theresa after she left home. He must remind her of Tony when he flops across her bed and says, "Sometimes I think, honest to God, I was better off in prison," for she pauses here to put the chain on the door. The entire basis for her affairs comes out again when Gary is fascinated by her scar, a fascination that embarrasses Theresa. Nevertheless, he must turn from her to arouse himself. Theresa's response is, by now, ingrained: "Maybe, maybe it's me. Whatever, it's not your fault. It happens." As with James, however, she is soon laughing at Gary, because he claims that women merely have to "lay there" while the man does "all the work." Gary starts getting rough to prove himself after she invokes the old rule about not sleeping over. In the ensuing scuffle, she tries to run out but cannot get the door unchained before Gary grabs her; the strobe starts blinking when it is knocked over, and in this intermittent light, we see Gary throw her on the bed, choke her, and rape her. She finally gasps, "Do it," over and over, and he reaches for a knife and stabs her repeatedly.[23] Gary kills her, but in the argument, the insecurity, the chain, the light, and the knife, James and Tony join in.

In discussing the novel, I used the metaphor of the two-way street that is really one-way. Picking up on one of Brooks's motifs, I would say the film portrays two doors that open on the same prison cell: the sexless mind or mindless sex, which is no real choice. Brooks thereby settles for a schematic presentation and "the simplistic, puritanical notion that indiscriminate sex leads to death."[24] In interviews, Brooks seems to have nobler intentions, but he clearly has not escaped the novel:

[Brooks] may have wanted to talk about the contradictory feelings he, as a good liberal, has about women. (They have the right to be independent and yet they need protection.) But what we get is a story of an insecure woman going after cheap thrills and getting in over her head: an ancient morality play.[25]

In other words, he has accomplished what Rossner does in her novel.

Brooks adds a few characters and deletes others. He creates new scenes, sometimes parallel to ones in the book, but he seldom shoots one exactly as it is in the novel. He moves the time from the entire sixties to one year in the seventies. The characterization in the film is, in general, psychologically more extreme. Yet, on the whole, these details in no real way keep the film from faithfully recreating the effects of the novel. Both employ a gritty style and an omniscient point of view with only partial effectiveness. Both devise a pathetic plot that moves from innocence to experience in an obvious and unenlightening fashion, all because Theresa's fate is determined by shallow, hackneyed psychology and characterization: Catholicism as ironbound repression; Irish parents as irrationally dogmatic idolaters; sisters as madonna and whore; men as dark hedonists or pale celibates; the protagonist as dual personality split into sweetness and fantasy by day and cynicism and abuse by night; and the surgical scar as feminine stigma, the root of all suffering. All these dichotomous forces, whether asserted to be natural or social, form the technical and formal foundation of novel and film. Upon this asserted foundation, the artists can build a story "bold" enough to show that, in life, there is good and bad.

The film, therefore, has no problem overcoming material differences to recover and recreate the effects presented in the novel. Fidelity to the novel, however, yields a meager success in this case. Faithful adaptations, if the novel is weak, represent a lot of time, money, and effort to imitate the worthless. And at bottom, the adaptation of *Looking for Mr. Goodbar* also compounds our ignorance of what brought Roseann Quinn to such a horrible death.

Damned if You Do, and Dammed if You Don't: *Deliverance*

> You can't understand. How could you?—with solid pavement under your feet, surrounded by kind neighbors ready to cheer you or to fall on you, stepping delicately between the butcher and the policeman, in the holy terror of scandal and gallows and lunatic asylums—how can you imagine what particular region of the first ages a man's untrammeled feet may have taken him into by the way of solitude—utter silence, where no warning voice of a kind neighbor can be heard whispering of public opinion? These little things make all the great difference. When they are gone you must fall back upon your own innate strength, upon your own capacity for faithfulness.
>
> —Marlow in *Heart of Darkness*

> Nature, Mr. Allnutt, is what we are put into this world to rise above.
>
> —Rose in *The African Queen*

In a passing reference to Brooks' film of *Looking for Mr. Goodbar*, Rossner calls it "uninteresting if not uncompelling."[1] With so many details—scenes, conversations, supporting characters—altered for the movie, Rossner might, of course, feel artistically betrayed. My point has been that, properly understood and evaluated, the novel and film do not differ that much. Had Brooks changed the title and the names of characters, his film would certainly have incited charges of plagiarism.

More typically, however, discussion of film adaptations focuses on cases wherein the film so alters the novel as to ruin the effect, a case in which any reader, let alone the novelist, would feel betrayed. In instances of this sort, many may wonder why the title

128

and names have not been changed as well. George Bluestone correctly assesses a few such examples, but, again, I think he errs in ascribing the differences in effect to the film medium. A film can have depth and development, but only if the film producers' intentions and capabilities allow for such depth and development.

Yet even today, when filmmakers can set their aesthetic principles above commercial interests, unfaithful adaptations persist, and readers and authors continue to feel betrayed; but now the argument over fidelity and relative quality becomes more artistically interesting because the causes are aesthetic, not commercial or political, choices. Moreover, these more independent filmmakers can attempt an adaptation that is not so much a cinematic rendering of but more a commentary on the original novel. In such an instance, questions of relative quality may pertain, but the two versions may sometimes seem not to be in competition. Either way, the conventionally unexamined ideas about fidelity must again give way. If, as in the case of *Mr. Goodbar*, a faithful adaptation does not guarantee a good film, neither does an unfaithful adaptation necessarily result in a relatively poorer film.

When an adaptation is not intended to be faithful, the deliberate infidelity may cause critical misunderstanding. The circumstances of adapting James Dickey's *Deliverance* illustrate this particular problem. In the afterword in his published screenplay, Dickey explains his intentions and frustrations. Admittedly inexperienced, yet asked to write the screenplay from his novel, Dickey set out to transfer "the essential story from one medium to another" in such a manner that his ideas would be preserved on the screen: "After all, it was my story, and no one else on earth could know it as I did."[2] The screenplay, as he submitted it to the studio, amply demonstrates that an almost totally faithful adaptation was possible; as Dickey hoped, reading his screenplay enables us to "see" the movie he wanted us to see. Nonetheless, the actual film turns out to be quite different. Holding no bitterness, Dickey states that "the director, John Boorman, the actors, and the crew did, I think, their honest best to come up with what they believe is a credible film version of the novel *Deliverance*"; and he adds, "I do not believe that my imagination or anyone else's could improve on the Chattooga River used in the film, or on cinematographer Vilmos Zsigmond's handling of it." Still, disappointed and somewhat confused, he mentions his unease on the set, where, unconsulted and therefore unaware of the aesthetic reasoning, Dickey could only watch as details, dialogue, and action were revised till "nothing but the bones" were left of his screenplay while ideas he thought to be "not only hopelessly but even laughably inadequate" found full embodiment on the screen.[3]

In the final film, Dickey receives sole writing credit,[4] and he plays the small role of Sheriff Bullard. Although I cannot say why Dickey was asked to write a screenplay, I think the film does not represent a repudiation of his talent or of his ideas. Boorman, instead, sees other possibilities in the same narrative circumstances. On the screen, Boorman's version of *Deliverance* does not repudiate Dickey's version so much as it develops an interesting variation.

The narrative that the two versions share involves four men on a float trip. Lewis Medlock talks Ed Gentry, Bobby Trippe, and Drew Ballinger into floating the Cahulawassee before it is dammed and thereby lost. The three days and two nights on the river are harrowing: two hillbillies sexually assault Bobby and are going to do the same to Ed when Lewis shoots one with an arrow; at Lewis's urging, they hide the body; back on the river, Drew falls in, possibly shot by the hillbilly who got away, and the two canoes capsize in the rapids; Drew is lost, and Lewis breaks a leg; fearful of their vulnerability, Ed scales the gorge wall and stalks and kills the other hillbilly; they hide this body, and, when they find Drew's downstream, they hide it also; believing that any evidence of foul play is buried for good, Ed concocts a story to explain Drew's disappearance and Lewis's injury (accidental capsizing in rough water), and the sheriff accepts it despite his deputy's suspicions. Both film and novel depict these events, but most similarity ends there.

Dickey notes that the "main entity the two versions will necessarily have in common is the river itself,"[5] but Dickey and Boorman emphasize different currents in their symbolic reading of this principle of nature. To Dickey, the river stands for rejuvenation, something that must be rediscovered by those accustomed to urban life. To Boorman, however, the energy tapped from nature is not as beneficial: once uncovered, it may grow threatening to civilized life; as Michel Ciment writes, the film "inverts the clichés of the ecological movement."[6]

The novel's theme of rejuvenation develops all the more clearly owing to Dickey's vividly descriptive style. Some reviewers have commented that Dickey, well known as a poet, does not use a "poetic" style in this, his first novel, implying, I suppose, that "poetic" means "difficult." In the novel's very first line—"It unrolled slowly, forced to show its colors, curling and snapping back whenever one of us turned [it] loose"[7]—Lewis is showing the other three men a topographical map of the river he wants them all to float; the literal description of the rolled-up map also suggests that the terrain and the river have an untamed life. Thus, whether or not one calls it poetic, Dickey's style conveys more than literal information.

Furthermore, Dickey employs metaphors well to give the precise turn of a phrase from described action to felt sensation, as in a passage that describes the dangerous excitement of running the rapids. In compounded syntax that matches the swiftness of the action that moves almost too quickly for description in words, Dickey compares the water of the rapids to "threads running through a loom," an image seen only "in a blinking leap," for the canoeists are moving so swiftly that little can be seen; instead, Ed's narration emphasizes what can be felt—the force of the water around his paddle that feels like "some supernatural source of primal energy" and his wild sensation of "unkillableness: the triumph of an illusion when events bear it out" (189–90). The image of the loom fixes in our minds the vortical danger ahead, and the brief figurative and descriptive details convey the disoriented glimpses Ed gets of this scene. With the river, though, Ed literally and symbolically rises to the occasion: after the ordeals of rape, murder, and burial upriver, Ed has grown fully in touch with this supernatural energy, and he realizes his power to survive and save the others—a realization so new that only a new word, "unkillableness," can embody the sense of his confidence.

Elsewhere, palpable description remains the key to Dickey's style: "How a man acts when shot by an arrow, what it feels like to scale a cliff or to capsize, the ironic psychology of fear"—these are the sensations we can feel through Dickey's careful prose.[8] He shows equal adeptness in suggesting the quiet eeriness of sleeping in the woods—"creatures with one forepaw lifted . . . eyes made for seeing in this blackness" (77)—and at rendering the more violent sensations, such as Ed's pain when he must remove an arrow from his side: "The flesh around the metal moved pitifully, like a mouth. . . . The woods and air were dizzy as with birds flying from all the trees straight into my face" (166).

Sensation, in fact, becomes a motif in the novel. From Ed's first step into the river, which he says seemed to grab him by the leg, to the time he takes his final leave by stooping for one last drink, the novel shows Ed's attaining a definite touch for nature and himself.[9] When the four men find the river, a twig sticks through the car window, and Ed notices "that one leaf was shaking with my heart" (62); wakened by an owl atop his tent the first night out, Ed touches one of the talons puncturing the material and then imaginatively hunts with the owl through the night; during the assault by the backwoodsmen, Ed's most telling emotion is that he had "never felt such brutality and carelessness of touch" (98); in his desperate scaling of the cliff to confront the expected killer, Ed's literal and figurative grasp saves him, for "strength from the stone flowed into me" (141); this "totally different sense of touch" (157) allows him to anticipate and defeat his foe; only when he touches the guitar callus on Drew's lifeless hand does Ed cry over his loss, but his wrestling with the last set of rapids returns him to concern for survival; and finally, when he has survived, Ed keeps the touch of the river inside himself.

This motif of tactile awareness corresponds to another motif of visual awareness and control. Ed works as an advertising executive, and he prides himself on his "ability to get the elements of a layout into some kind of harmonious relationship" (19). Even as Lewis shows them the map in the first scene, Ed is trying to "see" the river in the same way that he will later "see" the owl's hunting, "see" the river from atop the cliff before he has opens his eyes and looks, "see" his enemy before he arrives, and "see" Drew tumbling through the rapids after the fact. Also, Ed's visual imagination includes his ability to concentrate on and frame a subject. For instance, he has a peep sight attached to the string of his bow, enabling him to frame his target: "It isolated what was being shot at, and brought it into an oddly intimate relation with the archer. . . as though the target were being created by the eye that watched it" (32). Two important elements of Ed's rejuvenation come to him through such frames. First, his initial sight of the river is in a frame, an "ashen window" (63) made by Lewis when he pulls some limbs aside. And second, Ed's mortal enemy on top of the cliff appears, as he puts it, "within a frame within a frame, all of my making: the peep sight and the alleyway of needles" (163) that he had cleared from his perch in a pine tree. Ed comes to the woods with a basic visual talent, but once there, his sight and touch, especially among his senses, develop in a manner that allows him to survive in the wilderness and even take some of the wilderness home in his mind.

Dickey's vivid style and the sensuous motifs combine well, but some critics raise questions about the point of view. Warren Eyster states that Dickey certainly "responds to nature with intense personal depth," but "that his narrator, Ed Gentry, a second-rate art director who wants no more from life than to slide through it, 'to groove it with comfort,' to let life slip by with the least possible friction, should respond to the river with the soul of a poet is simply not convincing."[10] In that the trip awakens his senses, Ed's very sensuous narration of that adventure should be no problem. More troubling is Peter G. Beidler's objection that Ed's rejuvenation has value only to his deluded self, coming as it does at the cost of several deaths, burials, and lies.[11] Ed admits doubts, and Dickey allows ambiguities to remain, but not to the extent that we should suspect Ed's reliability.

In fact, because of Ed's reliability, Dickey takes on the challenge of winning our sympathy more than our trust in Ed's account of his ordeal and triumph. As one reviewer states, the point of view, "so effective in conveying the immediacy of experience, offers only tenuous support to the reader who suddenly wishes to distance himself from Ed Gentry, who feels that Gentry's triumph, no matter how intensely rendered, is earned by a callousness that is the antithesis of heroic."[12] The problem with the first-person narration, then, is not whether we believe in Ed's honesty, but whether we accept his actions as those of a man who grows in moral character.

As I hope to show, Dickey successfully meets the challenge of his technical choice. Boorman, however, poses the moral issue another way and, therefore, makes some different stylistic and technical choices. In the film, Ed does not undergo a sensuous awakening so much as he suffers a terrible trauma. The wilderness and the creatures have a certain appeal and an awesome beauty, but they contain no vitality, as in the novel, wherein even supposedly inanimate objects are not only animate but vivifying. Thus, whereas Dickey's style emphasizes the sensations in which Ed immerses himself, Boorman's style brings out the dangerous or ugly details of the surroundings.

One stylistic device that conveys this contrary sense is the obscured frame. In order, for instance, to film the scenes in the rapids as Dickey wrote them, Boorman would need to employ several point-of-view shots in which the camera would take Ed's place in the canoe; these shots would not have to be the exclusive choice, but they would serve best to make the viewer feel the excitement Ed describes. Boorman, however, seldom uses such shots during the canoeing scenes.[13] Instead, he uses a mix of close shots of the individual men and longer shots, some taken from the riverbanks and others from rafts in the river with the canoes. The close shots show the men's various reactions—exhilaration, fear, calm efficiency, or panic—and the water-level shots convey some of the speed and sudden falls with which the men contend. The telephoto shots from the side, though, show the most danger; from a distance, the telephoto shot, sometimes obscured by rocks in the foreground, conveys a stronger sense of danger because we see the threat while the men pass it unaware. These shots appear in the first running of rapids, but figure more prominently in the final running. In the novel, Ed's successful maneuvering through these last rapids triumphantly delivers himself and the two others from death; in the film, the passing of this last danger, with Bobby's help, looks more like an escape than a deliverance.

If the landscape is not so alive as in the novel, it still makes a definite impression in an awful way. Ed may not specifically see the rocks that dominate the foreground of the above images, yet he cannot avoid other sights. In particular, the presence of the corpse in the scene in which the four men discuss what to do with the dead man leaves a strong impression. Boorman's device here is not really an obscured frame because all the subjects are in the same plane. Nevertheless, the dead man, caught in the fork of a sapling and shot through with Lewis' arrow, seems to fill the foreground. The horrible sight impresses itself on Ed as well as the viewer. As Philip Strick notes, "The film is in fact very much concerned with images that refuse to sink out of sight. . . . In the scene of the first killing. . . Boorman allows us hardly one cutaway shot from the vacantly staring face and the shaft that has transfixed [the man's] chest."[14] Indeed, this lengthy sequence comprises many wide shots and close shots, but the corpse almost never leaves our sight, placed in the foreground, off to the side, or just next to a close-up of someone else; even when they start to bury the body, Boorman gives us a nearly ground-level shot of the grave site, which is suddenly obscured by the body's being dropped right in front of the camera.

Dickey and Boorman choose these different styles because they do not choose the same point of view. Dickey, wanting to show a suburban man's rediscovery of natural senses and strength under duress, appropriately has the character tell his own story in very sensuous prose. Boorman, on the other hand, sees more trauma than triumph in the journey, and he thereby uses a more omniscient point of view, so that we can see what Ed cannot see—yet. Boorman could have attempted first-person perspective, but in his version of the events, Ed does not grow to new awareness so much as he undergoes a terrible trial whose images he would rather avoid and suppress; therefore, Boorman's technical choice is appropriate, for his narrative still concentrates on Ed as the protagonist without allowing Ed's point of view to avoid and suppress what Boorman wants us to see about Ed's development.

These considerations should answer some critical objections to Boorman's adaptation. James F. Beaton asserts that the novel's technique, "consistently *expressive* of Gentry's interior life," challenges the filmmaker "to develop a cinematic technique that will register by its own means the same approach to experience, the same 'feel' for it, that a reader may discover in the novelist's prose."[15] Needless to say, Boorman's film fails for Beaton. However, the technique he calls for would be necessary only in a faithful adaptation: Beaton does not seem to consider that the filmmaker may choose deliberately rather than misguidedly. Thus, although the wilderness in Dickey's narrative is palpable and alive, the wilderness in the film is purposely not scenic; rather, the colors are desaturated, and the setting has, therefore, a "dark strange feeling" that is other-worldly.[16]

In another complaint, Charles Thomas Samuels claims that Boorman's dissolve-montage of Ed's scaling the cliff "reminds us that no human could perform this feat without interruption, hence it could not be photographed in a long take."[17] First of all, a long scene in a novel does not require a long take in a film to be rendered faithfully. More to the point, though, the scene in the novel goes on at length because it deals with Ed's struggle to put down his fear, to scale a sheer wall of rock, to open his senses, to enter the mind of his foe, and to discover the wherewithal to succeed on every count. In the film, the climb is a desperate move that may lead to survival; it is a smaller struggle. Consequently, Ed's sensuous description of pressing himself into the rock and being infused with its strength would prove too glorious for the film. The solarized images and the deep, muted roar of the river show Ed in nightmarish fear rather than moonlit triumph. Essentially, the stylistic and technical choices made by Dickey and Boorman result from different formal intentions—not from the latter's misapprehension of the former.

As I have suggested, Dickey intends that we view Ed as a good man who, taken out of his comfortable surroundings and placed in a world of lawless danger, manages to do the right things, violent as they may be, in order to survive as well as to rescue two companions. The form of this plot, in terms formulated by Norman Friedman, is the "maturing plot":

> The most common [plot of this type] involves a sympathetic protagonist whose goals are either mistakenly conceived or not yet formed, and whose will is consequently rudderless and vacillating.... [H]is character must be given strength and direction, and this may be accomplished through some drastic, or even fatal, misfortune.[18]

"Rudderless and vacillating" certainly describes Ed, as should be clear from Dickey's portrayal of Ed's boredom with the routine of his work and his life at home.

Ed's description of his job at the advertising agency recalls the lawyer's self-evaluation in Melville's "Bartleby the Scrivener": he boasts that his best qualities are his "prudence" and "methods," but he admits to tolerating the idiosyncrasies of his employees out of the "profound conviction that the easiest way of life is the best." Likewise, Ed states that he and his partner "ran a no-sweat shop" (15); they make good money, do not force their staff to be more than "earnest and on time," and deal with businesses that followed similar policies. Ed betrays no outward shame over this routine, as he readily admits to his more obsessive friend, Lewis: "I am a get-through-the-day man . . . mainly interested in sliding . . . finding a modest thing you can do, and then greasing that thing. On both sides. It is grooving with comfort" (39–40). Even when Ed first gets on the river, the regularity of paddling is easy because it reminds him of work that is familiar and therefore unthreatening. Despite the alleged satisfactions of this easy way at work, Ed knows he is really not happy at his job. He feels certain of his competence, even talent, at composing a layout, yet, after lunch, when the four men decide to go canoeing, Ed returns to his office in despair at having nothing of consequence to do.

Ed's personal life offers no more sense of completeness. He has no dream life and, sexually, almost nothing seems to interest, let alone excite, him. Walking back to the office from lunch, he feels desolated by all the women's stiff hair styles; he strains to find one "decent ass" in the lunch-hour crowd and succeeds, only to feel disappointed at the sight of her "barren, gum-chewing face" (17). Ed qualifies his sexist judgment when he goes on to admit to himself, "I was of them, sure enough" (17). This sexual ennui certainly contributes to Ed's feelings during the afternoon's tasks. The agency will be shooting pictures for the Kitt'n Britches account, a line of women's underwear. Ed had earlier rejected the suggestion of imitating the famous Coppertone ads, having a cat pull a model's panties down; instead, the photo will feature a model, wearing only the product, holding a kitten next to her face and looking over her shoulder at the camera. In the studio, Ed feels uneasy with the bright lights and the "pornography" of the situation. These commercial accouterments, like the hair spray and chewing gum before, destroy any genuine sensuality. Then Ed notices "a peculiar . . . tan slice" (21) in the model's eye, and when he touches her to rearrange her pose, he feels a thrill at a private moment in this garish setting: "The gold-glowing mote fastened on me. . . . [I]t was alive and it saw me" (22). Ed also feels the sexual arousal of viewing a woman as she modestly tries to cover her nakedness, but this subtle communication is what impresses him and stays with him.

This momentary thrill makes him feel his lack all the more. The next morning, before setting out to the river, Ed makes love to his wife. She is a generous lover to him, but Ed conjures up the model, seeing on her back "the gold eye," which represents to him "the promise of [sex] that promised other things, another life, deliverance" (29–30). Although loving, the brief motions that Ed and his wife go through have become routine. The hope for something more, the promise of "deliverance" comes from the infatuation with the model. Eugene M. Longen describes this promise as the idea that

> sex, in its nakedness and intimacy and physicality, is one of the few occasions left to civilized man when he can be in touch with his whole being—body and spirit—when he can shed the strait jacket of social conventions that dictate what he must do, where he must go, when, how fast, and how often, and when he can feel himself alive all the way to his fingertips.[19]

With the model, Ed only senses the promise, but does not fulfill it; and with his wife, he cannot quite break the routine of their lovemaking.

Clearly, Ed feels about his life a frustration that corresponds to the epigraph from Georges Bataille: "Il existe à base de la vie humaine un principe d'insuffisance." He may hesitate at the last moment, thinking he should play golf instead, but he goes with Lewis, because of the change, or, as Lewis would say, "breaking the pattern" (36). Thus, when he is on the river, he can take off his clothes, dive in the water, and think of letting go.

This theme of quiet frustration applies to civilization in general. Ed feels it in himself, but he also observes it around him, as in his comments on the lunch-hour crowd. Outside the city, frustration also pervades the landscape inasmuch as the fields and barns he passes all have signs promoting some religious or medicinal relief:

> From such a trip you would think that the South did nothing but dose itself and sing gospel songs; you would think that the bowels of the southerner were forever clamped shut; that he could not open and let natural process flow through him, but needed one purgative after another in order to make it to church. (37–38)

On the river and in the wilderness, Ed and the others could hope to leave behind such a landscape. Yet even after finding the river in the dense foliage and running their first set of rapids, they are brought up short. Ed says, "We were civilized again" (68), as they suddenly pass a bank covered with junk, including plastic, which Drew notes will never decompose. This immortal trash is a prelude to Ed's next sight, a section of the river polluted by the offal of a poultry processing plant: "A vague choked whiteness. . . . [A] chicken head with its glazed eye half-open looking right at me and through me" (69). These motifs of frustration, constipation, choking, and blocking—all symptoms of civilization's grip on the landscape—represent smaller versions of the dam that is going to quell the Cahulawassee. Goaded by Lewis, the other three suburbanites presumably want the same sensation: the feeling of something open and unchecked. In an interview, Dickey stated, "We all feel shamefaced about the vanishing of the wilderness, and we do feel like it is incumbent on us to get out there and see a little of it before it's all gone."[20] Ed's narration speaks for the others to the extent that they all want to break the pattern of their lives, if only for a weekend, but Ed is alone in what he actually does find on the river and keeps to himself back in civilization.

Boorman shares this view of civilization to some degree. In the montage of scenes accompanying the opening credits, civilization already spreads a deadly, ugly blight on the landscape. The first shot slowly tracks over calm water with half-submerged trees that give way to a view of bare hills in the distance. In voice-over, we hear Lewis pleading his case for the weekend trip: "You wanna talk about the vanishing wilderness? . . . Just about the last wild, untamed, unpolluted, unfucked-up river in the South. . . . Just gonna be a big, dead lake." The scene shifts to the dam project: noisy earth-moving equipment, a warning siren, and a dynamite blast on a barren hill. Boorman cuts to a panoramic shot of rolling, tree-covered hills, over which we hear the distant echo of the blast; then, in a similar shot, two cars pass in the foreground, carrying the four weekend canoeists. The title sequence ends as the cars pull into a dilapidated gas station, the camera panning over junk piled in the foreground. Bobby gets out and kicks at a pile of tin cans: "Christ, Drew. Look at the junk. . . . I think this is where everything finishes up. We just may be at the end of the line." The junk is not without its attachments for Bobby, though, as he spots an old car body and jokes: "That's my '51 Dodge. . . . Hoo! All my youth and passion spent in that back seat. All gone you see. All gone. Rest in dust." In this quick introduction, Boorman makes clear the destructiveness of the urban encroachment on the wilderness.

Nevertheless, the dam project does not, as in the novel, represent a larger version of individual frustration. Bobby may joke that his passion is gone to rust and dust, and the sex lives of the others may be hinted at in Lewis's promise to get them home in time for Sunday's football game: "You'll be back in time to see the pom-pom girls at halftime, 'cause I know that's all you care about." Still, if these men are getting away from it all, it all is not so bad. Without the extended "Before" section of the novel, the film shows no prevailing ennui in the people Ed finds around him, in the work he does, or in his marriage, nor does ennui motivate Ed to go on the trip. Against Lewis's argument about the dam, Ed notes the benefits of electric power and recreation, but, more importantly, he can tell his obsessive friend, "I like my life, Lewis." The difference is that, in the film, Ed is getting away from his routine without feeling that he *must* get away. The narrator of the novel needs the experience of the river because he is blocked and confused. The protagonist of the film, on the other hand, may be an average sort of fellow, but his day-to-day comforts cause him no consternation.

The Ed Gentry of the film gives no particular thought to his way of life and, to that extent, may take it for granted. Boorman will have him confront these thoughts only after he is on the river, not before. The plot of the film is not a maturing plot of character, but a testing plot of character: "The distinctive quality of this type is that a sympathetic ... character is pressured in one way or another to compromise or surrender his noble ends or ways"; giving in to the temptation could bring the protagonist wealth or even "save his neck, yet if he does he will pay the price of losing his own self-respect and our respect for him as well."[21] Boorman's film, therefore, differs substantially from Dickey's novel.[22]

Given this obvious difference, I think we can more reasonably assume that Boorman makes the changes in the service of his own different, coherent intention—not that he has somehow grossly misunderstood and betrayed the novel. In R. Barton Palmer's terms, the changes are "more ideological than narratological."[23] Dickey sends Ed down the river looking for something, and the question is whether he finds anything of value. Boorman sets Ed down in the river to meet a challenge to his way of life, and the question is whether he is equal to the challenge. The different answers lie in how the two artists view nature. That is to say, the term "nature" covers two distinct concepts: the idea of nature, whose chaotic energy resists taming by civilization; and the idea of human nature, whose instincts lose vitality as the wilderness disappears. At one extreme lies the amoral chaos of the jungle, and at the other, the immoral sterility of "civilized" materialism. Dickey and Boorman emphasize different—not contrary—senses of nature, and those different emphases dictate different resolutions when Ed confronts the choice between civilization and wilderness and must act like a "natural" man.

At the outset of the novel, Ed has in Lewis a mentor on the subject of one way of living naturally. Lewis wants Ed, Bobby, and Drew to float the river with him, but Ed senses more in the invitation: "A lesson. A moral. A life principle. A way" (8). Ed looks up to Lewis precisely because Lewis does not suffer the frustrations Ed does. Lewis is, Ed thinks, strong and thoroughly accommodated to the environment, and Ed wants to be transformed by that touch: Lewis's hand "seemed to have power over the terrain" (7), and, despite pushing forty, he remains "one of the strongest men I had ever shaken hands with" (9).

Despite this admiration, Ed should know better, for he already realizes how different Lewis and he are. Getting out of a daily rut hardly keeps pace with Lewis's obsessive drive: "He was the kind of man who tries by any means ... to hold onto his body and mind and improve them, to rise above time" (12). Riding with

Lewis into the countryside, Ed learns how fanatic Lewis can be and how their trip, more than just a weekend adventure, can prepare them for the apocalypse. Lewis insists that technology and politics will fail, and then "a few men are going to take to the hills and start over" (40); such a life would be full of suffering, "but you'd be in touch" (42). Bored with life, Ed feels attracted to the idea of getting "in touch," but he does not want to destroy his old way of life in order to attain a new one. Lewis challenges him, however, with the vision of a primal existence: "the last chance. . . . No price is too big" (42–43). Without really acquiescing to Lewis on this point, Ed finally tells him, feeling "so tanked up with your river-mystique," he has no doubt of "some fantastic change" (4) to come on the river. Indeed, the canoe trip does change Ed when the "systems" fail, but during that failure they both learn the limits of Lewis's extreme views of nature.

Those limits ought to become even more apparent to Ed while on the way to the river. Lewis tells Ed about a previous outing during which another friend got lost in the woods and broke a leg; a pair of backwoodsmen rescued them, illustrating the dependability of woodsmen, who know themselves and their environment. Lewis follows up on this story by recounting the time he had been fishing alone, had fallen and broken his ankle, and had to hobble out of the woods in extremis. In short, if Lewis welcomes the challenge of survivalism, Ed must realize that Lewis courts dangerous situations as much as excitement—"And I was damned well hoping that this wouldn't be another one" (44). Soon enough, though, Lewis is courting trouble, nearly coming to blows with a mountain man over pay for taking the cars downriver for them; although no fisticuffs ensue, Ed still gets a scare that he resents. With the price settled, Lewis speeds ahead of the local men and soon gets lost.

More dangerously still, as becomes obvious when they get on the river, Lewis ignores any warning that the river is impassable. When the four men capsize, Ed thinks that, aside from the possibility of a vengeful attack from above, floating that part of the river would have been impossible. Lewis's superior physical fitness and obsessive drive prove no match for the river: it carelessly tosses him and the other men out, and it incapacitates Lewis with a broken leg.

Ed's mentor has failed with his system too, and Ed must take over, deep in "the heart of the Lewis Medlock country," where "Everything around me changed" (137). Ed changes, but he does not go so far as Lewis would want to go. Although Ed adapts something primitive in nature so as to deliver Lewis, Bobby, and himself from danger, Lewis learns that he must change also. In the end, Ed can observe that Lewis "can die now" (235), having given up on immortality. Hence, the second epigraph from Obadiah. Lewis's obsessive survivalism, the "pride of thine heart," leads him to deceive himself and boast, "Who shall bring me down to the ground?" In Dickey's novel, Ed's ability to tap some of nature's energy helps him overcome the "principe d'insuffisance" of everyday life, but he does not follow his mentor, Lewis, so high into "the clefts of the rock" that he believes in his own indestructibility for long. The true natural man does not feel the oppression of the urban environment, but neither does he lord it over the wilderness.

Lewis had said, "No price is too big" (43), regarding the test of survival, yet his biggest fault comes from not admitting failure and death as possible payments. Ed shows Lewis that losing is a possibility also, thereby allowing Lewis to shed his pride. Ed's experience otherwise confirms Lewis's views of nature's power: Ed learns to live again, if not forever. In Dickey's screenplay, Ed's wife correctly, albeit facetiously, identifies Lewis with the remark, "Here's your hero."[24] By leading Ed to the river, he leads him in the right general direction and, therefore, deserves some of Ed's admiration (especially as it is tempered by a cautious skepticism of any extremes).

Lewis's character in the film, by contrast, deserves no such admiration, for the wilderness to which he leads Ed offers no liberation, let alone vitality. Boorman's different view of living naturally brings about several little variations in Lewis's characterization. As played by Burt Reynolds, Lewis remains just as fanatic in his views, but we forgive less because his bravado shows too much swagger—and, more important, the outcome is less heartening. Lewis certainly swaggers in the novel, but he seems to be aware of the show he makes. Asked why he wants to float the river, Lewis responds, "because it's there," but Ed adds that he said so "for my benefit" (59). Asked the same thing in the film, Lewis gives the same response, but he does so in all seriousness. The lack of self-consciousness tightens the screws on his fanaticism, which ironically makes him look even more ridiculous. Lewis even contradicts himself somewhat. Early in the film, he brags to Ed, "I never been lost in my life"; soon, however, he races ahead of the others to find the river, comes to a dead-end, retreats and pushes on, and finally finds it, intoning to Ed, "Sometimes you have to lose yourself before you can find anything."[25] Critics who call this line ridiculous, as well as the hackneyed, "Because it's there," are correct; yet, when they object to Boorman's including these lines, they miss the point by taking Lewis as seriously as he takes himself.

Lewis still makes his speech about the system's imminent failure, but the different context in the film tends to diminish his views. The conversation, in the novel, takes place at length on the way through the countryside; Lewis's naturalism, if extreme, looks appealing at least in comparison to Ed's defensive admissions about his easy, dull existence. In the film, the corresponding conversation takes place in a canoe; camp has been pitched nearby, and while Ed lies back and steadies the canoe, Lewis stands and hunts fish with his bow and arrow. Lewis talks as he takes aim: "Machines are gonna fail. And the system's gonna fail. . . . Then survival. . . . That's the game—survive." Lewis expresses essentially the same views as before, but Ed reacts with less defensiveness and admiration. While Lewis is speaking, Ed finishes a beer and pointedly pops the tab on another. Ed does not argue, but he does affirm himself: "Well, the system's done all right by me. . . . I like my life, Lewis." By not giving in to Lewis, Ed may be guilty of a little smugness, but he does not deny Lewis his own way; when Lewis spears a fish, Ed toasts him sincerely, "Here's to ya, Lewis." Ed will go with Lewis as a friend, but he is not prepared to follow him as a pupil.

Certainly, he should not set Lewis up as a model. In one way, Lewis behaves more consistently as a character in the film than in the novel: bow-hunting for fish and refusing any liquor are hardier signs of noble savagery than, as in the novel, bringing along steaks to barbecue and admitting that "going down white water about half drunk is not to be missed" (14). Hardiness aside, though, Lewis betrays inconsistency (as in getting lost) and even hypocrisy. When Bobby observes that the hillbillies are "pretty rough lookin'," Lewis tells him, "Can't judge people by the way they look, chubby." If Lewis cannot tolerate Bobby for being fat, his point about appearances holds up ironically, for his own tough-guy demeanor washes off easily. Ed sees him unmasked when, on their first morning out, he tries to wake Lewis for a little hunting; Lewis, curled up, moans like a schoolchild when nudged and cannot be wakened (despite his sudden alertness the night before to a sound no one else heard). Needless to say, a broken leg should reduce anyone to writhing pain, but Lewis does not bear up in the film as well as in the novel. Dickey's Lewis can still be aware of what the others are doing, telling Ed he is doing "exactly right . . . better than I could do" (194). In Boorman's corresponding scene, Lewis can only cry weakly that he understands what Ed is telling him and then fall back in pain. Lewis, to say the least, has little to teach Ed. When they first get on the river, Ed tells Drew, "Watch Lewis. Maybe we can learn something." Drew will later make the important point about Lewis's relationship with nature and the wilderness: "He learn[s] 'em, he doesn't feel 'em. That's Lewis's problem. He wants to be one with nature, and he can't hack it." According to Boorman's characterization, if and when Lewis's prophecy about the system's failing comes true, the others can turn to him for lessons only in fishing and paddling a canoe— not living more fully in nature.

Unfortunately, the system does fail. By the acts of rape and murder, indeed, two systems fail at once: the actual system of civilized justice and the mythical system of Arcadian life.

> There is no Garden of Eden, no American Adam, no noble savage; the two mountain men who would presumably be closest to the natural state are in actuality the most depraved and corrupt, the least moral characters in the novel. There is, in fact, no great immemorial forest to which civilized man might return.[26]

The men who attack Bobby and Ed are neither the easygoing types from the ad agency, nor the dependable, accommodating moun- taineers from Lewis's previous encounter. Ed may have hoped for Wordsworth, but he gets Conrad. In the novel, only his ability to adapt gets him out.

As should be clear already, Ed desires some transformation of his life, although he certainly would never willingly undergo the change necessitated by this weekend's ordeal. At first, we may be repulsed by the violence of this transformation; however, this "gut" reaction does not match Ed's own feelings, nor does the novel's tone offer support for it. Instead, Ed's violent behavior should be seen on further consideration as not only necessary under the circumstances, but also a healthy extension of Ed's natural talents rather than a murderous betrayal of his values.

Recall that Ed has a genuine talent for harmonizing the parts of a layout, but that his life generally bores him. Thus, he goes with Lewis in the modest hope of breaking his routine; anything more is too vague a possibility to be entertained for long. When Ed first reaches the river, he sees his reflection in the car window and is pleased with the image of himself as "a tall forest man, an explorer, guerilla, hunter" (62). Lewis had earlier told him that a fantasy life establishes the true measure of actual life. Ed defensively endures his quotidian existence, yet any transformation such as he will actually experience seems now to be no more than a fantasy or a flattering image. Still, the manipulation and realization of images are, if you will, second nature to Ed, and if not quite deliberately, Ed begins to realize that image of the forest man as soon as he gets on the river.

Ed adapts Lewis's naturalism to a second nature because he does not instinctively become a primitive so much as he mentally projects himself into the place of a primitive. The distinction is important, for the man of instinct, Lewis, breaks under duress, whereas "Ed's culture helps him effectively to adapt his quite human traits and skills to the immediate demands of the environment"; this cultural background includes Ed's visual and organizational talents as well as "models available in his local cinema."[27] For instance, Ed has no experience with a canoe, but sort of knows what to do from seeing films or other pictures. That night, he can imaginatively hunt with the owl, and the next morning he can hunt deer for real and get within fifteen yards of one by concentrating: "I was as invisible as a tree" (84). He is still enough of an outsider to get "psyched out" (87), lifting his bow hand and missing the easy shot, but he gets a shot. The small satisfactions of paddling a canoe and hunting in a forest do not relieve his frustrations, however. In these activities, he comes in touch with nature only to the extent that he is away from the office or the suburbs.

Further down the river, deeper into the wilderness, like Marlow in *Heart of Darkness*, Ed confronts a nature that, rather than merely diverting and relaxing, will be abiding. The ugliness and meanness of the two hillbillies who terrorize Ed and Bobby, who sodomize Bobby and intend to do the same to Ed, are horribly vivid in the lengthy rape scene. They do not represent nature, but they act as catalysts that force Ed into the real confrontation. Because the two hold a gun on their victims, Lewis must shoot the one covering the other's crime. Anyone would agree that Lewis acts justifiably in self-defense. The law of civilization begins to give way to the law of the jungle only when the men debate how to dispose of the body. Bobby, still in shock, does not participate.

Ed also cannot order his mind; at first, he expects some kind of showdown "in which Lewis would step out of the woods on one side of the clearing with his bow and the tall man would show on the other, and they would have it out in some way that it was hard to imagine" (103). The showdown, though, occurs between Lewis, "vivid" and "smiling easily" after his great shot, and Drew: Lewis speaks for the jungle, and Drew speaks for the law—but Ed will have to make the choice.

Drew asserts that the only thing to do is to turn the body over to the authorities and tell them the whole story. Lewis argues that going to the law would be a mistake, for the trial that would ensue would have a local jury disinclined to acquit any outsiders who shot one of their own in the back. As he listens, Ed feels the pull of Lewis's wilderness: "He had a point. I listened to the woods and the river to see if I could get an answer" (108). That is to say, Ed is turning away from what Lewis calls Drew's "conventional point of view" (109), the notion that civilization has all the answers.[28] When asked for his opinion, Bobby angrily kicks the dead body. Ed, however, has gone from initial shock and confusion to a willingness to hear the wilderness speak through Lewis. Drew pleads that concealing the body, a difficult enough task, will invite and seemingly corroborate accusations of murder. Lewis has a plan, though, and indicates in a sweeping gesture all of their surroundings as a good place to hide the body. The idea, of course, is that the dam will flood the entire scene, and anything buried under a lake "is as buried as it can get" (112). By now, Ed senses that Lewis is the only one in control of himself, and he admits to himself that he will go along—will have to go along— with anything Lewis does. As an ironic nod to lawful procedure, Lewis insists on a binding vote: Bobby wants the body—and the incident—buried; Drew tries to win Ed over by appealing to his suburban steadiness—"You're a reasonable man. You've got a family" (113)—unaware of Ed's unhappiness with his steadiness. Lewis's way prevails, and the four men are soon pushing deeper into the woods for a good burial site.

Having listened to the woods and river for an answer, Ed is now entering the wilderness and letting it enter him, feeling lost in a strangely reassuring way: "If you were in something as deep as we were in, it was better to go all the way" (115–16). After the burial, Ed notices a new isolation from the others, particularly Lewis, and a new comfort on the river that enables him to paddle "in long steady motions" and know "where the rocks were by the differences in the swirling of the water" (120). By following Lewis, Ed has set himself up for an ordeal he will face alone, but he has also found the natural wherewithal to do so successfully.

Ed feels isolated in his mind, and he is soon physically isolated too. Back on the river, Drew falls out of the canoe (Lewis will later insist that the second hillbilly shot Drew) and capsizes it. With his new feel for the river, Ed bodysurfs through the rapids to the calm water at the bottom of a gorge; when the other canoe hits the first, and Lewis and Bobby are pitched out, Lewis comes through with a broken leg. Because Bobby is not that fit to begin with, Ed becomes the leader, the one responsible for the others.

As such, Ed projects himself into the role quickly and draws well on his organizational talents. Believing that the second hillbilly will be stalking them from atop the gorge, Ed decides that he must scale the cliff, which looks "like a gigantic drive-in movie screen" (126), and, in accord with the Saturday matinee code, kill their enemy before he can kill them: "It's either him or us" (131). Lewis, otherwise helpless, encourages him when he reminds Ed that survival is everything. Ed surpasses anything Lewis would have done, however, for Ed does not just go hunting. Ed must enter the other man's head, make their "minds fuse" (154), so that once atop the gorge, he can know when the man will come looking for them and from what spot he will choose to shoot down on them. Apropos Lewis's survivalist philosophy, Ed realizes "that the forces he is dealing with are unconcerned and essentially physical and that his response must also be unconcerned and essentially physical."[29] Ed's superiority results from the fact that, in adapting himself physically, he is adapting himself imaginatively.[30] He is not hunting, as he did earlier for deer. Rather than looking for his quarry, Ed finds his spot and beholds his quarry even before it appears.

Thus, Ed does not so much descend to animalism as he rises to the challenge of projecting himself as an animal. He is not blind in primitive rage, but he is hypersensitive in visionary involvement with his task. Hence, his practically sexual possession of the cliff as he scales it; his wondrous view of the river without looking; his meticulous and vivid feel for his surroundings as he sets up his perch; and, despite his coming a moment later than when everything was perfect, his shot at his quarry almost exactly as he anticipated it.

His role must continue, though, for the two fire at each other simultaneously; Ed falls from his tree, is pierced by his own extra arrow, and knows that he has won only when his enemy comes at him and collapses at the last moment before shooting him. Later, after fainting in pain and relief, Ed cuts the arrow out of his side and goes after his victim who has crawled away, even feeling or smelling the blood when he cannot see it in the dark. When he finds the body, only then can Ed say, "His brain and mine unlocked and fell apart" (169), and he can quit the role he has projected so successfully.

Once he has shed the role of the hunter, Ed must confront the fact and the morality of taking a human life—an immediately harrowing confrontation, for when Ed sees his victim's face clearly, the toothless man who held a gun on him during the rape now has teeth. Despite discovering that these teeth are in a partial plate and noting the general resemblance otherwise, Ed admits he still is uncertain that he killed the right man. His uncertainty will be compounded when they find Drew's body downriver: Lewis will insist that a mark on Drew's head came from a bullet, not a rock, but Ed will leave the body underwater because an autopsy could raise too many questions. Therefore, Ed doubts whether he killed the right man and whether he had a legitimate reason to kill him regardless.

Ed's doubts should not influence readers to charge Ed with murder and unreliable narration after the fact:

> If Ed's assumptions about Drew's death and the possibility of being shot at again from the cliff were valid—and they are reasonable enough, given the bizarre premise of the original rape and killing—then it would have been dangerous not to act on them. The coincidence of having an innocent man appear at the time and place one expects a murderer is too improbable for the character, and, I suspect, for most readers. The effect of the ambiguity is disturbing for reader and character, but any taking of human life should be disturbing.[31]

If anything, the doubts show Ed again to be superior to his model, Lewis. Lewis gloated over the expertise of his kill, whereas Ed, although matching that expertise, retains his humanity by feeling anxiety over what he has had to do (the arrow in his side acting as a physical emblem of this mental pain). An animal would know no such regret as this, and Ed immediately overcomes any such animalistic tendencies. Regardless of his victim's identity, no one would ever know what happened, and Ed, able to do anything he wants to the body, contemplates sexual mutilation, decapitation, even cannibalism: "I waited carefully for some wish to come; I would do what it said." The "ultimate horror" does not arrive, however, and instead he sings a pop tune that comes to mind: "I finished, and I was withdrawn from" (170).[32] Ed will listen to the woods and river for what he must do, but his naturalization is not so complete that he can also hear what no sane human could not hear; like Marlow, he looks over the edge, but withdraws from stepping into the abyss.

Out of the ordeal, Ed's develops more than an ability to kill. Evidence of his rejuvenation comes before he is even out of danger. When he is climbing down with the body, the rope breaks and Ed falls into the river, where he feels the current flow through him, in and out of his every orifice. Before he was frustrated and blocked, but now the river has opened him completely.

Nevertheless, before Ed can put his restored sensibilities to good and honorable use, he must employ them to get off the river and away from legal investigation. First, he and Bobby sink the hillbilly's body in the river. Then, when they find Drew's body, they do the same. Finally, Ed must formulate a version of all the events so that there will be no conclusive investigation. In short, he must return to civilization with no overt traces of the wilderness.

When the four men entered the dangerous part of the river, the last sign of benign civilization was a farm with cows; the first sign that they have returned is the sight of another farm and cows. About their journey between these points, Ed will lie. After the last set of rapids, Ed makes Bobby look at the scene and agree on a story: these rapids capsized the canoes, causing Drew's disappearance and Lewis's injury; they never saw anybody else, and all evidence to the contrary would remain virtually inaccessible upriver. Like Marlow's reasoning, Ed's motive for telling the lie goes beyond self-preservation: the truth is too dark to tell. Nevertheless, as another image that he can now manipulate convincingly, the lie grows "so strong in my mind that I had trouble getting back through it to the truth" (227–28).

The lie contributes to the theme of living with doubts or ambiguities as a way of living. Ed learns "that morality is not grounded in absolutes, that there are circumstances under which even murder cannot be reduced to simple notions of right and wrong."[33] Lewis had no doubts because of his pride, and maybe only Drew gave such matters much thought. Ed's lie allows him and Lewis to reenter society with a chastened appreciation for all the other social "lies" that keep the wilderness away.

Ed's new awareness, coming at such an awful cost, becomes a source of satisfaction and new life. He implicitly rejects the possibility of a fulfilling life in the woods—the only place where, according to Lewis, "you'd be in touch" (42)—because he still needs other people; about the ambulance driver, Ed says, "Just that contact was what I needed most" (197). At the same time, he realizes the impossibility of a fulfilling life without his newly acquired contact with natural forces; the first night away from the river, he feels "too dry" and takes a shower in order to feel immersed in "river-water" again before retiring to a "night in brilliant sleep" (203), as opposed to the dreamless sleep he had known before. When he sees himself in a mirror, he is satisfied that he has more than matched the image of the tall, green mountain man, looking now like some survivor of a disaster. Everything Ed does thereafter confirms his new vitality. He looks forward to facing the sheriff, feeling "wounded and stronger" for "the stitches were pulling me together" (211).

And he is stronger. When the authorities find the broken canoe well above the point where their story had them capsizing, Ed coolly tells them that they misunderstood and has another version ready. When the deputy challenges him and suggests they know something about his brother-in-law, missing in the woods, Ed answers with indignation and challenges him to produce any evidence. Later, when Ed and Bobby are leaving to go home, Ed has one last confrontation with the sheriff, a scene he compares to a western in which the marshal runs the bad guys out of town. After one last question about having four life jackets—Ed tells him they had extras—the sheriff adds his recognition of Ed's natural ability: "You done good. . . .You'us hurt bad, but if it wudn't for you you'd all be in the river with your other man" (225). The only incident that haunts Ed somewhat is seeing the local cemetery being dug up for relocation before the flood.

He drives home, tells Drew's wife the bad news, reflects that the truth would not help her, and gives himself up to the loving ministrations of his wife but cannot tell her what is on his mind. He goes back to work and gradually relaxes as the finished dam covers his past. But his life has changed for the better because of the river. Society may dam up the river, but it remains in Ed's mind, where "it ran as though immortally" (234). Ed's archery, ad copy, and even some creative artwork improve, and he rehires and befriends an art enthusiast he had fired before because he was out of place in a commercial agency. Sexually, his interest in the model causes him to take her out to dinner, but she has become less real and therefore less fascinating, whereas his wife remains very real. He has a vacation home on a resort lake—not Lake Cahula, but similar to it—and lives happily, at work and at home.[34]

Ed completes his naturalization without its becoming excessive or obsessive. Ed has gone from being stifled by the tide of everyday life to tapping the energetic current beneath the tide. The violent baptism, as Dickey points out, requires only the one immersion: violence saves his life without becoming his way of life, for "he doesn't have to keep on doing it, and do these things again later in life—he's done it once and that's all he needs to do it. That's all he needs to know, that he's capable of it. And you can see in the last few pages, it's a quietly transfiguring influence on him."[35] The river gives him a natural strength that he channels into his natural talents. To that extent, the river restores Ed to life—and this restoration of nature through nature marks Ed's true deliverance.

As should already be clear, Lewis would prefer revolution to restoration. Nature for him should not only energize life; it should dictate a whole way of life according to a cruelly indifferent law of the jungle. Of course, as I have discussed above, Lewis lives to amend his views, and the change he undergoes serves to reinforce the validity of Ed's change—a validity further enhanced by reference to Bobby and Drew.

Bobby, an easy-going fellow like Ed, has no self-doubts. He is so unnatural and his life so unexamined that "he lives through the experience with the least physical injury and with the least amount of effort. . . . Despite his sexual encounter with the mountain man, Bobby remains essentially unchanged by his harrowing experience."[36] Bobby insists that the "creature comforts" (14) of liquor be brought along, and, in an already inexperienced bunch, he stands out as the worst canoeist—dead weight, except that he was so uncoordinated. During the cruel and senseless rape, Bobby shows embarrassment more than outrage, looking "like a boy undressing for the first time in a gym" (99). As weak as Lewis is strong, Bobby offers little more help than the incapacitated Lewis in getting them to safety. When Bobby fails to follow Ed's plan—to set out with Lewis just before daybreak while Ed waits for their enemy above—Ed picks up the dead man's rifle and yells that he should "shoot the hell out of you, Bobby, you incompetent asshole" (171). Ed resists, of course, but Bobby does not help later either. Running the last set of rapids, Bobby just sits low in the canoe and lets Ed fend for them all (in the screenplay, he even "flings his half-paddle away and gets ready to die, his hands over his face"[37]) In the end, Bobby's embarrassment and incompetence give an ironic comfort to Ed, who worries that Bobby might betray their story: the image of "himself kneeling over the log . . . howling and bawling and kicking his feet like a little boy" (227) would ensure his cooperation. Indeed, Ed sees or hears little more of Bobby. Inasmuch as Bobby apparently has no doubts about his easy life, the river's energy cannot give him any new strength, nor can its ravages inflict any new weaknesses. This inability to change makes him a survivor of sorts, but it also renders him inferior to Ed and the others, all of whom are capable of change.

Like Bobby, Drew has no apparent doubts about his way of life, but unlike Bobby and like Lewis, he does have convictions. Those convictions involve a lawful and a personal respect for other people and things rather than a self-centered survivalism. Thus, whereas Bobby teases the gas station attendant about his hat, Drew talks to him about the countryside and the river (only Drew seriously raises the question of whether they know what they are getting into). Drew winds up playing a country duet with the man's son (Bobby brings liquor; Drew brings a guitar). Drew reaches the boy—an albino with cast eyes, and an idiot savant on the banjo—through music, and although Ed is standing behind Drew, he says, "The back of his neck was sheer joy" (55). Once on the river, Drew also enjoys it, whooping it up and admitting afterward, "I've always wanted to do this. . . . Only I didn't know it" (75). He genuinely appreciates Lewis's introducing him to these experiences, but their convictions about survivalism and lawful respect clash after the killing of the hillbilly. Lewis argues, "There's not any right thing" that is certain, but Drew answers, "You bet there is. . . . There's only one thing" (107). Ed sides with Lewis, but from this point on, he starts to realize the limitations of both their convictions. Lewis's trust in his body will not save him from the rapids, and Drew's trust in respect for the law will not save him from the sniper. If Drew has any distinction in his favor, however, certainly his convictions show less pride and more humanity. He may die, but, unlike Lewis, he does not break in his beliefs as well as his body. Acknowledging this strength without denying the necessity of what he has done, Ed can later cradle

Drew's body and give him a sincere eulogy before letting him go: "You were the best of us, Drew. . . . The only decent one; the only sane one" (186). Nonetheless, these qualities prove useless in circumstances where decency and sanity are absent. Ed can act when Drew cannot, and for that, Ed saves himself and the other two. Ed regrets the circumstances, especially because of Drew's loss. However, after he lets Drew go and says, "We were free and in hell" (187), Ed is more in the right than he realizes: better damned than dammed up.

Ed's successes, his survival of the horrible ordeal as well as his ability to prosper afterward, would have been impossible without the feelings of ennui that afflict him at the outset. Lacking real satisfaction with his life, Ed needs a rejuvenating experience, and when that experience turns ugly, he still gets through it for the new life at the other end. The Ed Gentry of the film, however, exhibits none of this ennui; his life is comfortable, if unexamined. In fact, the film's Ed seems to take his life for granted, and owing to this fundamental difference from the novel's protagonist, the ordeal of the river offers, not a challenge to start a new life, but instead a test of the life and values he already assumes to be worthwhile.

Lewis mentions several times that the river will soon be gone, turned into a "big, dead lake," and at the beginning of the film, he places the blame on the suburban living Ed and the others enjoy: "You push a little more power into Atlanta, little more air conditioners, for your smug little suburb, and you know what's gonna happen? We're gonna rape this whole flat damn landscape—we're gonna rape it." These four tourists, then, if not from the power company (as the gas station attendant believes at first), come from the outside, where the landscape is expendable. Do they know anything about what is to be sacrificed? We hear Bobby ask, "Any hillbillies up there anymore, Lewis?" and we see him in mock amazement over the junk that preceded them. Bobby cares less, but his ignorance may represent all of them.

The only characteristic that sets Ed apart in these early scenes is his feeling of being out of place, an embarrassment over his health and comfortable existence. The excursion to the wilderness allows the novel's Ed an escape, and he immediately responds to the natural surroundings. On the other hand, the film's Ed may want to enjoy himself, but he cannot escape the awareness (as Boorman's camera emphasizes) of his being out of his element so far from home. At the gas station, James F. Beaton writes, the attendant and the few other mountain people seen are, in stark contrast to the weekend canoeists, "impoverished, inscrutable, and literally degenerate."[38] Whereas Bobby and Lewis are condescending and Drew is friendly, Ed alone seems distant and uneasy. While Drew is playing his banjo duel with the boy, a hillbilly comes up behind Bobby and Ed, gruffly asking, "Who's pickin' a banjo here?" Ed cannot bring himself to answer, although the man means no harm; he joins the music by whistling. At the garage where they hire drivers for the cars, we share a point-of-view shot with Ed as he looks through a window: inside, a very old woman watches over a dwarfish, open-mouthed, expressionless child; the reaction shot shows Ed's shock and embarrassment over his intrusion. In the novel, Ed talks about the general deformity he has noticed in country people, but in the film, Ed's embarrassed silence, the way he stands off from the others, and the addition of this scene looking through the window—all serve to emphasize his being an intrusive outsider.

Soon, Ed feels vaguely threatened by the surroundings he does not know. When they finally put in on the river, Ed takes a last look up on the bank to see the three men hired as drivers; in this point-of-view shot, the men, moving off in the dense foliage, look like threatening shadows because they are lit only from behind. (This dark effect anticipates the first glimpse Ed gets of the two who attack them.) Right after this scene, the canoes float under a footbridge from which the retarded boy with the banjo stares down. Despite Drew's waving and mimicking of guitar playing, the boy does not react other than to watch them pass below. Ed takes one last look behind at the boy and his banjo swinging like a pendulum, and he is clearly unnerved by the boy's vacant stare.

Ed probably would rather not see these disturbing images, but what he cannot see may scare him as much. The first night in camp, Lewis suddenly walks into the darkness, reappearing in a moment, saying, "I thought I heard somethin'." Frightened, the others ask, "Some*thing* or some*one*?" Lewis, brave and enigmatic, answers, "I don't know," and he laughs at their fright. This incident briefly stirs up the uneasy feelings brought on by contact with the mountain people. Seen or unseen, then, things in the wilderness put Ed on edge.

After passing the boy on the bridge, Ed can enjoy the rest of the day; they see no one else to disturb them. In the first stretch of white water, Ed and Drew handle their canoe very smartly and look exhilarated. Even so, for Ed, the trip is recreation, not recreation. That first afternoon, when Ed and Lewis are drifting and fishing, Ed seems self-assured. Lewis gives him the spiel on how the system is going to fail, but Ed answers, between sips from his beer can, "Well, the system's done all right by me." Lewis tries to make Ed's comfort seem shallow: "Oh, yeah. You got a nice job. Got a nice house. Nice wife. Nice kid." As he is nocking his arrow, Lewis presents a picture of a strong, wilderness hunter, and his repeated use of "nice" clearly mocks Ed. Ed says, "You make that sound rather shitty, Lewis," but, undaunted, he still asserts that he likes his life. When Lewis asks why, then, go on these trips with him, Ed replies, "You know, sometimes I wonder about that." Whatever disturbing feelings have come from the sights he has seen in the hills, Ed clearly has not brought any serious doubts with him from work and home. He goes with Lewis to go; he does not require an important reason for being on the river. Before going to sleep on the first night, a drunk Ed says, "No matter what disaster may occur in other parts of the world, or what petty little problems arise in Atlanta, no one can find us up here." Rather than celebrate a communion with nature, this little ode merely acknowledges that they are away from the phones. Ed will be sleeping it off rather than hunting with owls this night. The difference from the novel is somewhat representative: the film's Ed may be living in a daze (although I do not think we are meant to be too hard on him), but more significantly, he is not hunting for something so deep in the wilderness that only through an owl can he see it, let alone catch it.

Ed's lack of any deep yearning for renewal literally unfits him for hunting the next morning. In the novel, his prowess and his desire lapse only at the final moment when he lifts his bow hand as he releases the arrow. In the film, the problem is more like fear of killing. When Ed nocks his arrow and comes to full draw, a hum rises on the soundtrack. His hands start to shake, and he starts to sweat. His shot flies well off the mark. When he retrieves his arrow, Ed looks a little relieved, but still uneasy enough to slip on the damp leaves in the forest. The novel's Ed barely misses the deer because he has not yet quite attuned his natural powers to his surroundings. In the film, Ed feels no strong need to be in touch with nature; therefore, he cannot shoot the deer because he does not really want to kill it.

Back at camp, Ed does not admit getting a shot, let alone missing it (unlike the novel's version in which Ed tells Lewis that he would not have missed such an easy target), but does almost tell Lewis something that he cannot get out. I think he wanted to say that he knows no reason to kill a deer for himself. In one day on the river, Ed has asserted the value of his way of life (albeit from a reclining position with a beer cooler at hand), and nothing he has seen will convince him of the superiority of Lewis's survivalism in the woods; if anything, the waste and deformity of wilderness living has convinced him of the opposite. He may want to tell Lewis that wasting another deer would serve nothing, but, cannot out of embarrassment. Ed is embarrassed by his health in front of the country people, and, conversely, he is embarrassed by what Lewis would see as weakness. In both cases, Ed takes the easy step of standing aside and keeping quiet. This humanly natural reaction will lead Ed into more trouble than he could suspect.

As in the novel, the real conflict for Ed starts with the assault by the two mountain men. Ed's quiet reticence, relative to the novel's version of the scene, continues. Bobby speaks more to the men at first (lines that Ed spoke in the novel), and when Ed does try to talk to them, he speaks more politely: "This is ridiculous. Excuse me" rather than, "Shit . . . I don't know whether you're making whiskey or hunting or rambling around in the woods for your whole fucking life" (96). Ed's nervous reactions around these two do not differ much from his reactions to the other mountain folk, although these two are truly threatening.

Given that genuine danger, Lewis's killing of the one man is again a justifiable homicide.[39] Also as in the novel, the ensuing debate occurs between Lewis and Drew. Drew almost frantically asserts that the "one thing to do" is turn the body over to the police and tell them exactly what happened; he shouts, "It is a matter of the law!" Lewis coolly and dispassionately makes his case that a jury trial is not in their interests: "Shit, all these people are related. Be goddamned if I wanna come back up here and stand trial with this man's aunt and his uncle, maybe his momma and his daddy sittin' in the jury box." Lewis also answers all of Drew's questions the same way he does in the novel: he tells them that, if the incident comes out, "this thing's gonna be hanging over us the rest of our lives"; and he reminds them that the lake will bury the incident "about as buried as you can get." The argument, once more, pits the law of civilization against the law of the jungle.

Because Bobby is too disturbed to take part, Ed again must decide. In the film, however, his reactions and reasoning change—

even if the decision does not. Ed's decision in the novel, although made under pressure and with reservations about Lewis's attitude, develops gradually as Ed listens to nature and comes to see Lewis as a strong leader in such circumstances. No such orderly thinking affects his decision in the film. With the ghastly corpse in such plain sight, Ed's expression remains scared and confused. When Lewis first asks his opinion, he stammers: "I don't know. Uh, I really don't know." Bobby, as before, wants everything buried and hushed up, so when they vote, Ed is under the gun once more. Drew pleads with him: "For God's sake, you got a wife, you got a child. . . . Think about your family, Ed." Ed shouts, "Yes!" but the disturbed cry does not really assent to Drew's point. Drew goes on: "We gotta do the right thing. Ed, we're gonna have to live with this the rest of our lives." Drew has repeated Lewis twice here: his mention of Ed's family recalls Lewis's mocking of such a "nice" home, a mocking that Ed rebuffed; and his warning about living with the incident "the rest of our lives" echoes the same line Lewis uses in the service of a different argument. Out of these arguments, Ed's answer comes naturally: "Right! I'm with Lewis." Drew cannot know Ed's self-satisfaction and comfort at home, so he cannot anticipate the more apparent threat to that comfortable life: not a guilty conscience for the rest of his life, but a possibly life-long legal entanglement. Lewis wins Ed over with the possibility of burying the incident and thereby avoiding the consequences. Ed has seen rural poverty, has faced a man with a gun, and has witnessed the rape of his friend—and each time he could do nothing but stand aside and observe. Given the chance to do something, Ed stands aside in deference to Lewis. Whereas, in the novel, Ed's following of Lewis begins his rejuvenation in nature, here it concludes a giving in to human nature, taking the apparently easy way out.

Unlike the novel, then, the film does not show Ed's becoming one with nature, at ease in the isolation of the wilderness. Instead, the haunting implications of what he has done arise immediately. The grisly sight of the dead man's face figures prominently in the sequence in which they carry the body into the woods and dig the grave. The most notable difference from the novel's treatment of the burial involves the dead man's hand: while the four men push dirt over the body, one hand sticks out of the ground; we see Ed in a close shot react, and after he pulls himself together, he pushes the hand under the loose dirt, the camera tilting down on the very spot.

Ed will become isolated in the ordeal to come, but the concomitant responsibilities represent less a challenge to be met than the consequences of a test already failed. Compared to the novel's version, the men's actions in the film betray more panic after the burial. In the novel, they remain calm enough to redistribute the gear in the canoes, giving Lewis's canoe the heavier load, and they travel for an hour before coming to the rapids where Drew falls out and they all capsize. Not so in the film. Having run back to the canoes, Ed asks, "What's the plan, Lewis?" Lewis says to himself, "Plan?" before telling the others that they will just complete the trip and get home; obviously, he has not given any thought to events that may come after the burial. The four of them push off in a hurry. Immediately, the river's sound grows louder and deeper. Ed shouts at Drew to put his life jacket on, but Drew's dazed expression shows that he does not hear or does not care. Very quickly they hit a stretch of white water surrounded by high stone walls. Lewis sees something atop the cliff and yells for them to get going. Ed must yell to Drew to keep paddling, but amidst the roar of the river, Drew acts disoriented and stupefied. Suddenly, from Ed's point of view in the rear of the canoe, we see Drew shake his head, shake it again, and keel over into the river. The ensuing tumble—Lewis flying head over heels, Bobby tossing about, Ed trying to grab a rock and slipping away, Lewis screaming in pain, Ed finally rolling over the falls into the calmer bottom of the gorge—gives no impression of Ed's being any more in touch with the river than the others are. A couple of point-of-view shots of rolling over the falls show us the confusion they all must feel; in addition, four consecutive shots of Ed calling for Drew—a low-angle shot of him with the cliff behind, a wider shot of the gorge, a high-angle shot of the gorge, and a higher-angle shot of the entire scene—emphasize their desolation. Ed voted with Lewis because, he must have reasoned, Lewis's law of the jungle promised the easier way out of their predicament. Now Ed must realize that such reasoning cannot hold in the jungle.

Inasmuch as Ed has involved himself in Lewis's kind of nature out of desperation, his relationship to that nature has little chance for development. He has not come to the woods looking for something to enliven his suburban existence, and therefore, from the outset, he has not been refashioning his natural surroundings to create that something; he is just along for the ride. Now, when that ride has been so rudely interrupted, his new role of deliverer, in contrast to Ed's role in the novel, cannot further develop that creation, cannot become a task he projects himself into, thereby completing his naturalization. Instead, he must accept the role as the only, desperate choice available because of other desperate choices. Lost in the gorge, with Drew missing and Lewis saying Drew was shot, Ed thinks that they are all sitting ducks for the gunman. In anger, he shouts: "Lewis, what are we gonna do, Lewis? You're the guy with the answers. What the hell do we do now?" Lewis replies, "Now you get to play the game." Ed says, "You're right, Lewis, you're right," echoing his assent to Lewis's plan before, but now his tone has turned from panic to despair. In both novel and film, the role of deliverer is thrust upon Ed, but in the latter, he accepts it as a last chance without his counterpart's "joy at the thought of where I was and what I was doing" (137).

In a sense, therefore, this desperation makes the task much simpler. Ed does not adopt an elaborate animal cunning to anticipate and kill his foe. He tells Bobby, "Well, if he knows where we are, then we sure as hell know where he's gonna be: right up there." "Up there" is the top of the cliff, so he must climb the cliff and wait. Boorman's simpler portrayal of Ed's climb reflects the simpler nature of the task.

In another sense, however, Ed's mission is not simpler in the film than in the novel. The novel's Ed feels fear, but he also draws strength from his surroundings, eager to outdo himself and to become something more than he was. In the film, Ed knows the same fear, but he is further diminished by the losses he has suffered and now must act against his own inclinations to escape even more suffering or loss. Thus, on the way up the cliff, Ed draws momentary sustenance from a wallet photo of his wife and son. Then he nearly slips, and in so doing, drops his wallet; he must set aside his normal values and kill this man, or he will not live to enjoy these values again. James F. Beaton scoffs at this scene:

> The poignance and artificiality of such a moment is wholly out of keeping with the novel's enthusiasm; there, one senses Gentry's pride in having at last become a calculating and determined hunter, one who methodically clears away an unobstructed firing position in a pine tree ... and anticipates carefully the suspected attacking riflemen's strategy.[40]

Of course, the scene differs from the original, but it betrays no false emotions because it fits the drama of this version. Boorman's intention results in Ed's finding himself in a different kind of conflict: Ed must not so much adapt himself to the role as lose himself in it.

Appropriately, then, Ed does not vanquish his enemy with skillful dispatch. Once atop the gorge, he does not need to calculate his foe's plan and painstakingly set an ambush for him at the anticipated spot; Ed simply nocks an arrow and fights off sleep—unsuccessfully. The hillbilly's appearance startles Ed awake, although the man does not see him at first. Ed draws down on him, but the hum on the soundtrack and his shaking, as before with the deer, increase; he tells himself, "Release," but he cannot kill the man any more than he could the deer. Only when the man sees him and fires his gun—only in honest self-defense— does Ed shoot back at the same instant. In the novel, Ed concentrates too long and hard on his shot, giving the hillbilly a chance to fire back. Here, Ed can hardly concentrate at all; when he lets loose, the shot will have to be lucky. Both versions have a moment of suspense when the hillbilly approaches, raises his gun, and then collapses with the arrow now clearly visible sticking out of his back. In the film, however, Ed has less control of himself because his fear outweighs almost all else. Earlier, Ed gave in to human nature by trying the seemingly easy way of avoiding confrontation, and now when he cannot avoid it, human nature causes a nearly immobilizing fear.

This fear keeps Ed from fainting away in this version: he has to jump up and make sure that the man is really dead. When he looks, he gets a new fear. He grabs the man's face and sees the teeth that his attacker did not have before. The man is wearing false teeth, as Ed discovers, much to his apparent relief, but later, with Bobby, he will not say for certain that it is the right man. [41]

The tension does not break for Ed. In the novel, when he tracks his victim and finds him, their minds unlock; the rope's snapping while Ed lowers the body to the river corresponds to this break. For Ed here, on the other hand, the fear and uncertainty do not allow him such a release. When the rope snaps, rather than entering the river and feeling its strength flow through him, Ed plunges into a dark pool where he becomes entangled with the rope and the ghastly embrace of the dead man. Sinking that body in the river does away with one fear, but uncertainty grows. When they find Drew's body, Ed and Bobby cannot decide if he has been shot, and they do not ask Lewis for his educated guess. Again to avoid legal questions, they sink Drew's body also. Bobby says,

"Oh, God, there's no end to it." Unlike in the novel, Ed cannot respond confidently: "Yes, there is. . . . This is the end. This is all we have to do, but we've got to do it right" (186). No conclusive evidence resolves this doubt for us and Ed—"was he shot by the surviving hillbilly or was his death an accident or possibly suicide?"—thereby robbing "the outcome of any sense of triumph."[42] Ed can do it right in the novel and make a personal triumph out of his ability to kill an enemy and then manage the legal questions afterward. Ed, in the film, has had doubts about almost everything he has done since getting on the river, and getting off the river will not dispel them.

They ride through the last set of rapids, and Ed sees a sign that they are back in civilization—a junk car on the shore. Ed concocts the same story for the authorities—that everything happened in these last rapids—but he does not reflect that the lie will protect the civilized as much as it will protect them. He lies simply because he realizes that "we're not out of this yet." As they paddle to their destination, we see a slow dissolve-montage of trees half-covered by placid water and of distant hills on which trucks are dumping more dirt for the dam: the cover-up is beginning.

They reenter civilization with less difficulty than Ed feared. Everybody is kind and helpful. He finds the cars where they are supposed to be, and the boy at the gas station (who resembles the retarded boy from before) shows genuinely patient concern despite Ed's difficulty in responding. In the hospital, Ed tells the nurse he is glad to be among "nice" things again: "Oh, chromium, paper tissues, hot water—nice." At the boarding house, when Ed enters, everyone around the dinner table stops talking out of respect for his hardship. Quietly, they pass him dishes of food, and they look on in sympathy when Ed momentarily breaks down and cries, probably for their kindness as much as his sadness. Bobby breaks the spell by commenting, "This corn is special, isn't it?" and hospitable conversation resumes all around. Even the sheriff holds no threat for him. When the deputy raises the same contradictions as in the novel, Sheriff Bullard calmly tells him that there is not any good evidence: "We don t have a thing. Let's just wait and see what comes out of the river." (James Dickey, who plays Bullard generally well, delivers this last line with a bit too much gravity.) All this kindness seemingly renders the lie unnecessary "because the sheriff . . . proves to be . . . more judicious than Ed, or the other survivors, would believe, despite the protestations of Drew."[43] The townspeople in the novel behave kindly also, but the film, especially with the expansion of the dinner scene, emphasizes their hospitality—their sharing of certain values with Ed. Later, as a languid cabby tells Ed and Bobby that the coming inundation will be the "best thing that ever happened to this town," they see a small church being towed out of town, its bell ringing. Ed must realize the expense at which he has preserved his comfortable life. He has betrayed the values he would keep, and the burial of this hospitable town symbolizes that betrayal. Ed knows for whom the church bell tolls.

Ed's lie still holds, but he does not get any satisfaction, let alone new vitality, out of the experience. In the novel, "the experience on the river becomes a sacred memory to Ed, and he seems to undergo a spiritual awakening as a result of this communion with darkness"; in Boorman's version, however, the "conclusion is much harsher" for "the journey has no purpose; nothing is achieved, nothing gained."[44] During his last talk with Sheriff Bullard, Ed salvages a little self-respect by not adding to the lie. Bullard asks about the extra life jacket, and Bobby tries to interpose, "Didn't we have an extra one?" They did have spares in the novel, but here Ed answers firmly, "No, Drew wasn't wearin' his." Asked why not, he replies, "I don't know." This exchange, which ended in the novel with the sheriff's telling Ed, "You done good" (225), ends here on a different note, when Bullard tells him: "Don't never do nothin' like this again. Don't come back up here. . . . I'd kinda like to see this town die peaceful." Thus admonished, Ed goes to get the canoe, and he sees the graveyard (shot through a little window in the foliage, like his first view of the river) where men and machinery are disinterring all the graves. The sounds match those of the equipment used by the authorities to drag the river. Rather than the energy of the river, Ed will take with him his sensation of discovered death.

The experience will continue to overshadow the comfortable life he has lived. Ed's return home includes no scenes in which we see Ed as a better man at work, a better husband at home, or a better archer at the lake with Lewis. Rather than the lovingly concerned nursing from his wife, Ed comes back to a brief, silent embrace, after which his wife sits idly in a chair away from him and their son. Then, as the soundtrack increasingly reverberates with an electrically distorted version of the banjo theme, the scene dissolves to a placid lake on a blue night: suddenly, a stark, white hand breaks the surface, and the scene quickly switches to Ed's bolting upright in bed and shouting, "No!" The dead hand could belong to any of the three corpses left under the lake. Clearly, Ed has not gotten in touch with his senses by developing a feel for nature; instead, he has capitulated to his human nature and left himself in the grasp of deathly guilt. He has delivered himself from one evil to another.

Unlike the protagonist of the novel, Ed here does not begin in doubt and end in affirmation. Just the opposite: he begins in self-assurance (albeit unexamined) and ends in doubt. Dickey's Ed passes his achievement test far better than we could have expected, whereas Boorman's Ed lacks the moral strength required to pass his test of character. Nature enhances the capabilities of one; human nature daunts the other.

Ed's diminished stature in the film fits other changes Boorman has made in characterization. As I have argued above, Lewis is a bit more fanatical and ridiculous in this version. Consequently, if Ed emerges from the ordeal as superior to Lewis, he has not surpassed much; more significantly, though, if the experience humbles Lewis, we see no evidence that Ed's example has anything to teach him.

Bobby's character features other important changes. Whereas Dickey's Bobby is so dull and easy-going as to be outwardly unaffected by any of the awful incidents, Boorman uses Bobby's character as a parallel that reinforces our view of Ed's character. At first, Bobby appears less tolerant and considerate than Ed. He teases the gas station attendant about his hat, he seems condescending in his mockery of the little hoe-down started by Drew and the boy, and he dismisses the whole scene, when the boy will not speak, by telling Drew, "Give him a couple bucks." He also falls way short as an outdoorsman. Lewis has to tell him which way is downstream, and the only pleasure Bobby takes in sleeping outside comes from his air mattress: "Well, I'll say one thing for the system—the system did produce the air mattress, or as it's better known among we camping types, the instant broad. And if you fellas will excuse me, I'm gonna go be mean to my air mattress." The declaration comically echoes Ed's statement that "the system's done all right by me." (Bobby's later remark, "I had my first wet dream in a sleeping bag," is a line spoken by Lewis to Bobby in the novel; the switch here reinforces both Bobby's lack of earnestness and Lewis's fanatical purity.)

We start to care more for Bobby, however, because Boorman makes him more sympathetically vulnerable. When he teases the man about his hat, the man tells him, "You don't know nuthin'";

this exchange follows the novel, but now Bobby turns away as if snubbed and hurt. The same reaction occurs when Bobby tries to express his excitement at riding through white water for the first time: "Yeah, we beat it, didn't we? Didn't we beat that?" But Lewis's reply—"You don't beat it. You don't beat this river"—dismisses that excitement, just as Lewis always dismisses "chubby." He is turned away once more when he tries to be friendly to the two hillbillies: he greets them, "How goes it?" but is snubbed by the mean answer, "What the hail ya think you're doin'?" This gesture of turning away hurt may demonstrate that Bobby's mocking behavior covers a nervous defensiveness: otherwise, why would he be hurt by rejection? Like Ed, he lives, perhaps, too comfortably, but instead of Ed's embarrassed silence, Bobby puts up a front of jollity or cynical humor to cope with those who lack such comforts.

Of course, Bobby's rape evinces that vulnerability most clearly. Here, too, Boorman makes Bobby more sympathetic by making the attack uglier. He displays the same sense of embarrassment at having to undress for the men, but we also perceive his fear when we hear him praying to himself—"Lord, deliver us from all"—and see him try to run with his pants half-down. Thereafter, the rape, if such can be imagined, inflicts much more humiliation than in the novel, with Bobby vainly trying to get away, pleading and groaning for the man to stop, and being forced to "squeal like a pig."

This added vulnerability has a definite function in the film: relative to the characterization in the novel, Bobby here functions much less as a foil to Ed; he becomes more dependable in spite of suffering more. Bobby does not fail to do what Ed tells him. In the last set of dangerous rapids, Bobby does not cower in the bottom of the canoe; rather, he keeps control of himself, paddles strongly, and collapses in relief after they reach safer waters. Bobby also stands up to the authorities with more steadiness. In the film, Ed accuses him of getting scared and telling the truth, but he has held firm; furthermore, Bobby has a scene in which he answers the deputy as firmly as Ed talks to the sheriff. When the deputy scornfully accuses, "Yeah, well, that's a goddam lie," Bobby does not turn away. Finally, when they are leaving, Bobby has enough strength to offer to drive Drew's car if Ed would rather not. Overall, although a less physically fit person, Bobby resembles Ed in that he comes to the woods in comfortable self-satisfaction, and he is leaving in chastened doubt. He tells Ed, "I don't think I'll see ya for a while," and we sense that Ed wants it this way also. Ed has nothing to be proud of in this trip, and he needs no extra reminders of his experience.

If Ed's character is not enhanced relative to Bobby's, it certainly diminishes in relation to Drew's character. Drew, once more, appreciates other people and the rights of law, and he remains firm in these convictions. In the duelling banjos scene, the boy is not hustled out by his father; instead, he and Drew find each other by strumming and responding to each other. Drew comes nearer, tells him, "Come on, I'm with ya," and the music takes off. When the boy's playing outraces him, Drew looks into his grotesque grin and says, "I'm lost" (in sharp contrast to Lewis's boast), although he strums the last chord with him. Rather than a friendly exchange of names, as in the novel, this scene ends with the boy's turning away from Drew's offered hand; Drew smiles and shrugs. All four of the men will be touched by this madness found in rustic beauty, but Drew's duet and friendly (if confused) smile demonstrates an openness superior to Lewis's bravado, Bobby's cynical insecurity, and Ed's embarrassed reticence.

Throughout the trip, Drew's openness allows him to be more appreciative of others. After running the first rapids, when Lewis sermonizes that the "first explorers saw this country . . . in a canoe," Drew responds, "I can imagine how they felt." Upon seeing that Lewis has speared a fish, Drew gleefully says, "Goddam, he got one!" (Bobby intones an ironic, "Terrific, Lewis," and then adds quietly, "I hate him.") Nevertheless, with no disrespect to Lewis or Ed, after Ed returns from deer hunting, Drew states, "I don't understand how anyone can shoot an animal." Drew hates purposeless violence. Shooting a fish for dinner or shooting a man in self-defense serves a worthy purpose; shooting a deer for sport serves nothing. Worse, burying the dead man betrays the law and serves no purpose, for it unjustifiably denies and hides a justifiable act. Drew's friendly appreciation for others is bounded by a civilized respect for all life, friendly or not.

As the one who holds these values most strongly, Drew suffers the most after their betrayal. He looks almost insane in the way he helps dig the grave, and his distracted mind certainly contributes to his death (whether or not a bullet grazed his head, he probably died by drowning—a fate he might have avoided if he had had his life jacket on). Ed acknowledges these values when he commends Drew's body to the river: "Drew was a good husband to his wife, Linda. And, uh, you were a wonderful father to your boys,

Drew—Jimmy and Billy Ray. And if we come through this, I promise to do all I can for them. He was the best of us." Only this last sentence comes from the novel. With the additional lines, Ed recalls home and family, the life Ed wants to preserve. In the novel, his eulogy expresses regret that Drew had to die, and nostalgia for values that were of no use in the wilderness. Here Ed must realize that Drew's values are his values, that he betrayed them both, and that Drew's death is unnecessary. Around the campfire, Drew sang, "The world's just a bottle / and life but a dream; / and the bottle, when it's empty, / it ain't worth a damn." In the loss of Drew, Ed feels most acutely the carelessness of how he has lived and the waste of what he has done: neither his comfortable life nor his crimes to preserve it are worth the cost of dam or damnation.

Boorman's film obviously adapts Dickey's novel unfaithfully, yet charges that he misses Dickey's point miss Boorman's point. The definite changes Boorman makes clearly serve a different, coherent intention. Dickey's bored, rudderless protagonist finds in the wilderness the means to rejuvenate good and valuable capacities within himself. The most challenging detail of this characterization involves its violence. Dickey succeeds in making the violence necessary without celebrating it. Ed must do what he does in order to survive, and the humane value of that violent deliverance comes out in his creative channeling of his renewed energies. Ed survives by violence in order to live fully according to the worthy abilities that were growing dormant before.

Boorman sets aside this protagonist in favor of another who may be as easily found in suburban living: not a man plagued by doubts, but one whose unexamined comforts keep him away from all doubts. New surroundings and sudden, random violence afflict this protagonist differently, but the power of the drama is not diminished by its new direction. In fear and panic, Ed tries to preserve himself by the easiest means at hand: covering up the incident and attempting to forget it. The vanity of this endeavor and the betrayal of the values it is meant to protect become manifest with powerful irony, for Ed did not have to fail and suffer the consequent degradation. In the novel, all the evidence suggests that, despite Drew's lawful pleading, the other hillbilly would still have been there to shoot at them. The condensed duration of events in the film, however, implies that, had they followed Drew's civilized impulse, they would have been downriver before the other hillbilly could get in place to threaten them; they would have still had to contend with the river, but they would have been at full strength.

Strength marks the difference in the protagonists. Dickey's Ed draws strength from nature without adopting nature's amoral law of the jungle. Boorman's Ed does not have the moral strength to withstand human nature, and, thereafter, no feat of physical strength can recover that loss. The differing currents, however, move with equal power: Dickey's story of creative growth and Boorman's story of self-betrayal have the same ability to carry us swiftly and emotionally to their separate ends. The river forks at the beginning, and arriving at either destination, one cannot say with justification that Dickey or Boorman is the better navigator.

Walking Around in Harper Lee's Shoes:
To Kill a Mockingbird

> All joy or sorrow for the happiness or calamities of others is produced by an act of the imagination, that realises the event however fictitious, or approximates it however remote, by placing us, for a time, in the condition of him whose fortune we contemplate; so that we feel, while the deception lasts, whatever motions would be excited by the same good or evil happening to ourselves.
>
> Our passions are therefore more strongly moved, in proportion as we can more readily adopt the pains or pleasures to our minds, by recognising them as once our own, or considering them as naturally incident to our state of life. It is not easy for the most artful writer to give us an interest in happiness or misery, which we think ourselves never likely to feel, and with which we have never yet been made acquainted.
>
> —Samuel Johnson, *The Rambler*, No. 60

The type of adaptation yet unexamined seldom—or supposedly never—occurs: the film that faithfully recreates the powers and pleasures of an excellent novel. More often than not, those who would claim that great novels make for poor adaptations point to masterpieces in print. Thus, *Wuthering Heights*, *Moby Dick*, *Ulysses*, and *The Great Gatsby* have undone those filmmakers who dared to adapt them. These adaptations and others like them may have some fine, even outstanding, qualities, but they pale by comparison with their originals. Such "failures" do not, I think, result from any theoretical or material necessity. As should be clear from my introduction, supposed barriers to adapting novels to film arise in practice, not in essence.

If I had to explain why so few great novels have been made into equally great films, I would suggest that the best filmmakers do not look to the best novelists for inspiration, for they can find that in themselves. Shakespeare, rather than adapt Chaucer's *Troilus and Criseyde*, rewrote *Troilus and Cressida* as his own play; and Orson Welles may have once wanted to film Conrad's *Heart of Darkness*, but, once that project stalled, ideas for motifs and themes easily found their way into *Citizen Kane*. No one accuses Shakespeare of losing Chaucer's effects and betraying the original, and, based upon Robert L. Carringer's descriptions, I think no one should regret that Welles had to move on to another project.[1] Just so, we should not be surprised when an artist such as Jean Renoir or Stanley Kubrick does not—or should not—attempt to serve the works of Herman Melville or James Joyce. Nevertheless, the choice to serve remains possible, as we can see in a few adaptations of excellent novels by very talented, if not powerful or dominating, filmmakers.

Robert Mulligan's adaptation of Harper Lee's *To Kill a Mockingbird* fulfills such a choice. Mulligan's career may not stand equally beside those of the world's best directors, but when Alan J. Pakula acts as his producer and his subject matter involves children or adolescents and their anxieties, his films display a worthy talent. Bring these circumstances together with a screenplay by Horton Foote, and the result is a minor masterpiece.

Lee's novel has been a favorite in high school English classes since its publication in 1960. Amy Lawrence notes that a recent survey placed the novel among the top ten most frequently taught literary texts in high schools.[2] Edgar H. Schuster points out, however, that students too often focus only on the racial injustice, ignoring the fact that Tom Robinson's trial on trumped-up rape charges figures prominently in less than half the book.[3] Likewise, the film, released in 1962, received "several awards for its 'decency' in the presentation of racial injustice in the South; in the heightened climate of the Civil Rights Movement, *To Kill a Mockingbird* was taken primarily as a moral exposition of the plight of blacks in America."[4] If the trial and the racial injustice do not comprise the whole purpose of Lee's plot, dwelling solely on these elements for the film would vindicate the all-too-typical charge that adaptations reduce and simplify the original novels. Mulligan's film does not vindicate that charge, for, if it does not preserve every character and event, it does maintain the emotional power of Lee's education plot in which we watch a young heroine learn to see beyond herself.[5]

Harper Lee announces this purpose fairly early in the novel. Recounting her story from maturity, Scout Finch, our narrator and protagonist, tells how her first days of school brought difficulties in getting along with her teacher and classmates. Ready to give up the entire enterprise of education, she allows it another chance when her father, Atticus, grounds her real education in a fundamental lesson: "If you can learn a simple trick, Scout, you'll get along a lot better with all kinds of folks. You never really understand a person until you consider things from his point of view ... until you climb into his skin and walk around in it."[6] Thereafter, with the fine example of Atticus, the children— primarily Scout and her brother, Jem, but also their friend Dill— learn the importance of sympathy.

Mulligan's film preserves Scout's point of view in voice-over, and, early on, she encounters the same difficulties and hears the same lesson from Atticus. Thereafter, the children will gradually attain the same education in sympathy.[7] The film does not include some supporting scenes or as much detail about some characters, but its plot maintains Scout's learning to overcome childish superstition and prejudice by seeing things from another's point of view.[8]

Before Foote's screenplay based on Lee's novel can achieve anything, Mulligan must make us believe in the characters. Getting good performances out of Gregory Peck or Robert Duvall presents little challenge; what Mulligan deserves great credit for is directing his young actors (Mary Badham as Scout, Phillip Alford as Jem, and John Megna as Dill) through very naturalistic performances. In just the opening scene, Scout speaks her lines while gliding in a tire swing, sitting on the railing of some steps, and climbing a pole—behaving, in short, like a child at play. Scout's first day of school begins with other fine touches: Jem's suppressed giggle at her dress, Scout's dejected posture and behind-the-back snarl over breakfast, and their noisy banging in and out of the screen door when they leave. These child actors manage to get into the skins of their characters, making the efforts of Lee, Foote, and Mulligan come to fruition.

In both versions, Scout contains more than one point of view within herself. She narrates the novel clearly in retrospect, after "enough years had gone by to enable us to look back on them" (7), the days of the Depression in Maycomb, Alabama. Just as clearly, the voice-over in the film is spoken by an adult voice.[9] From this perspective, Scout can recall the central events in her education and see herself before she learned sympathy. Along the way, she recounts the incremental realization of her mature self, sadly noting, as well, those who do not or cannot learn and teach the same lessons. This maturation comes about sensitively, but without sensation or forced angst; in an article written while she was in college, Lee satirized the typical modern novel that must feature "a sadistic father, an alcoholic mother," and a southern setting where an "annual race riot full of blood & gore" would drive the "sensitive" hero to agonize over the hypocrisy of "the holy-rollers" and other townspeople.[10] That is to say, Lee has no interest in recounting life in Maycomb from the perspective of Boo Radley or Mayella Ewell; when she reads Faulkner, she must feel curious about the Compsons' more normal neighbors, rejecting the notion that all happy families are alike. Nick Aaron Ford writes that Scout's narration in the novel represents "the most vivid, realistic, and delightful experiences of a child's world ever presented by an American novelist, with the possible exception of Mark Twain's *Tom Sawyer* and *Huckleberry Finn*"[11]; Twain's work, unfortunately, has yet to find as sensitive a filmmaker.

Mulligan underlines the poignancy of his narrator's view of the world by developing a motif that links the sense of time to certain objects that measure its passage. One scene begins with Scout on a tire swing, moving like a pendulum and counting with the toll of a bell that marks the time Atticus will be coming home. In a later scene, when Jem goes back to the Radleys' barbed wire fence to retrieve his pants, he tells Scout he will return by the count of ten and leaves through a loose plank in their fence; again, she counts with the plank's diminishing pendular swing, and, as she reaches ten and the loose plank ceases, a shot suddenly rings out—a sudden alarm that briefly heightens our fear for Jem's safety. Furthermore, for both children, a prized possession is their father's watch, inscribed with the love of their dead mother, whereas a gift they receive (left anonymously by Boo Radley) is a stopped watch. The sad difference between the Finch and Radley households is that time has stopped in the latter.

Lee embodies much of Scout's education in the contrary examples of others. One such "teacher" is Scout's Aunt Alexandra, Atticus's sister who stayed home on Finch's Landing, which estate could provide the family, despite the leveling poverty of the depression, an all-important "background." An early encounter with her aunt puts Scout in the awkward position of causing a family argument: Aunt Alexandra thinks Atticus should make

Scout wear a dress. Scout overhears Atticus, and she says that this occasion was the only time that she could recall his speaking sharply to anyone; in view of the conflicts to come, his vociferous defense of his children is notable. Confronted directly by Aunt Alexandra about becoming a lady, Scout makes no more headway: she claims that a dress is impractical, only to find herself surrounded by her aunt's circular reasoning that anything requiring pants is nothing for good girls to be doing. Later, when Aunt Alexandra has moved in—mostly to watch the children while Atticus is busy with the trial, but also, she adds, to give Scout "some feminine influence" (129)—she becomes involved with many of the ladies of Maycomb and thereby endeavors to teach Scout the social graces: proper dress and manners by decree, gossip and intolerance by example.

Both Scout and Aunt Alexandra learn something. The intolerant gossip that Aunt Alexandra favors turns against her when Mrs. Merriweather expounds on "some good but misguided people"— that is, Atticus—who stirred up the black people. Scout has only a dim awareness of what the ladies are talking about, but she can perceive the icy rebuke Miss Maudie delivers to Mrs. Merriweather and the gratitude Aunt Alexandra unexpectedly shows to Miss Maudie. Scout does not comprehend what exactly has happened, but she can understand her aunt's feelings—and realizing that she has feelings adds to her education. Moments later, when Aunt Alexandra and Miss Maudie must carry on despite the news that Tom Robinson has been killed, Scout adopts her aunt's ladylike manners to help: "I carefully picked up the tray and watched myself walk to Mrs. Merriweather. With my best company manners, I asked her if she would have some. After all, if Aunty could be a lady at a time like this, so could I" (240). In time, Aunt Alexandra returns the favor. During the tumult following the assault on Jem and Scout, Aunt Alexandra brings her some clothing, the previously hated overalls. Scout says that if she had noticed her aunt's action at the time, she would "never let her forget it" (267), but that promise comes from the mature Scout. She can have this retrospective chuckle, because both learn from the experiences about being "ladylike." If Aunt Alexandra is too old to change much, she yet learns to see through the unladylike attitudes; and if, in the end, Scout does not have to give up her unfeminine ways completely, she learns to respect the civilizing effect of "ladylike" manners.

This relationship parallels and expands upon a much briefer one with Uncle Jack. He too is concerned to have Scout be more ladylike, although his reason stems from the fact that she has begun to test adults with some salty language. When he takes it upon himself to spank her for her behavior—beating up and cursing her cousin Francis—he later regrets not listening to her side of the story: Francis had called Atticus a "nigger-lover." Uncle Jack admits to Atticus what Aunt Alexandra never says aloud, admitting that he does not understand kids and that Scout had to be the one to make such a lack clear to him. Whether her teachers admit it or not, in Lee's school of ethics, the more Scout learns, the more others may learn from her.

Aunt Alexandra and Uncle Jack do not appear at all in the film, and other characters from whom Scout learns lessons appear relatively briefly. A somewhat negative example comes from Mrs. Dubose, also known as "plain hell" (11), an only slightly less fearsome neighbor than the unseen Boo Radley. Many children go out of their way to avoid her house, for she would sit on her porch and lambaste anyone passing on the sidewalk; one time, she adds her voice to the chorus telling Scout she should be wearing a dress. Atticus tells Jem that he must "hold [his] head high and be a gentleman" and "not let her make [him] mad" (104). Atticus even demonstrates before his children how to disarm Mrs. Dubose by speaking up first, doffing his hat, and telling her, "Good evening, Mrs. Dubose! You look like a picture this evening" (104). Even so, Mrs. Dubose gets to Jem one day: she scolds the two kids for being out, for causing mischief, and for having a father "lawing for niggers" (106). Jem cannot abide this last insult, and he returns to cut the blossoms off all her flowers. Part of his reparation involves reading to her.[12] Scout accompanies him and observes how Mrs. Dubose, always looking horrible and sickly, initially behaves as cantankerously as ever and then slips into a sort of stupor. One day, they become aware of the fact that Mrs. Dubose has been stretching out their visits, taking gradually longer to go into one of her "fits," as Scout calls them. When she finally dies, Atticus informs Jem and Scout that the reading served merely to distract her while she struggled to beat a morphine addiction contracted in her illness. For all her insults and contrariness, Atticus states that her ability to die on her own terms makes her worthy of respect for great bravery beyond the sort of activity that usually denotes courage. Scout once said that Atticus "was the bravest man who ever lived" (105) for facing Mrs. Dubose's torments; in coming to understand the old lady's torment, Scout learns to understand another kind of bravery.

The film keeps Mrs. Dubose as a visible counterpart to Boo Radley, another terror flanking the children's street. Her illness and defeat of her addiction have been cut. One key scene remains in which Atticus becalms her as she is scolding the children for a lack of respect. With Scout, Jem, and Dill hiding behind him, Atticus greets her effusively and waxes ecstatic on the "showplace" her garden makes. Mrs. Dubose forgets whatever was bothering her as she sits quietly mollified. Thus, although the character has certainly shrunk in scope, her role still supports the narrative's central lesson, that of getting along with people by seeing them from the inside.

Miss Maudie, a friendlier neighbor, also helps the children see things more clearly. In the novel, she has more scenes—reacting stoically to the loss of her house in a fire, and holding off the gossips at Aunt Alexandra's tea party—but her most important scenes remain in the film. When Scout and Jem complain that Atticus cannot do anything—by which they mean anything that looks attractive to children, such as driving a dump truck or playing football—Maudie reminds them of other important talents: making an airtight will, primarily. They remain unimpressed in both novel and film. A more significant discussion comes when the town seems to have turned on Atticus for defending Tom Robinson. Maudie enlightens the children after the verdict has, incredibly, gone against him: "Things are never as bad as they seem. . . . I simply want to tell you that there are some men in this world who were born to do our unpleasant jobs for us. Your father's one of them" (218). She says almost exactly the same thing in the film and thereby retains her character's most important function, that of helping to explain the adult world to them.

Calpurnia provides some lessons by formal methods and others by example. In the novel, Scout mentions that part of her difficulty with her schoolteacher stems from already knowing how to read and write (just not according to the teacher's methods); she reads with Atticus, and Calpurnia, who schooled her in writing, must share the blame for using uncertified methods. Since Scout's mother has been dead for many years, Calpurnia acts essentially as the children's mother—a relationship Atticus insists that Aunt Alexandra respect. Thus, her teaching Scout to write, showing her around the kitchen, or scolding her for misbehaving seem natural.

Scout may want Atticus to fire Calpurnia after she punishes her for being rude to Walter Cunningham—Walter is having lunch with them and his rural custom of pouring syrup on his meal elicits a shocked response from Scout—but the anger does not differ from what a child might feel for a scolding parent.

As a black servant, however, Calpurnia can broaden the children's education in a way parents rarely can: she can take them into another world. One Sunday she brings Jem and Scout—in a starched dress—along to her church. Some blacks make plain their disapproval of the intrusion, but others join Calpurnia in showing them the same hospitality that Calpurnia wanted Scout to accord Walter. Once inside, they observe how the mostly illiterate congregation can be led in song from one hymnal and how the poor folks can come up with a bountiful ten dollars to help Tom Robinson's wife. Equally illuminating is Calpurnia's switch to black dialect, which she uses so as not to appear affected to her friends: Scout feels a bit of wonder at Calpurnia's straddling two worlds—of the second of which she knew almost nothing—and she has to admire what she regards as Calpurnia's "having command of two languages" (128). Calpurnia's education has come from others rather than a book, and she is passing the same gift on to others in the same manner.

Although the film reduces Calpurnia's role by cutting the scene at the church, her place in the family and in Scout's education nevertheless remains essentially intact.[13] Because Aunt Alexandra does not appear in the film, Calpurnia's role as the children's mother expands slightly. More importantly, Calpurnia anticipates more directly Atticus's golden rule. As in the novel, Scout embarrasses Walter Cunningham at the dinner table and receives the same scolding and swat on the backside. Immediately thereafter (rather than later that night), she sits with Atticus and pours out her frustrations of the day. Atticus's advice to see things from the other person's point of view puts into other words Calpurnia's rebuke about how to treat company in the house.

Overall, these supporting characters introduce Scout to new ways of seeing. All of them want to shape Scout's education in some manner, although not all offer her worthwhile lessons deliberately. Whenever the lessons are worthwhile, they serve to reinforce the words and deeds of Atticus. For this reason, the editing of these characters, either to eliminate them completely or to shorten their roles, does not necessarily imperil Lee's intended effects. Neither padding nor necessities as wholes, these characters function as supporting illustrations of Lee's educational theme. Cutting their roles back, without cutting them out, leaves Scout's world populated by a sufficient number of models who variously approach or fall short of Atticus's standard of moral behavior. In both versions, then, Scout is not only told about this golden rule, but she can observe and emulate others in accord with their failure at or achievement of a sympathetic education.

Of course, Scout learns the most from Atticus. She observes in him some of the simplest common sense, as when he rescues Miss Maudie's rocking chair from the fire, saving "what she valued most" (74). He also instructs the children in lessons such as seeing things from inside another's skin or never shooting at mocking-birds because, unlike other targets for a child's gun, "they don't do one thing but sing their hearts out for us" (94). If Calpurnia or Aunt Alexandra sometimes show too much reticence or fear in educating the children—when asked, for instance, to explain "rape" or "nigger-lover"—Atticus knows the children need a clear understanding lest they get a slanted one. Thus, given the diffi-culty of defending Tom Robinson in a racially charged rape trial, Atticus refuses to hide his problems from the children and care-fully explains his motivations for taking an impossible case.

Atticus finds himself in a paradoxical position. He explains to Scout that, if he avoided the case, the chain of consequences would first involve his self-respect, which in turn would entail his capacity to serve as the county's representative in the state legislature (that is, entail his capacity in his own mind, not necessarily in the minds of all the voters) and his capacity to discipline his children. Admitting frankly that he cannot win, he yet asserts, "Simply because we were licked a hundred years before we started is no reason for us not to try to win" (80). As he says later, "Before I can live with other folks I've got to live with myself. The one thing that doesn't abide by majority rule is a person's conscience" (109). His reference to the "hundred years" of history shows his understanding of the obstacles in his way, but he reacts with what Fred Erisman calls a "tolerant skepticism." The skepticism leaves him "unfettered by the corpse of the past" and thereby "free to live and work as an individual"[14]; answering only to his own conscience gives him a kind of freedom not available to those who would remain bound by prejudice and tradition. On the other hand, that individualistic need to "live with myself" makes more difficult his living "with other folks," so tolerance allows him to remain in the community whose prejudices he confronts and whose ostracism he consequently suffers (that is, he tolerates their reactions as much as they tolerate his actions). Although Atticus tries to explain these difficulties to his children, his life clearly justifies as well as exemplifies the lessons he teaches more explicitly.

He speaks to Scout and Jem because they ask him questions about the case, but he knows their curiosities and needs before they ask. When the case is only beginning and the children know nothing about it, Atticus tells Uncle Jack what he will later tell them about his reasons for taking it. He then adds that he hopes the children will not be afraid to come to him with questions about what they might hear around town—and only then discovers Scout, who has been eavesdropping. Sent off to her bedroom, Scout tells us, "But I never figured out how Atticus knew I was listening, and it was not until many years later that I realized he wanted me to hear every word he said" (93). The trial will be an ordeal in many ways, and, like a good lawyer, Atticus lays the groundwork for his case outside as well as inside the courtroom.

His talent as a lawyer owes much to his ability to understand people; in court, he simply must reveal more of what he understands than he might otherwise wish to do. Such understanding comes out in his explanation to Scout of why the community exempts the Ewells from some rules: living "like animals," they do not have to attend school because such an ordered environment would merely oppress them further, their father may hunt out of season because he wastes his relief checks on cheap liquor, and no one "begrudges those children any game their father can hit" (35). The county allows this compromise rather than punish the Ewell children. Likewise, after Atticus has exposed the brutality of their family life in court—and made plain that Mayella Ewell's loneliness and Bob Ewell's violent temper have conspired to put Tom Robinson on trial—he refuses to retaliate when Ewell spits on him. He explains to Jem, "I destroyed his last shred of credibility at that trial. . . . So if spitting in my face and threatening me saved Mayella Ewell one extra beating, that's something I'll gladly take" (221). Atticus misunderstands only to the extent that he thinks Ewell will be satisfied with spitting on him.

Some skins may be too vile to be entered sympathetically, but no one else lives beyond Atticus's understanding. He can forgive Mr. Cunningham's coming to lynch Tom, because he knows that "Mr. Cunningham was part of a mob last night, but he was still a man" (160). And, aside from anything to do with the trial, Atticus can understand the supposedly unspeakable horror of Boo Radley. All his educational methods come into play again. Explicitly, he instructs the children to stay away from the Radley house and not to torment Boo. When, at Dill's urging, the children nevertheless try to spy on Boo one night, Atticus keeps his counsel in the ensuing ruckus, letting Scout know only much later that he knows "shadows that leave size-four bare footprints" (245) were what Mr. Radley was shooting at that night. And in the end, when Boo Radley has come to their home, Atticus takes him to the front porch rather than the living room, an act that Scout now quickly understands as sympathetic to Boo's sensibilities: "The livingroom lights were awfully strong" (274). With everyone he meets, in word and deed, Atticus exemplifies the sympathetic life Scout grows to understand as the only life worth living.

Even with fewer scenes, his character suffers no significant reduction in the film. All his lessons and admonitions remain, as do his explanations of why he and others must act the way they do. As an example of one change in the film, no scene occurs wherein Atticus tells the children Mr. Cunningham's joining the mob should be forgiven. Instead, the film offers a new scene at the outset (new inasmuch as the film dramatizes it whereas the novel reports it) in which Mr. Cunningham brings a bag of hickory nuts in partial payment to Atticus for an entailment. Summoned by Scout, Atticus accepts the nuts graciously, but when Mr. Cunningham has gone, he says, "Scout, I think maybe, uh, next time Mr. Cunningham comes, you better not call me. . . . I think it embarrasses him to be thanked." He can then explain to her how the depression has hurt the rural people more, much as he explains the differences between the Ewells and other people. More so, however, the little incident sets up the way Mr. Cunningham will be embarrassed by Scout again: when she innocently brings him to himself and out of the mob. His recovery suffices to earn any forgiveness, and the drama has not been diminished in its effect.

A couple of other scenes serve, if anything, to enhance Atticus's nobility. Scout overhears a great deal of adult conversation in the novel—only some of which she fully comprehends—and the film once turns that technique around to have Atticus overhear his children. Tucked into bed, Scout questions Jem about their mother: how old they were when she died, whether she was pretty and kind, whether they loved her and so on. The scene dissolves to Atticus, seated on the porch, and at this moment, when he is listening to his children's poignant feelings and knowing the difficulty of rearing them without their mother, Judge Taylor stops by, makes brief small talk, and then asks if he has heard about Tom Robinson's case: "Yes, sir." The judge says he realizes that Atticus must be busy with his practice and the children, and, when he pauses, Atticus says, "I'll take the case," before the judge asks. The judge says that he will see Atticus in court—"Yes, sir"—and leaves with a thank you—"Yes, sir." Under the circumstances, having the excuse of being a widower with children, his immediate acceptance of the case and his obedient refrain of "Yes, sir" show how highly Atticus values the morals he has set for himself.

Later, the film enhances his stature not so much in what it gives Atticus to say, but in how it portrays his speech. His summation to the jury remains virtually intact from the novel. After some initial remarks, this speech occurs in practically one very long take. Only two brief cut-away shots are inserted: one of Tom when Atticus refers to Mayella's transgression of tempting and kissing a young Negro man, and an ironic cut to the gallery restricted to black observers when Atticus notes that all people should be equal in a courtroom. Otherwise, the speech's passion and force come uninterrupted, a choice that would obviously mean little on the stage, but that, in a film, adds dramatic impact (and perhaps helped Gregory Peck win an Oscar for his performance). Such emphases serve, despite the cutting of some scenes, to maintain the force of Atticus's wisdom, and the sympathetic morality that his character embodies in the novel remains undiminished in the film.

An insight of Amy Lawrence's places the forcefulness of speech at the center of the film's treatment of characters. She sees the narration as potentially problematic because Scout's voice has become disembodied: her narration "authorizes . . . the writing out of her own body," a process that begins with the "'writing out' of the mother" (although Lawrence later acknowledges that the mother's absence "might also be autobiographical").[15] In this scheme of things, Atticus represents a "patriarchal ideology," and he even shares more than we might suppose with Bob Ewell: "Both fathers are repressive; it comes down to a matter of degree." Ewell's oppression of women takes the obvious form of beating his daughter; Atticus figuratively beats Mayella in court, thereby making it "the woman who is guilty, and what she is guilty of is desire."[16] I do not go along with this analysis, for, if his cross examination of Mayella is rough—a man who suffers at least equal oppression has his freedom on the line—his treatment of her father is simply dismissive; and when Atticus, in his speech to the jury, says, "The defendant is not guilty, but somebody in this courtroom is," I think he is pointing his finger at Bob Ewell more than at Mayella.

Even so, Lawrence makes the fine point that Mayella rebels in full, ungrammatical voice: before leaving the stand—and as the camera tracks in for an emphatic close-up, much as it will do when Tom Robinson struggles with his testimony—she attacks the courtroom decorum of the "fancy gennelmen" who have insisted on this vain legal exercise. In this instance, Mayella means that they should simply accept her word about the attack and get on with the conviction and punishment, but I would add that her accusation that "it don't come to nothin'" also refers to her entrapment: she may or may not be seen as a perjuror, but either way, she will return to her isolation in her father's house and remain subject to her father's wrath.

If I may extend this insight, I would suggest that the outburst may add to Scout's education. As Lawrence points out, Scout and Mayella share some traits—hair in the eyes and absent mothers, for example. I would add that they both have outcasts looking out for them: Tom Robinson, the black man who pities Mayella and offers help with chores, and Boo Radley, the mysterious subject of superstition who secretly stands guard over the children. But Scout has the good fortune to have Atticus as her father, a man whose sympathies practically eliminate the possibility of anyone's being an outcast to him, so her rebellion need not be shouted. Instead, when she later understands the necessity to tell Atticus that the law will not avail—in the case of Bob Ewell's death, the entrapment she perceives involves Boo, who, but for the "perjury" of a false report by the sheriff, would not be able to return to the safe isolation of his house—she moves away from Boo so that she can quietly state her case. The film underlines this contrast in the manner in which the different fathers touch their daughters at these moments: Bob Ewell grabs Mayella as she tries to run from the courtroom and, in mock indignation, puts her down in a chair; Atticus, on the other hand, picks up Scout and stands her on a chair so that he can speak to her without looking down—and then Scout is the one who really does the talking.

In that summation, Scout puts Atticus's own words against him (and she employs the metaphor of the mockingbird, a verbal performance that contrasts with Mayella's usage), precociously exhibiting the mature result of the education that Atticus provides. For his character, and the supporting roles, to be truly edifying in this education plot, first the children must be childish. Not to be obvious here, but the lessons discussed heretofore cannot be credible if learned as easily as my summary may suggest: children, who must learn to see beyond their self-centered world and get into another's shoes, should be wearing morally small shoes at the outset.

Scout behaves well and has intelligence, but she still acts just like a child for much of the story. More than once she hears someone tell her she is too young to comprehend whatever is going on—which usually reflects the truth. For instance, when Jem goes to retrieve his pants that became tangled in the Radley's fence, he overrules Scout's fear by saying he would rather face Mr. Radley's shooting at intruders than get "whipped" by Atticus for the first time. Scout says, "Sometimes I did not understand him, but my periods of bewilderment were short-lived" (61). Indeed, she does manage almost to keep up with Jem. At the trial, when Reverend Sykes suggests the testimony may be unfit for the children, Jem assures him that she does not understand, which leaves her feeling "mortally offended" (175). Later, the Reverend again wonders if Jem's review of the laws on rape may not be proper for Scout's ears, and Jem again responds that she does not understand what they are talking about. This time, Scout protests, "I know every word you're saying," but then reflects that she did not get to learn more because her rebuke was "too convincing" and "Jem hushed and never discussed the subject again" (212). Scout learns plenty before the novel's end; along the way, however, she retains enough childishness to act as though she knows more than she does.

Her childishness also suffices to lead her to disobey Atticus occasionally, notwithstanding the wisdom of his admonitions. On the matter of fighting with other kids, she "soon forgot" (79) that he would punish her if she got into more fights and that she should be old enough to know better. A talk with Atticus about the trial enables her to withstand the taunting from a classmate, but soon thereafter comes the trip to Aunt Alexandra's and "disaster struck": the encounter with cousin Francis and the fisticuffs to follow.

Fortunately, childishness includes innocence, and this latter quality in Scout allows her to disarm a violent mob bent on the kind of fighting she once favored. Curious to see what Atticus is doing out at night, Scout, Jem and Dill come along just when a lynch mob confronts him at the jail to prosecute Tom Robinson in their own way. Scout spots Mr. Cunningham in the crowd, greets him, and proceeds to explain that she knows his son Walter: "I beat him up one time but he was real nice about it." When he does not respond, she tries Atticus's advice about discussing what other people are interested in, "so I tackled his entailment once more in a last-ditch effort to make him feel at home" (156). She slowly realizes that something is wrong and figures she is to blame, but Mr. Cunningham tells her he will pass along her greeting to Walter and takes the mob away with him. Only the next day does she realize what might have happened: "Jem was awfully nice about it: for once he didn't remind me that people nearly nine years old didn't do things like that" (158). Of course, nine-year-olds do act that way, so mistakes will happen—and innocent mistakes may be a blessing.

We can measure Scout's behavior relative to Atticus's lessons and example, but we also have Dill and Jem for comparison. Dill befriends the Finch children during his summer visits to his Aunt Rachel, their neighbor. He has a rather fragile constitution, but an extremely healthy imagination. The first time he meets Jem and Scout, he announces himself, "I'm Charles Baker Harris. . . . I can read." The announcement does not impress them, for Scout can already read without having been to school and, besides, Dill looks "right puny for goin' on seven." Dill recovers, "I'm little but I'm old" (11). This aging occurs mostly in his own mind and shows in his fantasies and tall tales. For instance, his second visit to Maycomb begins in "a blaze of glory": he brags that he rode the train alone and saw Siamese twins along the way; he also reports that his father, whom he would not discuss before, is taller than Atticus, has a pointed beard, and is president of the railroad—adding with a yawn, "I helped the engineer for a while" (40). Nonetheless, Dill experiences some genuine aging. When he runs away from home and comes to the Finches, his story includes woes such as being "bound in chains and left to die in the basement . . . by his new father," traveling with an animal show as a camel tender, and arriving in town "clinging to the backboard of a cotton wagon" (142), but the fact remains that he got from Meridian, Mississippi to Maycomb, Alabama somehow. He similarly embellishes their confrontation with the lynch mob—"It's all over town this morning . . . all about how we held off a hundred folks with our bare hands" (160)—but the fact is that the mob went away.

These wild stories appeal more to Scout than to Jem, yet they also serve to distinguish her from Dill. Without a loving home life, Dill's experiences make him grow old before his time; similar trials make Scout grow up. Scout learns to live with others, whereas Dill expects he will become a clown to mock them. An absent parent affects Scout so much less because Atticus provides a good home anyway. Dill's misfortune stems from having Atticus as only a temporary refuge, and his other means of accommodation takes him inward—further into his own skin, rather than sympathetically into another's.[17]

Dill functions in the film much the same way: the screenplay preserves their meeting, gives Dill an overactive imagination for bragging and for instigating adventures, and eventually shows how Scout matures relative to him. Again, Scout has the fortune of a loving home that keeps her from suffering Dill's escapism. Mulligan emphasizes the point in one touching juxtaposition. Right after the exchange with Mrs. Dubose, we see Atticus go into his home with Scout and Jem on either side of him; a moment before this long shot dissolves to the next, Dill enters on the right, watching alone as the family goes in to dinner. The scene that this one dissolves to shows Scout sitting up in bed, reading with the help of Atticus, which, as Lawrence notes, represents the "private time" that Scout "values most,"[18] and which, of course, Dill can never share with either of his parents.

Contrasts between two of Dill's arrivals provide evidence that such love and warmth have an influence on Scout. Soon after his first appearance, he is bragging about his father's railroad and his opportunities to run the train. Scout seemingly accepts whatever he says, whereas Calpurnia kindly humors him: "Is that so?" Upon his arrival the next summer, he bursts in on their breakfast and boasts that now his father is a pilot and will come give him a ride soon. This time, however, Calpurnia need say nothing, for Scout's reaction shot clearly displays skepticism. Dill's plans to become a clown do not figure in the film; nevertheless, his static— albeit rambunctious—characterization still points up the growth in Scout's education.

As the older brother, Jem anticipates some of Scout's growth: he, after all, goes through it before her. His progress involves more than his run-in with Mrs. Dubose or Mr. Radley and his running commentary on the trial. From the outset, he occasionally displays the sympathy that Atticus encourages in them. Early on, he must redress whatever harm Scout has brought about. For instance, when Scout presses Dill about his father—"Then if he's not dead you've got one, haven't you?" (12)—Jem hushes her to save Dill any further embarrassment; Scout, whose experience of an absent parent offers only death as the cause, fails to understand. Jem also separates Scout and Walter Cunningham during their fight, and he invites Walter to dinner. Much later, he helps forestall another fight when he goes to the jailhouse with Scout and Dill. At first, Jem contents himself with watching from a distance and goes into the mob only to catch Scout and bring her back. Once before the mob, however, Jem understands what is going on and refuses to leave. Scout obviously does no harm here, despite what she thinks. More important, she does not comprehend why Jem, in disobeying Atticus, has managed to help make things right.

The difference is that Jem has begun to understand Atticus sooner. Recall that the children think he can do nothing interesting: they tell Miss Maudie that he cannot even beat either of them at checkers, and she answers, "It's about time you found out it's because he lets you" (95). Soon thereafter, when a mad dog wanders into the neighborhood, Sheriff Tate balks at shooting it, deferring to Atticus who dispatches it with one shot. The children are amazed at the scene and at the news that Atticus has always been known for his marksmanship. Miss Maudie explains his modesty, noting that "people in their right minds never take pride in their talents" (102). Scout is beaming with pride, though, and she looks forward to telling everyone at school—until Jem stops her: "Naw, Scout, it's something you wouldn't understand. Atticus is real old, but I wouldn't care if he couldn't do anything. . . . Atticus is a gentleman, just like me!" (103). Although, like Scout, he will have his moments of backsliding, he sees the value of Atticus's wisdom and thereby provides another good example for Scout.

This example does not always please her, of course, for what older brother has always pleased his baby sister? At one point, Jem even joins the legion of those trying to make a lady of Scout, yelling at her after another altercation, "It's time you started bein' a girl and acting right!" (117). She appreciates him more in the end when she realizes the comfort of his mature understanding: her role in the Halloween pageant has proved disastrous, but he shows sympathy, downplays her mistakes on stage, and generally understands her emotions without having them explained explicitly: "Jem was becoming almost as good as Atticus at making you feel right when things went wrong" (261). And becoming as good as Atticus is as good as one can get.

At the outset of the film, Jem appears unfinished in his education. He sits in a tree house—sort of on strike because Atticus cannot do anything, such as, presently, play football for the Methodists. Meeting Dill, though, he again quickly hushes Scout's prying questions. From this beginning, Jem's development follows much the same line as in the novel.

One scene adds a detail to his protectiveness of Scout. In both versions, the children play by rolling inside a tire, and in both, Scout rolls into the Radley yard. The novel has her run out of the yard, forgetting the tire; Jem then shows his bravado by recovering the tire. In the film, he shows the same courage by running onto the porch and slapping the house—but only after he has pulled Scout out of the yard first.

The film also adds to Jem's confrontation with the adult world by having him face some matters alone. The children do not accompany Calpurnia to her church, so their introduction to the black people's way of life occurs in a ride with Atticus when he goes to see Tom Robinson's wife; Scout falls asleep, however, so Jem alone witnesses the approach of Bob Ewell and his drunken shouts of "nigger-lover!" Again, on a similar trip to inform the Robinson family of Tom's death, Jem alone witnesses Ewell's spitting on Atticus, an event only reported in the novel. The frightfulness of these sights clearly weighs on Jem's mind, and the film underlines the point after the first trip. Back at home, Atticus tells him that some ugly things in this world cannot be avoided. When he leaves Jem to watch the house while he takes Calpurnia home, Jem hears scary sounds, and shadows play across his face. Running up the street, he turns to find a little medal in the knothole of the tree in front of the Radley house. In the novel, Scout found little gifts in the tree first and soon shared them with Jem. Here, Jem keeps the medal to himself and will do the same with several other gifts left in the tree, telling Scout only somewhat later. By not allowing Scout knowledge of these details, the film places more responsibility on Jem for protecting her from the adult world while also showing him hints of additional protection for them both.

In the adult world of this community, prejudice—both racial prejudice and a not-so-subtle caste system—presents the biggest obstacle to achieving genuine sympathy. The caste system varies, being sometimes reasonable and sometimes unreasonable. For instance, Aunt Alexandra's habit of pointing out "the shortcomings of other tribal groups to the greater glory of our own" (131) would lead her to foolish notions about "better breeding" in Maycomb families than in rural ones. To Scout, the caste system works another way:

> The older citizens, the present generation of people who lived side by side for years and years, were utterly predictable to one another: they took for granted attitudes, character shadings, even gestures, as having been repeated in each generation and refined by time. (134)

Such predictability, as she eventually learns from Atticus, allows her to understand, for example, the behavior of the Cunninghams, without looking down on that behavior. She begins to learn this lesson early in the film, when Atticus explains to her how, despite being poor, they do not experience the same kind of poverty felt by "country folk, farmers."

Atticus tries to instill in her a sense of differences among people that makes no unwarranted judgments about them. The lesson presents difficulties and causes confusion for the children. Scout innocently thinks that "there's just one kind of folks" (230). Jem answers that he once thought so too, but events have made him wonder why, if people are all just "folks," they cannot get along with one another and even seem to make an effort to hate each other. The confusion stems from the way adults twist castes into prejudices. Atticus wants Scout and Jem to respect the individual differences in other people, but the children see some adults ignore individual traits in favor of assigning undesirable traits to groups.

The most obvious instance of such ignorance involves the trial of Tom Robinson. Well before any appearance in court, Atticus admits the obstacle: "The only thing we've got is a black man's word against the Ewells'. . . . The jury couldn't possibly be expected to take Tom Robinson's word against the Ewells'" (92). Atticus knows that the Ewells fall lower in the castes than his family, and he sympathizes with the harshness of their existence. Even so, he would never assume they were lying, whereas others, appraising the same difference in caste between Tom and any Ewell, would never fail to assume that Tom was lying. This prejudice means that Tom cannot win. After Scout listens to Tom's testimony about Mayella Ewell's advances to him, she comes to "understand the subtlety of Tom's predicament: he would not have dared strike a white woman under any circumstances and expect to live long, so he took the first opportunity to run—a sure sign of guilt" (197). Once the jury has reached its foregone conclusion, Atticus can only describe, not explain, to the children why:

> Those are twelve reasonable men in everyday life, Tom's jury, but you saw something come between them and reason. . . . There's something in our world that makes men lose their heads—they couldn't be fair if they tried. In our courts, when it's a white man's word against a black man's, the white man always wins. They're ugly, but those are the facts of life. (223)

Even here, frustrated in his endeavor to have justice prevail, Atticus does not reply in kind. He understands the men of the jury, sympathizes with them, and refuses to hate them. Having his children feel likewise recovers what little justice remains in the case.

These prejudices and frustrations recur in the film, of course. In fact, Mr. Ewell himself confronts Atticus on the issue of credibility. Following the initial reading of the charges, Ewell faces off with Atticus to tell him, "Somebody told me just now that, uh, they thought that you believed Tom Robinson's story agin' ourn," a report Ewell laughs off as "dead wrong." When Atticus states his intention to defend Tom, Ewell incredulously yells, "What kinda man are you?" In the event, Tom's situation remains impossible. Cross-examined by the prosecutor, as in the novel, Tom states that he often helped Mayella Ewell because he "felt right sorry for her." Here, before the prosecutor can pounce on such presumption, we can hear some snickering in the courtroom, and Mulligan inserts a worried reaction shot of Atticus. Tom is telling the truth, and everyone knows it is convicting him of a lie.

The children see through these lies, but they do not see adults correcting the consequent injustices. Atticus tells the children that they would have acquitted Tom because: "So far nothing in your life has interfered with your reasoning process" (223). Fred Erisman reads this line as illustrating Atticus's "Emersonian quality" of maintaining "the clarity of the childhood vision": "In the unsophisticated vision of the child is a perception of truth that most older, tradition-bound people have lost."[19] The film cleverly uses the set of the courtroom to exhibit the children's level of understanding. As the trial proceeds, Jem rests his head on the gallery railing, and his expressions show that he can feel the emotional ebb and flow of his father's case. Scout sits on the floor, peering impassively through the railing, as if behind bars. Her lack of expression fits her lack of understanding, partly of the proceedings, but mostly of the forces that will govern the inevitable outcome of the proceedings. After the guilty verdict, however, when everyone in the gallery stands to honor Atticus, Scout's rising above these bars also suggests her initial glimpse over the barrier of childhood innocence.

These children would certainly have acquitted Tom Robinson, but Lee hardly wants us to think that children are all born with clear reasoning and unfortunately grow up to take on adult prejudices. Their sorts of lapses have another name: before prejudices come superstitions. Some are rather general, such as Jem's belief that Indian head pennies "come from Indians" and have "real strong magic" and "make you have good luck" (40). Others are more specific, such as the widely accepted rumor that Mrs. Dubose "kept a CSA pistol concealed among her numerous shawls and wraps" (103–4). The subject of their wildest imaginings dwells out of sight within the Radley house: Boo Radley—his name is actually Arthur, but Boo is the *nom de scare* given him by the kids—inspires many legends, and their ability eventually to see through those legends measures and confirms their ability to see through adult prejudices.

At the novel's beginning, the children believe Boo Radley to be "a malevolent phantom" whose yard must be avoided; no one touches the pecans fallen off their tree, for "Radley pecans would kill you" (13). The legend, as Jem and Scout pass it on to the excitable Dill, goes back to some rather harmless delinquency of several boys, including Arthur Radley; the country boys were sent to industrial school, but Arthur was released to his father and "not seen again for fifteen years" (15). One day, according to one neighbor, while cutting and pasting items for his scrapbook, Arthur calmly stabbed his father in the leg, pulled the scissors out, and went back to his scrapbook. Arthur had a brief stay in the courthouse basement—his father did not want him in an asylum—and Jem assumes that Mr. Radley keeps "Boo out of sight . . . chained to the bed most of the time" (16). Sometimes, though, Boo gets out, as Jem explains: "When it's pitch dark. Miss Stephanie Crawford said she woke up in the middle of the night one time and saw him looking straight through the window at

her . . . said his head was like a skull lookin' at her." He further
edifies Dill with a complete description:

> Boo was about six-and-half feet tall, judging from his tracks; he dined
> on raw squirrels and any cats he could catch, that's why his hands
> were bloodstained—if you ate an animal raw, you could never wash
> the blood off. There was a long jagged scar that ran across his face;
> what teeth he had were yellow and rotten; his eyes popped, and he
> drooled most of the time. (17)

These details outstrip even Dill's imagination, and he instigates
the plan to draw Boo out; in their endeavors, they see nothing but
a hulking shadow on the Radley porch, and Mr. Radley shoots at
them, thinking they are thieves.

Given what they are looking for, their failure to see anything
should not surprise us, but Boo does make several appearances
that they fail to note fully. The first time Jem runs up to the Radley
house just to answer a dare from Dill, "we thought we saw an
inside shutter move. Flick. A tiny, almost invisible movement, and
the house was still" (19). Also, when Scout, in the tire, accidentally
rolls right up to the Radley porch, she alone knows that "someone
inside the house was laughing" (45). Such indirect signs continue
in the gifts left for the children and the shadow that kindly
withdraws.

So intent are they on spotting a monster that they do not realize
they are being watched over by a guardian angel of sorts. The
night Miss Maudie's house burns, Scout finds herself wrapped in
a blanket that Boo put on her without being noticed in the
excitement. Most fortunately, Boo watches over and saves them on
the Halloween night Bob Ewell attacks them. Scout, by this time,
has come to regret any torment she caused Arthur and fantasizes
only about making small talk with him, like real neighbors. Still,
she thinks, "We would never see him" (245). Perhaps because she
no longer looks for a monster, she finally sees him that Halloween
and discovers that, despite his "sickly white" (273) pallor, Boo is
no hobgoblin. She later tells Atticus, in regard to a scary book of
Jem's, that the supposed demon "was real nice." Her words could
refer to Boo Radley or any other victim of superstition or
prejudice, and she has learned fully, as Atticus reminds her, "Most
people are, Scout, when you finally see them" (284).

Mulligan carries these superstitions over into the film, where
Jem and Scout still illuminate Dill regarding the pistol-packing
Mrs. Dubose and, more excitedly, the horrific Boo Radley. In fact,

the film more firmly establishes the link between these childish notions and the inexcusable prejudices of adults. As Jem describes Boo's monstrous appearance, Dill's aunt comes up behind them and gives Dill quite a fright; that she, and adults like her, are the real source of fear becomes clear when she tells Dill to believe everything Jem has said and embellishes the story with her own version of the incident with the scissors.

Of course, as in the novel, Boo presents no threat to anyone. Mulligan, however, does not keep many of Boo's "appearances" in the film. During the children's attempt to sneak up to his house, we still see a large shadow approach and, when they cower in fright, withdraw. Otherwise, the film lets us—and the children— discover Boo's true horror in its absence.

For instance, while the children are approaching Boo's house the night they want to spy on him, a loud bump startles them, but they can see no one on the porch. Later, on the night Jem has witnessed Ewell's confrontation with his father and then been left to watch the house alone, Jem hears that bump again; now, looking twice at the empty porch, he seems to realize that the porch swing makes the noise in the wind. Turning to go back to his house, he finds the first gift Boo leaves for them in the tree; in telling Scout about these gifts, he recalls how his pants were untangled and left folded for him on that first night of spying. Later, Scout also looks at the empty porch again, taking note of the empty swing that contrasts so much with the familial occupation of their porch. All in all, the more they do not see Boo, the less they fear what he might do to them.

In addition, the children believed the stories of Boo's looking in windows to scare people, and the film uses this superstition as a motif. To begin with, Mulligan preserves the irony of the children's looking through Boo's window. Furthermore, the scene wherein Scout asks Atticus whether Boo spies on her begins with a tracking shot in from the darkness to her bedroom window, through which we see her and Atticus; obviously, no spooks hide outside this window on this night. If Boo does not lurk at windows, though, other malevolent characters may sit there nonetheless. At the Robinson home, while Atticus goes inside to discuss the case with Tom's wife, Jem stays in the car. As he shrinks back in the seat, Jem sees Ewell come right up to the front window and peer in on the sleeping Scout. Everyone knows the awful life of his family, and now Jem also sees Ewell as the monster lurking in the dark. Boo, on the other hand, shows himself to be the opposite: everyone thinks he stalks prey in the night, but no one actually knows much about the Radleys. When he rescues the children from Ewell, we see that he does want to look into Jem's window. His innocent intentions are clear, however: his shy peak at Jem's room, like his wish to touch Jem's face, betrays no more than a curiosity about how other, more normal people live. This curiosity resembles that of the children except that, rather than morbid thrills, Boo looks for that life his family has been sadly missing; the horror of Boo Radley involves, not what he does, but how he must live. In any case, the true identity of the monsters in Maycomb has become as clear as glass.

Scout, for one, realizes this truth and acts on it immediately. In both the novel and the film, Ewell's death presents Atticus with a moral problem. At first, he thinks Jem must have stabbed Ewell in self-defense and that Jem will have to prove his innocence in court. Sheriff Tate makes him see that Boo stabbed Ewell, but he states that his report will say Ewell fell on his knife. Atticus wants to rely on the courts, but Tate wants to spare Boo the consequent publicity of his act. Scout overhears this conversation on the porch—much as Atticus overheard his children from the porch on the evening when the case began—and she is ahead of him when Atticus starts to explain what he regards as a minor conspiracy. She knows that no crime has been committed, she now understands the mob mentality of some of the community, she can put herself in Boo's place, facing this community, and she recalls Atticus's lesson about not killing a mockingbird. As Jem once did for her, she helps make things feel right for Atticus. Scout takes Boo home and stands on his porch to see what Maycomb looks like from his perspective; more importantly, she has completed her education in her heart, and she can put herself in his skin before she steps onto his porch.

Technically and formally, the filmmakers have accomplished the same with Lee's novel. The actors have inhabited the skins of Lee's characters, and the writer and director have entered the author's mind and realized her intentions again on the screen. A number of choices have not matched those of Lee, and some characters and several scenes find no counterpart in the film. Nevertheless, the kinds of choices, not the number, matter the most. In both versions, Scout's education assumes the same shape, and we arrive at the same satisfaction with the achievement of her sympathetic mind.

Back Where We Started:
2001: A Space Odyssey

I am part of all that I have met;
... and vile it were
For some three suns to store and hoard myself,
And this gray spirit yearning in desire
To follow knowledge like a sinking star,
Beyond the utmost bound of human thought.

—Alfred Lord Tennyson, "Ulysses"

I mean *Negative Capability*, that is when man is capable of being
in uncertainties, Mysteries, doubts, without any irritable
reaching after fact & reason—... This pursued through
Volumes would perhaps take us no further than this, that with
a great poet the sense of Beauty overcomes every other
consideration, or rather obliterates all consideration.

—John Keats

What is the ape to men? A laughing-stock or a painful
embarrassment. And just so shall men be to the Superman: a
laughing-stock or a painful embarrassment. ...
I entreat you, my brothers, *remain true to the earth*, and do
not believe those who speak to you of superterrestrial hopes!
They are poisoners whether they know it or not.
They are despisers of life, atrophying and self-poisoned
men, of whom the earth is weary: so let them be gone!

—Friedrich Nietzsche, *Thus Spoke Zarathustra*

Up to this point in my argument, I have been trying to
demonstrate two fundamental flaws in the theories of George
Bluestone and those who still show his influence: material and
technique make for poor categories on which to base claims about

an adaptation's fidelity to a novel; furthermore, fidelity to the novel makes for an equally poor criterion on which to base evaluative judgments of an adaptation. Nevertheless, if these theories seem too reductive to me, perhaps they have the excuse of dealing with a very young medium. Cinema has just reached the century mark, and "talkies" have been around just over sixty-five years. If we remember that, while James Joyce was breaking literary ground with *Portrait of the Artist as a Young Man* and *Ulysses*, D. W. Griffith was breaking cinematic ground in "The Lonedale Operator" and *Birth of a Nation*, well, we can understand how literature in print gained the critical reputation of occupying the higher ground. This topography has not remained stable, however, and the progress of cinematic art has brought about plenty of leveling.

In an interview focusing on *2001: A Space Odyssey*, Stanley Kubrick has even claimed a certain superiority for film: "I don't have the slightest doubt that to tell a story like this, you couldn't do it with words. . . . There are certain areas of feeling and reality—or unreality or innermost yearning, whatever you want to call it—which are notably inaccessible to words."[1] Kubrick's statement runs contrary to Bluestone's claim that "The rendition of mental states—memory, dream, imagination—cannot be as adequately represented by film as by language."[2] I think both overstate the case. Bluestone's sample of films might fall short of the adapted novels in the subtlety with which they render mental states; but, as I have argued before, his sample does not represent film's potential and, therefore, does not warrant theoretical conclusions about all films. Likewise, Kubrick's *2001* may be very subtle and provocative, but the assertion that words cannot represent certain feelings that film can represent strikes me as unsupported and, finally, insupportable. I cannot accept Bluestone's conclusion that literature alone can portray mental states, and by the same token, I cannot accept Kubrick's contrary claim: tested inductively, broad premises ruling out effective adaptations of novels to film do not merit validation, but neither do equally broad premises that would claim certain unique capabilities for film.

In an odd turnabout, this issue of a medium's unique capabilities has become more important because of adaptations in reverse: today, along with screen versions of novels, we also see adaptations of films to print (known in the pithy patois of the business as "novelizations"). Like too many of the film adaptations, these "novelizations" embody little more than a commercial instinct to exploit a hot property, in these cases, popular films. 2001 was planned and written simultaneously by Kubrick and Arthur C. Clarke, although their motives do not seem to have been so commercial.[3] Implicitly, Bluestone's book warns that the usual sort of adaptation cannot substitute for reading the novel. I doubt that many people, upon the release of a new film today, decide to wait for the "novelization," but in the case of 2001, many felt compelled to consult the novel when it came out. Jeremy Bernstein, who wrote a number of features about the film while it was in production, says, "After reading the book, I realized that I hadn't really 'understood' the film."[4] Certainly the film has a reputation for confusing its audiences, and second viewings were necessary to win over some critics.[5] Clarke has written, "If you understand 2001 on the first viewing . . . we will have failed"; he adds, speaking of the enigmatic ending, "You will find my interpretation in the novel; it is not necessarily Kubrick's. Nor is his necessarily the 'right' one—whatever that means."[6] Clarke's novel presents little difficulty on the first reading, and his "interpretation" differs from Kubrick's. I would not say that one or the other is "right" (each may be right relative to his intentions), but in their difference, I would have to say Kubrick's surpasses Clarke's by far. In fact, the novel "explains" the film only to the extent that it simplifies and reduces an ambitious work of cinematic art.

According to Clarke, the collaboration began in 1964 when Kubrick wrote to him to suggest developing a film that would involve two main interests: "(1) The reasons for believing in the existence of intelligent extra-terrestrial life. (2) The impact (and perhaps even lack of impact in some quarters) such discovery would have on Earth in the near future." Very quickly, Clarke settled on his story "The Sentinel" as a suitable beginning.[7] Briefly, the story recounts a discovery by a geologist and moon-explorer of the late 1990s. One day, he sights an unusually bright object on a distant lunar mountain, and, when he and a colleague climb the rock face to examine it, they find a pristine pyramid, a structure that he immediately realizes must have been placed there by aliens. As he tells the story, twenty years after the discovery, the pyramid has finally been penetrated, by atomic power, and found empty. The narrator then speculates that it was a sentinel: a device left there millions of years ago to send signals to its alien owners and, when its signal was interrupted, to tell them that the potential for intelligent life on Earth had proven itself actual by crossing space. The account of the mission reenacts, in microcosm, that crossing and ascent, and the story ends on a note of expectation: waiting for the aliens to respond. From this same germ, the discovery of other intelligence in the universe, Kubrick's version of 2001 emphasizes the spectacular impact such a symbolic meeting has on the teleological growth of human intelligence, whereas Clarke's version emphasizes the hopeful impact such an actual meeting has on the survival of human beings.

Kubrick's style in 2001 impresses even most of the film's detractors. Of course, those detractors complain that the style conveys no clear meaning. Asked to clarify his film's message, Kubrick rejects the need for any explanation: "I tried to create a *visual* experience, one that bypasses verbalized pigeon-holing and directly penetrates the subconscious with an emotional and philosophic content."[8] Kubrick, like many artists, refuses to pronounce his theme, but, again, I think he misrepresents or overstates the capabilities of "visual" communication. More to the point of the audience's confusion, he does not address here the issue of simple continuity, the simpler question of "What happens?" The film opens with scenes depicting prehistoric ape-men, leaps forward to lunar explorers, and suddenly leaps forward again to an expedition to Jupiter. The crucial question remains whether these "chapters" represent disconnected, albeit awesome, tableaux, or logical, albeit elliptical, episodes in a unified plot. John Russell Taylor, citing the effects of television on audiences, says the movie succeeds with the popular audience precisely because it "is a succession of vivid moments, not an articulated plot" (130).[9] Thomas Allen Nelson, on the other hand, claims that Kubrick's "audacious course" proceeds by "ellipses," challenging the audience to "fill in the gaps" of the plot by "visual attentiveness and subliminal penetration."[10] I agree with Nelson, and examination of Kubrick's style does reveal unifying and purposeful elements in his unusual yet comprehensible plot.

Perhaps the most spectacular motif is the recurring image of celestial alignments. The film's very first shot, mounted on an interplanetary crane and accompanied by the triumphant swelling of Richard Strauss's *Thus Spake Zarathustra*, rises over the moon to reveal the Earth behind it, and rises further to reveal the sun beyond the Earth: a lunar eclipse seen from the far side of the moon.[11] Kubrick outdoes himself in fulfilling his personal dictum "that the first shot of the film should be the most interesting thing that the audience has seen since it sat down."[12] These alignments occur again when the monolith first appears to the ape-men, when the monolith gives off its piercing signal on the moon,[13] and, with Jupiter and its moons, when Bowman follows the monolith "beyond the infinite." Each instance marks a beginning: a first use of tools, a first interplanetary journey, and a first interdimensional journey.[14] But what of the first shot? By backward extrapolation, we might say that this alignment marks *the* beginning, the creation. In part, I am thinking of these alignments as a variation on the *magnus annus*, a period of birth, apocalypse, and rebirth, the duration of which measures the time it takes the heavenly bodies to return to the positions they had at creation.[15]

If this motif does mark the boundaries of what Yeats would call gyres in history, it lends significance to a motif that resembles these alignments in a lesser way. In the space sequences, men gracefully but mechanically glide into alignment with various destinations. As the Orion approaches the revolving space station, we see the pilots' visual displays of the navigational grids lining up and matching; similar shots occur during the Aries's approach and landing on Clavius, and during the moonbus's arrival at the TMA site; lastly, Bowman uses the same matching grids to pursue and lock on to Poole's body. All involve wondrous feats of navigation, but in the absence of grand or mysterious music, their mechanical precision looks rather humble next to the cosmic alignments. Kubrick's motif suggests, then, a diminution of sorts when mechanisms enact these alignments. Bowman, as a Star-Child in the final shots, will be a heavenly body unto himself, coming into alignment with the Earth as the *Zarathustra* theme announces his birth; this rebirth, as I will show, comes only after he removes the mechanisms between himself and the heavens.

Kubrick's spectacle also impresses us in its scale. The long-take shots of the landscape early in "The Dawn of Man" convey one kind of timelessness—immeasurable because no intelligence exists to measure it—and long-takes and slow tracking shots in the Louis XVI room at the end convey another kind of timelessness— immeasurable because time has so contracted "beyond the infinite" that Bowman sees himself arrive at points in his aging before he ages.

In between these timeless sequences, Kubrick maintains the impressive scale by expending so much film time on several scenes, notably the two legs of Floyd's trip to the moon, both accomplished in waltz time to the tune of "The Blue Danube." Kubrick's camera glides through space, following the curves of the Earth, the moon, the space station, or the ship's trajectory. One pair of shots especially shows space travel as dance: as the *Orion* approaches the space station's central landing bay, we see in a long shot the ship matching the roll of the station; in the next shot, from inside the *Orion's* cockpit, we see the landing bay, now seemingly motionless. With the dance partners in sync, the waltz music ends as the *Orion* lands.

These sequences proceed at such length in order to establish the beauty of the dance in outer space. Other sequences, such as some aboard *Discovery* objected to by critics, linger so as to establish the inexorable routine. Originally, Kubrick had the two EVA scenes at the same length. Bowman's preparation of the pod, the opening of the pod bay door, the slow ejection of the pod, its gradual rising and turning, and finally its glide back to the radio dish—all these maneuvers, in the film's initial release, were matched when Poole ventured out. In cutting the film after its previews, Kubrick shortened the latter sequence, although some critics still felt both could be reduced. However, Kubrick's attention to each little action has its purpose: "This laborious preparation may appear initially repetitive until Poole's computer-controlled pod turns on him and murders him in space, thus justifying the prior duplication by undercutting it with a terrifyingly different conclusion."[16] The accumulation of detail, even in the cut version, works because of this sudden interruption in the routine.

In these sections of the film, Kubrick's deliberate pacing has two functions. Aboard *Discovery*, the pacing conveys the lull of standard operating procedure—even amidst the decidedly non-standard setting and journey. During Floyd's trip to Clavius, the pacing allows us to see the spectacle of space flight, a spectacle ignored by all the characters. On both legs of his journey, Floyd sleeps, and cabin attendants get dinners and watch inane television. From the space station, Floyd makes a nearly pointless phone call home (no E. T., he), oblivious to the stunning sight of Earth rolling in the background. Travel in space offers many wonderful sights, but only the audience appreciates them: standard operating procedure prevails among turn-of-the-century men—at least until its mechanical failure.

The spatial orientation of Kubrick's shots can be as spectacular or disturbing as the temporal orientation of his pacing; but, again, the characters seem unaware. Nelson remarks that the language, aside from its obvious lack of color or expressiveness, remains "timebound and linear": the characters "ignore the fact that in space directional terms like 'forward' and 'backward' or 'up and down' no longer have the same meaning as they do within Earth's gravity." As John Charlot puts it, humanity has yet to accommodate itself to space exploration, for despite "living in space, man still thinks as if he were on earth."[17] Indeed, we alone see space redefined: the four sides of the space station's landing bay, each with men visible through windows, but for each of whom the landing bay is "up"; the flight attendant who walks up a wall and exits "up-side-down" on the ceiling; the interior of *Discovery's* centrifuge, first seen in a seamless pan as Poole jogs around it, running toward the camera on the "right" wall, then away on the "left" wall, and "up-side-down" and back again to the "right" side; and a shot that begins with Bowman looking straight up into the camera, which then pulls back to reveal Poole standing on the same plane as the camera—ninety degrees perpendicular to Bowman's "floor." As I have indicated, though, only the audience is floored by these displays. The only time a character becomes aware of his unearthly surroundings occurs when Floyd ponders the mysteries of the zero-gravity toilet.

The distance between us and the characters results from Kubrick's point of view. The wonderful spectacle and the disorientation in time and space establish the bases of the film's style, but to the characters, almost nothing that impresses us impresses them. That is, in no way could most of these sights come through any character. Kubrick, however, does not employ an omniscient camera; therefore, he has no access to their unspoken ideas, knowledge, or perceptions, let alone background information. We see the prehistoric ape-men, but Kubrick does not describe their existence; nor does he describe the space ships, moon bases, or any technological accessory. The film presents these objects, but without an omniscient point of view—without a camera that wanders and explores for its own sake—we can get no explanations of their functions, let alone specifications of their construction.[18] Obviously, the characters do not discuss these matters because, to them, such objects exist almost invisibly in the familiar, quotidian world. As for Kubrick, he does not linger over or zoom in on mechanical details so much as he allows his camera to watch, at length, the objects in motion or the objects deployed by the characters. Essentially, but for a few inserts, he employs a dramatic point of view.[19] In Friedman's terms, the information we get comes from "what the characters do and say," and the rest is "wholly scenic" in presentation.[20] Such a presentation fulfills Kubrick's wish to reach his audience visually without resort to overt manipulation. More importantly, it allows the audience to see the characters in their surroundings and, thereby, to perceive the characters' unstated lack of wonder, for the spectacle that so impresses the audience goes unnoticed by the characters.

The few departures from this dramatic technique thereby stand out: each one, a selectively omniscient view through one character's mind, signals the presence of a conscious intelligence—conscious relative to the blasé reactions so common among the characters. Therefore, Kubrick's style and technique open a gulf between our conscious wonder at the achievements of turn-of-the-century technology and the unconscious routine of those living and working in the retooled universe.

Clarke's style and technique could hardly differ more from Kubrick's. Whereas I would characterize Kubrick's film as expansive, elliptical, and mysterious, Clarke's novel deals in irony, suspense, and speculations that explain rather than mystify. Clarke fills all the gaps in the narrative. For example, the leap from ape-men to spacemen—accomplished by Kubrick's brilliant match-cut from the first tool, a bone, to the latest in tools, a spacecraft—becomes in the novel a brief run-through, in one chapter, of man's gradual evolution. Throughout, Clarke presents no setting, no action, no technology without a lengthy explanation. Thus, we read of the ape-men's day-to-day existence; we learn how the signal from TMA-1 is relayed through the solar system; we review how hibernation works in interplanetary flight; we follow Bowman through one day's routine aboard *Discovery*; we set the plot aside to indulge in space probes of an asteroid and Jupiter; we get a full accounting of HAL's failure; we read Bowman's lengthy and philosophical speculations on what the aliens will be like; we read what they actually are like; we tour the passage between our solar system and theirs; we learn why the room at the end is decorated as it is; and, finally, we get an explanation of what happens to Bowman and what he is up to at the end. Unlike the film, the novel leaves no questions unanswered (and may therefore be mistaken for the answer to any question left open in the film) because "Clarke combines these evocations of exploration and wandering amid the lonely expanses of space with an elaborate substructure of explanatory material, which subordinates the idea of 'mystery' to the speculations of science."[21] The novel even neglects the film's only joke, Floyd's consternation before the operating instructions for the zero-gravity toilet, in favor of several paragraphs to explain how and why "everything moved in the right direction, in the one place where this mattered most."[22]

Of course, both share the quality of lengthy treatment, but they have different effects in mind: Kubrick's film, seeming to suppress the events of the plot, invites us to contemplate spectacular or awesome sights, whereas Clarke's novel, deliberately interrupting the plot, takes us along as it delves into complicated processes and esoteric concepts. Clarke can thereby achieve a "plausibility of effect" that seems so essential to "the SF art of credible future,"[23] but Kubrick is interested less in how the future will work and more in how humanity will realize its future.

In the novel, then, all the mysteries and elliptical passages involve much smaller issues: mysteries in the sense of suspense, or "What happened next?" Therefore, Clarke often uses what must be a favorite stylistic trait: an ellipsis to elicit thought, or a dash to indicate interrupted speech. When the monolith tests the ape-men's dexterity, Clarke writes, "On the planet Earth, the first crude knot had been tied . . ." (22). Or again, when Bowman and Poole launch a probe at an asteroid, he writes, "They are aiming at a hundred-foot-diameter target from a distance of thousands of miles . . ." (107). In each case, the ellipses perhaps give us pause to contemplate how far humanity has come—and to wonder how far we might go—but they also hold us in suspense about whether the challenge will be met. The dashes, on the other hand, raise only immediate concerns. Poole's frantic shout, "Hal! Full braking—" (141), and Bowman's exclamation, "Just a minute— that's odd—" (190), both leave us hanging on what happens next; in these cases, we soon realize that Poole has been attacked by his pod, and Bowman has glimpsed infinity through the star gate.

Moreover, Clarke commonly uses a one-line paragraph, a hook, to end a chapter—another stylistic touch that maintains interest in the plot by teasing us with suspense: What is so important on the moon? What does the signal mean? Is HAL malfunctioning? Will Bowman be able to carry on alone? Are the aliens satisfied with the human result to their experiment? and What are they doing to Bowman? Clarke is obviously fascinated by the subjects of space travel and alien intelligence, and he wants us to feel that fascination also. His style, however, is calculated, not to inspire our own philosophical awe, but to have us join him in imagining the technical and practical realities such an exploration would entail.

To enter into one man's version of these speculative realities, we also join the characters through whom the exploration is conducted. Thus, rather than simply observing the ape-men, we have Moon-Watcher singled out because, compared to his fellows, he has curiosity and imagination. Floyd, Poole, and Bowman, unlike their film counterparts, have not only consciousness, but feel stimulated by and interested in all they do: they seek the same answers that we seek. In the novel, then, we get information from all the characters, and we get information they cannot learn. That is to say that Clarke's point of view is omniscient. We have access to the characters' minds as they search for answers, but the narrator can also give us access to history and to the aliens so that we get answers the characters will not learn, at least not immediately. Moreover, although Clarke never refers to himself, he tends to intrude sometimes as a narrator of editorial omniscience. For instance, when Moon-Watcher decides that the monolith must be a mushroom despite lacking any resemblance to a mushroom, the narrator wryly offers that "greater and later philosophers than Moon-Watcher would be prepared to overlook equally striking exceptions to their theories" (19). Much later, when Bowman travels through the star gate and sees equally baffling sights, the narrator allows that "it was too much to expect that he would also understand" (207). Overall, though, the omniscient narrator—ironic, teasing, suspenseful—bridges the distance between us and the characters, for we and they want to learn the same things. This narrator will not efface himself and show the search; he has much to say, and he tells us the answers.

In his telling, one of the things Clarke tells is a story: long ago, aliens visit Earth and teach ape-man a few lessons; at the turn of the twenty-first century, the human result of those lessons leaves the planet to meet the teacher. Regarding the film, we may ask whether Kubrick—through his spectacular style and objective, dramatic point of view, but minus some narrative links—portrays this same story. The answer, I would argue, is no. Clarke has not adapted Kubrick's story—obviously suggesting that I think that Kubrick's film has a comprehensible story, that the film does have a structure, a unified purpose, to make meaningful each wonderful sight and each sudden leap forward in the action.[24]

Perhaps the most confusing effect of Kubrick's method results from the fact that the audience cannot readily identify a protagonist who holds all the events together. Obviously, no single character qualifies. Alexander Walker finds unity in a theme: "If one can isolate any dominant thematic core in *2001*, it is the film's concern with the concept of intelligence." W. R. Robinson and Mary McDermott, in a variation on this theme of intelligence, assert that "the eye" is the film's "main character": the plot proceeds

> through the increase in size and power of the yellow eye that first appears in the predatory leopard among the apes, enlarges into the ubiquitous, objective, rational yellow, red and blue eye of the computer HAL during the astronauts' space travel, and finally during the light trip in Part III expands to fill the entire screen and blink through a series of psychedelic colors in a very "elaborate" performance of self-perception, self-cleansing, and self-reincarnation.[25]

I would say that, abstractly or figuratively conceived, human intelligence acts as the practical protagonist, for Kubrick symbolically organizes his action around an idea, not events.

Nevertheless, that protagonist does have physical embodiment—and as more than simply an eye—for, in the four sections of the film, intelligence develops in an aggregate portrayal: "Each higher capacity for intelligence—ape, man, computer, superman—indicates that the preceding ones were finally limited." Not every development marks a final improvement, however. Despite the technological prowess of men and HAL, they yet fail to demonstrate any spiritual or emotional growth: "The film would therefore open with a true step in biological evolution, then portray two further 'progressions' as limited, deceptive, before an authentic progression in the finale."[26] The aggregate protagonist—Moon-Watcher, Floyd, HAL, and Bowman/Star-Child—personifies intelligence in various stages, and Kubrick examines its growth, regression, and final excellence. On the level of an exemplum, the film follows an education plot, which involves "a change in thought for the better in terms of the protagonist's conceptions, beliefs, and attitudes."[27] Intelligence, born out of inspiration, changes for the better when, having exhausted itself in rational science, it returns to inspiration.

In the film's opening section, "The Dawn of Man," whatever the intelligence of the ape-men, it proves ineffectual: extinction may not follow imminently, but neither will propagation or evolution. Shots of the bleak landscape include bones of several animals;

each fade to black leads to another such landscape. The shots, like the inhabitants of this scene, do not progress so much as they simply come and go. When we first see the ape-men, they are grazing the same scarce vegetation as several tapirs. An ape-man growls loudly at a nearby tapir, but it does not react in the least; a similar growl moments later elicits a reaction only when accompanied by a shove. Soon, a leopard springs from some rocks and claims an ape-man while the others scatter. These creatures exist, but they control nothing of their existence. Even among themselves, they assert or acknowledge no real authority. The shouting match over the water hole merely marks the leaving of one group and the coming of another; no territory will be held, and both sides get their drink. These ape-men make a loud noise, but they remain subject to the silent landscape by day and, wakeful in their caves by night, also fear the purr or growl of the unseen leopard.

Into this existence comes the monolith, as sudden as the leopard, one morning at their cave, more immovable than any tapir, totally unresponsive to their shouting and foot stomping. Moon-Watcher (for the sake of convenience, I will adopt Clarke's name for this particular ape-man) raises the alarm and, after much tentative dancing, dares to be the first to touch it: gingerly at first, then carefully stroking it in wonder. The music of György Ligeti's "Requiem" accompanies this appearance (and all further scenes of the monolith but the last), but, although the piece sounds other-worldly, we should not jump to conclusions. Carolyn Geduld thinks that "the apes are manipulated" by the monolith, which "programs intelligent life on Earth for millions of years."[28] I do not think we can ascribe too much to the monolith's intervention, for we do not see the monolith ever again at the cave, and the ape-men take no note of its disappearance. Where it remains is in Moon-Watcher's mind. Soon after the appearance, Moon-Watcher is looking at a pile of bones and picks up a skull—perhaps some poor Yorick he once knew. Immediately there follows a flash-cut, the low-angle shot looking up past the monolith to the sun and moon overhead. In another low-angle shot, Moon-Watcher picks up a large bone and notices its leverage. As the *Zarathustra* theme swells on the soundtrack, a slow-motion montage shows Moon-Watcher smashing other bones, intercut with shots of falling tapirs: he is realizing what he can do with this tool. The low angle shows his authority, the music signals a birth, and the flash-cuts of the monolith and the tapirs indicate thought. Kubrick can briefly depart from objectivity now that there is a subjectivity present to enter. The question remains where such consciousness comes from: the monolith or Moon-Watcher? Clearly, the monolith gives no instruction in the fact of death, let alone the physics of levers as a means to forestall death. At the most, the vision of the monolith beneath the eclipse inspires Moon-Watcher. The notion of something different—different from the day-to-day struggle he knows—literally dawns on him, and his original discovery leads to a new life that eclipses the old. In this sense, the monolith stands not merely as an artifact, but also as "a symbol . . . of that inspirational force through which life eternally renews itself."[29] Intelligence arrives not through instruction or infusion. It comes through inspiration.

In this Genesis, if the ape-men do not reside in a Garden of Eden, they at least have a land of plenty, once they learn to eat meat. Their knowledge, however, also makes possible the misuse of knowledge. No serpent tempts them, so they take its place: Moon-Watcher and his fellows supplant the leopard in his role as predator, when they come off the rocks and club to death the leader of their rivals at the water hole. When he discovered the tool that would put off death, Moon-Watcher threw it in the air in joyful realization. When he uses that tool to bring swift death to his enemy, Moon-Watcher again throws the bone in the air, now in assertive strength. From this latter instrument, Kubrick match-cuts to the satellites of the future: perhaps an initial suggestion that technology can get out of hand.

This match-cut shows the tremendous progress born out of that original tool, an advance in technology that is startling even given the centuries of time. Nevertheless, while humanity's tools have become more complex, intelligence has not kept pace. Humans seem to have control of the natural environment yet remain subordinate to the technological environment built in order to subdue the natural. Moreover, their language remains as ineffectual as their ancestors' grunts. Rather than the impressive satellites floating in space, Kubrick could just as easily have cut from the bone to Floyd's pen floating in the weightless cabin of the *Orion* while Floyd sleeps: the pen, less wondrous than the satellites, yet marks quite an advance in sophistication over Moon-Watcher's bone, but instead of being tossed skyward in triumph, this little instrument has merely slipped through the fingers of another spaceman bored with the routine of space travel.

As with this pen, a relatively simple device for written

communication, no one seems to grasp tools of communication. On board the space ships, we see film programs that are available to the passengers: a sappy love scene set in the front seat of a car, and a wrestling match—that is, soap operas and Wide World of Sports, like cockroaches, will survive forever. Also, the telephone has added pictures to its transmission, but Floyd's obligatory call home does not reach out and touch anyone. His wife is not at home, so he talks to his fidgety daughter. Asked what she wants for her birthday, she automatically responds, "A telephone." Floyd tells her, "We've got lots of telephones already," although their ready availability has not helped these two talk to each other. On second thought, she wants a bush baby, a creature that, as in the ape-men's clans, could be held and cuddled in the absence of mom, dad, nanny. As for Floyd, his medium is the message: "Tell mummy that I telephoned. . . . And that I'll try to telephone again tomorrow." Actual communication matters less than the use of the tool.

From this inane conversation, Floyd steps into another, with the Soviet scientists in the space station's lounge. Of course, Floyd says nothing, even when asked, about the goings on at Clavius, for he has the excuse of state secrecy. Such security does not excuse the emptiness of the rest of the chat: "You're looking well too"; "Well, when you do see him, be sure and give him my regards, huh?"; "Now, I really must be going"; and "Don't forget you have a standing invitation if you ever get to the States." Clive James writes that the language in the film consists of nothing but "jargon,"[30] but that term describes only the way in which life has been drained from all communication between pilots and their ground controllers—a situation in which one might expect jargon, especially during such missions as a first flight to Jupiter. More disturbing, despite such exciting times, family members and acquaintances have nothing to say: on or off the phone, human speech has grown from grunts to the exchange of automatic pleasantries.

The real test of human speech comes with the appearance of something dramatic about which to talk. A kid's birthday or a chance meeting with old acquaintances may not turn anyone into a Churchill. How about a chance meeting with an alien artifact buried around the time of mankind's birthday? Well—as Floyd would probably say—even on this matter the talk remains distinctly unanimated. When Floyd addresses the scientists at Clavius, he affects a cheerful—and unconvincing—outlook for the benefit of those upset by the quarantine imposed for secrecy. Then he adds his congratulations for their discovery, "which may well prove to be among the most significant in the history of science." The so-called TMA-1, humanity's first evidence for the existence of alien intelligence, cannot inject any excitement into Floyd's response. Later, in the moonbus en route to the excavation site, Floyd chats with two scientists over coffee and sandwiches: Floyd asks, "I don't suppose you have any idea what the damn thing is, huh?" and one answers, "I wish to hell we did"; Floyd then concludes with a chuckle, "Well, I must say, you guys have certainly come up with something." Several critics were appalled at the banality of these conversations, especially in view of the dramatic circumstances. Stanley Kauffmann, for one, hoped that Kubrick was kidding. He failed to see the satiric point, believing instead that Kubrick forgot the screenplay in favor of special effects. F. A. Macklin argues, to the contrary, that even if the banality is not obvious enough, one could hardly miss the two scientists' complimenting Floyd's pep talk: "You know, that was an excellent speech you gave us, Heywood. . . . I'm sure it beefed up morale a hell of a lot."[31] No one who heard the speech could believe it was excellent, and the persistent questioning of the need for secrecy provided no indication of improved morale. In the year 2000, the crisis of human intelligence has no more obvious symptom than in these insipid communications—even about the most historic of events.

The crisis of intelligence has come about because humanity no longer uses its intelligence. Having fashioned many tools, like the video-telephone, humans now use them instead of their intelligence. In this routine mechanization, however, the simplest human functions are taken over by and subordinated to tools. As Floyd experiences it, going to the bathroom has become a rather daunting task. Food appears in just a package with a picture to identify the taste one sucks, or in evenly cut shapes that look and taste like chicken or ham sandwiches. If technology can intervene in the human alimentary system, it can do the same to the human mind. Confronted, therefore, by something so plain and obvious as the monolith, these moon-explorers still show no more intelligence than Moon-Watcher; in fact, their technology, in their space suits, literally comes between Floyd's hand and the monolith. Moon-Watcher could touch it, and it inspired him. Floyd, with the advantage of centuries of progress, cannot grasp it, and he joins the others for an uninspired snapshot next to the monolith. The little awareness that Floyd does achieve (after the monolith catches their attention with its ear-splitting signal, not unlike the ape's having to hit the dull tapir to get its attention) leads to the *Discovery's* mission to Jupiter, a leap forward, whether or not Floyd fully appreciates its significance.

A title tells us that this mission to Jupiter comes "18 Months Later." The crisis of intelligence, having come to a head in 2000, will now be resolved in *2001*, the beginning of a new epoch. The *Discovery*, in spite of its name, yet seems an unlikely setting for such a revolution: the men aboard suffer from the same intellectual and spiritual atrophy, and the crew's functions are subordinate to the ultimate tool, HAL. Floyd merely dozes during his flights, but three of the five crew members here are in deep hibernation. Of course, the hibernation has the practical effect of conserving food and air, but the deliberate choice of unconsciousness, the mechanical appearance of the hibernators, and the explanation that hibernation is "exactly like being asleep" except that "you don't dream"—all these details seem to comment on the kind of men so encased.

The food eaten by the other two, Bowman and Poole, looks pasty and tasteless; appropriately, their conversation also lacks any spice. In the interview with the BBC reporter, Bowman and Poole get only mechanical questions—How is everything going? and Why use hibernation and what is it like?—to which they give pleasantly mechanical answers. HAL, on the other hand, gets to talk about itself. Asked about its self-confidence and its relationship with humans, HAL waxes positively effusive:

> No nine thousand computer has ever made a mistake or distorted information. We are all, by any practical definition of the words, foolproof and incapable of error. . . . I enjoy working with people. . . . I am putting myself to the fullest possible use, which is all, I think, that any conscious entity can ever hope to do.

HAL can talk about itself so expressively because it has a "self" to talk about. (Our first encounter with HAL is a point-of-view shot of Bowman passing one of HAL's "eyes," a shot that, as Carolyn Geduld notes, establishes HAL's "vitality as well as its paranoid watchfulness"[32]; with the presence of a viable consciousness, Kubrick can and does employ several subjective shots. HAL has no real "self," however, and we get an indication of this lack of actuality in the distortion and discoloration seen through its "eye.") When the interviewer turns again to Bowman and Poole to ask their personal views of HAL as a thinking being, they have no definite opinions: HAL "acts" like a human, they say, but "whether or not he has real feelings is something [they] don't think anyone can truthfully answer." We may speculate in which direction they are leaning by noting the easy use they make of the personal pronoun in reference to HAL, a usage that is common in most of the writing about the film (and that, I admit, requires a struggle to avoid).

Bowman and Poole lack individuality and personality because neither is a complete man. They somewhat resemble one another, and they both exhibit the "*programmed* . . . machine-like" behavior that obviously comes from astronaut training,[33] but we should see them as more than mechanical humans who stand in ironic contrast to the human-like machine, HAL. These two astronauts also comprise fractional complements of a potential whole. During the interview transmission, each watches his own viewer, turned slightly away from the other. Poole jogs and shadowboxes to pass time[34]; he also rests under a sunlamp, presumably to keep a healthy appearance. The body has no soul, however. At the non-physical game of chess, HAL forces him to resign, and he responds to a taped birthday greeting from home with complete listlessness. Conversely, Bowman makes sketches, drawings of his hibernating colleagues, to pass his time. Notably, HAL engages Bowman in conversation about its misgivings concerning their mission: the "rumors" of the incident on the moon, and "the melodramatic touch" of putting the others in hibernation. Bowman is not very forthcoming in this talk, but he does seem thoughtful at least compared to Poole. After HAL has, they think, erred in its analysis of the unit controlling the antenna (ironically, their communications tool, never put to effective use, still turns out to be a serious vulnerability), Poole simply concludes that they have no "choice but disconnection"; Bowman agrees, but he also sees the logistical problems that would result and wonders about HAL's reaction: "Well, I'm not so sure what he'd think about it." Because these two seem divided into physical and mental halves, and because human mentality has degenerated, one would think that Bowman and Poole would be no match for HAL if a match is what HAL wanted.

HAL would be favored because, next to its human colleagues, it appears complete, even perfect. Several critics have remarked, in this respect, that HAL's character comes across as the most human in the film: it certainly is the most expressive. Even so, HAL also remains incomplete, and we must not be taken in by appearances. I think we can see HAL's lack most evidently in the question of motivation.[35] HAL will later tell Bowman that it will not let any human jeopardize the mission by disconnecting it, but that does not explain its original mistake with the antenna unit. HAL may appear to be plotting, but the appearance of a human trait does not prove its actual existence. On the contrary, HAL's lack is precisely that it is not human, and therefore, its actions really have no human motivation. HAL ironically offers the best explanation: "It can only be attributable to human error. This sort of thing has cropped up before, and it has always been due to human error." As human intelligence and spirit atrophy in humans, they try to program these qualities into machines. It cannot be done. The act itself only demonstrates further degeneration. Matched against HAL, moreover, humanity could complete its surrender except that one of the men aboard ship makes himself whole.

As HAL sets out to dispatch the human crew, it cannot know that the struggle will bring about the revival of inspired human intelligence in one of them. The violence, as several critics have noted, strikes us as especially chilling because it is so mechanically distant—that is, inhuman. While Poole is attempting to replace the antenna unit, HAL directs the pod to turn on him. We see the pod wheel about and approach with its mechanical arms reaching out, but the camera cuts away from the actual attack: four flash-cuts of HAL's looming "eye" on the pod, a sudden cessation on the soundtrack of Poole's breathing, and an insert of HAL's "eye" inside the ship. This last shot, suggestive of a murderer looking on quietly and coolly as the crime proceeds, disarms us all the more effectively because the consciousness behind that "eye" is false, is not really there: how cool can you get? and what a getaway! In any case, the killing is real, and Bowman rushes out to attempt a rescue. Left alone, HAL can do away with the hibernating crew simply by stopping their life-support systems. Poole, attacked from behind as was the shrieking ape-man taken by the leopard, succumbs in silence. The three men in hibernation also make no sound; instead, their machines shriek for them, beeping and pulsing, flashing "Computer Malfunction" and "Life Functions Critical," until they too succumb in silence, "Life Functions Terminated." Tearing the air hose on Poole's space suit and unplugging the hibernators, HAL has mechanically killed them by killing their machines.

Meanwhile, although done with the pod's potentially lethal arms, Bowman retrieves Poole's body quite gently. The cradling of the body appears rather tender, the only such tenderness we see, aside from the ape-men's holding their young. In his haste to save Poole, Bowman leaves behind his space helmet. Several critics have remarked that he effectively loses his head, that panic and anger then awaken him emotionally. Leaving the helmet, while not a calculated move on Bowman's part, results in his regaining his head. When HAL refuses to let him back aboard, HAL sounds confident of prevailing. Bowman says he will use the emergency air-lock, and HAL replies, "Without your space helmet, Dave, you're going to find that rather difficult." HAL thinks that a human cut off from mechanical support is a dead man; with most men of the time, it would be correct. In its mechanical way of thinking, though, HAL fails to account for human ingenuity. When Poole made a poor move in his chess game, HAL gently lectured him: "I'm sorry, Frank, I think you missed it." Poole lacked HAL's mental agility. Now HAL has missed the next move because it lacks imagination. Unable to use his helmet, Bowman uses his head: with the explosive bolts on the pod's hatch, he can propel himself through the vacuum and pressurize the air-lock before his lungs collapse. This time the machines shriek like ape-men to ward off the human attack: as the hatch is set to explode, a deep warbling is heard and a siren sounds. From inside the air-lock, these warnings and the penetrating explosion are rendered silent in the vacuum, and the rushing sound of pressurization, followed by Bowman's respiration, signals the human victory.

To finish off his opponent, Bowman must disconnect HAL and thereby restore tools to the status of utility, not mock consciousness. John Charlot writes that the "humanizing of HAL is an attempt to resolve the dualism between man and his tools," a clearly "bad solution" that Bowman corrects when the "'humanity' of HAL is deprogrammed."[36] We see Bowman's superiority in the low-angle shot of him as he descends on HAL— the first such use of this perspective since the triumphant view of Moon-Watcher. This termination, in contrast to those immediately preceding it, has no coldly mechanical quality, for Bowman lays his own hands on HAL and throttles it. Again, several critics have remarked that HAL's "death" affects us as the most touching demise seen in the film.[37] As Bowman stalks HAL's Logic Memory Center, HAL certainly seems contrite: "I know I've made some very poor decisions recently, but I can give you my complete assurance that my work will be back to normal. I've still got the greatest enthusiasm and confidence in the mission, and I want to help you." Well said, but HAL's euphemistic repentance—four murders passed off as "very poor decisions"—has as much heartfelt emotion as Floyd's affected excitement over the discovery of the monolith. The important difference remains that Floyd's heart has atrophied, whereas HAL's program never actually included a heart. The same must be said of HAL's behavior in extremis. With the disconnection of each system— several miniature monoliths—HAL claims to feel the reduction of electrical activity. In a calm, but gradually degenerating voice, HAL pleads: "Stop, Dave. I'm afraid. I'm afraid, Dave. Dave, my mind is going. I can feel it. I can feel it. My mind is going." Even so, HAL feels nothing; instead, noticing the shut-off of certain functions, its programming merely calls it fear and sensation— quite a refinement on shrieking or flashing lights.

I do not mean to say the scene should leave us unaffected altogether. The emotional impact comes not from HAL's death throes[38], but from Bowman's reactions. His anxious expression and labored breathing show that, false or not, exterminating any consciousness greatly taxes the emotions. Reduced to the "childhood" of its first program, HAL wants to state its name and sing "A Bicycle Built for Two" ("Daisy, Daisy . . . I'm half crazy all for the love of you"). Bowman's sympathetic pity confirms that his emotions have reawakened, here in expressing the difficulty of finally severing the tie between humanity and the convenient, but false humanity of "user-friendly" machines. Bowman's ability finally to feel these emotions, even as he struggles with their mechanical manipulation, gives this scene its true emotional power. Such awareness demonstrates genuine progress over the likes of Moon-Watcher, a more cold-blooded killer.

With the antenna presumably out of order (Poole was replacing the aiming mechanism when attacked) and with HAL's cognitive functions disconnected, Bowman goes on utterly alone. A message from Floyd suddenly appears. Embedded in HAL's memory, it had been meant for the arrival in Jupiter's orbit, but it comes on now because that part of HAL's programming has been shut off and can no longer withhold it. Again, some critics have written that this withheld message explains HAL's mistakes. Nelson, for instance, speculates that this message out of HAL's "unconscious" represents "the secret that drove him to madness."[39] But again, the metaphor strikes me as too anthropomorphic, too willing to admit

HAL's humanness. I think the message, like so much other communication in the film, tells us more of significance in what is not said. Floyd reports the discovery of "the first evidence of intelligent life off the earth" and goes on to explain that, but for the signal aimed at Jupiter, "the four-million-year-old black monolith has remained completely inert." Although the message must continue, the last line we hear is, "Its origin and purpose: still a total mystery." We do not hear the probable commands for the mission around Jupiter: search for artifacts, collect data, and if possible, make contact. Also unspoken are the deficiencies of such a mission: the desire for something tangible. Floyd cannot realize that, along with the monolith, mankind's powers of inspired thinking have also been inert. Fortunately, cut off from deficient men and debilitating machines, Bowman can, like us, not hear the orders to search for things; he can pursue the more intangible mysteries.

Thus, in the ensuing sequence titled "Jupiter and Beyond the Infinite," when Bowman arrives in Jupiter's orbit and sees the monolith alternately gleaming and fading from sight above the planet, he does not monitor it or send probes; rather, he goes with it. His orders have brought him to Jupiter, but Bowman goes "Beyond the Infinite" on his own. His ability and initiative to do so indicate a distinctly more active intelligence than could be found in those who would give or follow the mission's tentative, mundane orders.

Ironically, Bowman's journey after the monolith yields the contact Floyd had probably hoped the crew would make. In other words, once Bowman's intelligence outgrows the mission, he can fulfill it in a way unimagined before. The rushing, colored lights, the exploding nebulae, the viscous and cloudy shapes, the multicolored landscapes—these visions, to judge from Bowman's frozen reaction shots, beckon and terrify him. Soon, however, the visions alter his eye; seen in several extreme close-ups, Bowman's eye, his means of perception, changes colors and adapts to these visions. Only at his seeming destination, the white room decorated in classic French style, does his adapted eye regain its original color.

In a film that confounds so many viewers, here we can all agree on the important questions: Where has he arrived? and why has he come? Walker says that such questioning may not help: "It is no use seeking rational explanations for metaphorical or allegorical situations. The process of events in the room is more important than the end products of its furnishings."[40] In any event, the film offers the bewildered viewer little evidence for answering these questions with confidence. What we do have is the pod parked in this bedroom. From Bowman's point of view (roused consciousness allows for subjective shots again), through the pod's window, we see Bowman in his space suit; in close-up, Bowman appears much older. We follow Bowman into the next room—the pod having disappeared—where he finds a sink and two bathtubs. On the soundtrack, his breathing is joined by sounds from the bedroom. From his point of view through the doorway, we see Bowman, older yet and dressed in a comfortable robe, eating at a table set for one. This seated Bowman turns, comes forward, and finds no one; meanwhile, the sound of his respiration in the space suit has ceased. Back at the table, he upsets his wine glass, which shatters on the floor. Leaning over to pick up the glass, the sound of difficult breathing attracts his attention to the bed. There lies Bowman, now greatly withered with age. He reaches out his hand, pointing, and we see the monolith at the foot of his bed. Bowman, without touching the monolith, has made contact.

Still, the question remains, What has he discovered? In this setting, time disappears; but unlike Moon-Watcher's prehistoric setting, where time did not exist because no consciousness felt its passage, here Bowman has full awareness of passing beyond time, like an Einsteinian traveler watching himself arrive. As he continues to meet himself, he sheds himself. The pod and the space suit disappear much as the monolith disappeared from the ape-men's cave. So will his body leave. The setting provides a room for cleansing, a table for nourishment, and finally a bed for passing on to the next world. This death is not final. His body breaks like the wine glass, but only the physical container is lost. When Bowman reaches toward the monolith, he becomes a fetus on the bed. From this new being's position, the camera tracks into the monolith: the fetus penetrates the monolith, and Bowman thereby becomes the first whose grasp exceeds his reach.

Sent to find aliens, Bowman instead finds and renews himself. When he enters the monolith's blackness, he comes out over the Earth. In the last image, accompanied by the *Zarathustra* theme, the fetus turns its wonderful gaze on us. Nelson says that these glittering eyes are "mutely imploring the audience to ponder [their] mystery," and Walker notes the image's "richer allusiveness" that is "open-ended, yet oddly comforting in the way that dream imagery can be to an awakened sleeper gratified by the echoes and associations lingering in his conscious mind."[41] Bowman, if he could speak here, might say that he found no aliens. (Those who think the monolith is some kind of other-worldly device controlling evolution would do well to consider the film's attack on the vanity—as witnessed in HAL—of such attempted control.) The monolith—simple, opaque, and always present at these intellectual thresholds—represents that principle of inspired intelligence that has brought mankind from the caves to the stars. This intelligence, however, must surpass these environments. Untethered to particular place or time, intelligence can comprehend more than a body can. When Bowman, as the Star-Child, enters the monolith, he penetrates the universe and comprehends it in himself; after realizing everything within the self, nothing can be alien. Bowman, at the zenith of human intelligence, beckons us to this mysterious journey in which we would travel so far in time and space only to arrive where we began and know the place for the first time.

Kubrick's allusive style, dramatic technique, and mythic structure in *2001* all make for a very ambitious and challenging film: the dramatic (i.e., the showing rather than telling) portrayal of the educational development of something as abstract as human intelligence. To the extent that the dramatic manner expands rather than contracts the plot, Kubrick depends on the willing involvement of his audience—an appropriate decision, for a film about intelligence, to be truly satisfying, ought to exercise the viewer's intelligence. The film certainly rewards the effort to be so involved, which, I think, further sets the measure of its success and greatness.

As I have stated earlier, Clarke's printed adaptation of this story demands considerably less of its audience. The novel is not diminished simply because it tells rather than shows. On the contrary, Clarke selects the point of view appropriate to his intention. Clarke, however, intends nothing so ambitious and daring as to treat the development of human intelligence: he concerns himself with the survival of humanity as physical beings—an obvious contingency for the existence, let alone growth, of intelligence. Clarke, therefore, using the same aggregate protagonist, invents a didactic action, not to examine how intelligence should excel, but to tell us how the race survived and evolved from prehistory, and then to speculate on how the race must evolve in order to continue to survive. Rather than the quality of human thought, Clarke contemplates the mental maturity of beings faced with threats to their physical existence. Clarke's exemplum then follows a "maturing plot of character" in which the aggregate protagonist's "goals are either mistakenly conceived or not yet formed," and in which the protagonist "must be given strength and direction."[42] In contrast to the film's education plot, the development of humanity comes down to, more simply, a matter of experience—and, significantly, a proper upbringing.

As the novel begins, a millions-year-old drought has brought the ape-men to the brink of extinction. Moon-Watcher may have latent intelligence, but this latency stands as a minor problem compared to the death of the species. Ironically, the ape-men are surrounded by sustenance on the hoof—if only they could recognize it. For the ape-men in the film, although their life and surroundings appear bleak, stagnation, not extinction, threatens their existence. Thus, in the novel, the monolith makes a more fortunate and necessary appearance because the ape-men face an immediate and life-threatening problem, and they have no time to wait for inspiration. Moon-Watcher takes the monolith for an inedible rock and lets it go at that. In fact, the monolith has been sent from outer space, a probe in search of potential intelligence. It hypnotizes Moon-Watcher's tribe, shows them pictures, and examines their minds and bodies; tests include tying a knot or, for Moon-Watcher, throwing rocks at a target. Moon-Watcher, one of the few who succeed, gets another lesson, a picture of a family group who have had plenty to eat; he feels a new "dissatisfaction with his life" as the monolith manipulates and twists his "simple brain . . . into new patterns" (25). Finally, Moon-Watcher can go on to the field test: almost against his will, he is compelled to find a heavy stone, approach an unsuspecting pig, and bash its brains in: a simple lesson by cosmic standards, but it suffices to save the race.

The monolith presides over the removal of one other threat, the leopard. Having shown Moon-Watcher pictures of comfortable cave life, the monolith plants the seed for Moon-Watcher's own thinking: using "an immense effort of imagination," he realizes that eating his prey "in the safety of his own cave" (30) will keep him out of harm's way. The leopard, though, follows the scent of dead meat into the cave. Now the ape-men accidentally learn another lesson: in a dark cave full of armed ape-men, a leopard puts itself at a mortal disadvantage. Moon-Watcher has grown so that he no longer exists at the mercy of his surroundings, and the monolith, its work completed, may decamp.

This monolith symbolizes no principle of inspiration that causes man to pull himself up the ladder of intelligence. Rather, in the world of the novel, it exists as a tangible artifact that acts as a fortunate savior of the race. Rather than mere salvation, John Hollow remarks that, inasmuch as the monolith actively starts man's evolution, "what we have is something very like creation," and the story "is about the relationships between creator and created, about the fact and implications of that moment of contact between two levels of being."[43] The monolith as creator has awakened the ape-men's intelligence; once given, the knowledge may be used for good or ill.

Left on their own after the monolith is satisfied that extinction no longer threatens, the ape-men, like pupils out of the teacher's sight, put their lessons to ill use. In the new garden of plenty, "two blemishes" remain: the leopard, and another tribe from the other side of the river. The monolith, of course, has left instructions that will see to their safety from the leopard, and the other tribe, with whom Moon-Watcher's clan merely exchanges shrieks, poses no serious threat. Threat or no, the others still present an annoyance Moon-Watcher will not abide; thus, they terrorize the others with the leopard's head impaled on a stake, and, while the others are paralyzed with fright, Moon-Watcher clubs their leader to death. "Now he was the master of the world, and he was not quite sure what to do next" (34). In the hands of the immature creatures, the means of survival can be turned into the means of destruction. With their first evolutionary step, they have moved from one threat to another.

Nevertheless, Clarke keeps the emphasis on mastery, and the new threats result as the inescapable complications that attend any progress. Before moving on to Floyd in the year 2000, Clarke inserts a chapter to outline these implications. Ape-men develop their dexterity, which allows them to make better tools, which then allow the development of limbs and brains—"and at its end was Man" (36). The mastery of each level of being brings new dangers: new technologies for good can also make for bigger, more devastating weapons. Clarke says the technology is necessary to conquer the world, but it leaves man "living on borrowed time" (37). The human race thereby confronts a problem other than a crisis of intelligence in which humanity allows tools to take over while the brain atrophies. Instead, they must remain alert to the contingent dangers of their progress and overcome them by continued growth.

With the leap forward to 2000, Floyd and others then face the questions of whether they are, indeed, alert and whether they are prepared to make further advances. The answer is yes and no. The world is in transition, for the terrible knowledge of the atom has also opened up the universe. Like Moon-Watcher's leopard and rival tribe, Floyd's world suffers from being "dominated by two problems": the rival tribe has become a population explosion and consequent food shortage, and the leopard has grown into dozens of antagonists with nuclear capability. The Chinese, suffering the worst population growth and food shortage, only exacerbate the problem by their willingness to sell nuclear weapons to any country; some hope that the Chinese simply need the capital, but others fear that they have developed superior weapons. On the other side, exploration and colonization of the moon offer some potential for relief, and martial technology thereby can have peaceful applications. The narrator says, "Man had at last found something as exciting as war," but he immediately adds, "Unfortunately, not all nations had yet realized that fact" (64). Devastation and thriving survival stand as equally available choices.

Floyd, for one, has the mental and spiritual vigor to understand the problems and their potential solutions. In great contrast to his film counterpart, Floyd has not been lulled by technology. When we first see him setting out for the space station, he tells himself, "No matter how many times you left Earth . . . the excitement never really palled" (41). Throughout the journey to Clavius, Floyd's awed appreciation of scientific and aesthetic wonders remains evident. He does not fail to see the spectacle of the Earth behind the space station; he contemplates the "Newspad" as near "perfect communications" (57), admitting that it would yet be surpassed by something even better; a flight attendant enchants him with "zero-gravity . . . Balinese dance movements" (58); over the moon, he practically chokes up at the sight of a man-made beacon; and he is struck at how the "flashing binary impulses" (60) of machines could make this space travel into "a normal, routine flight" (61). Everything that the film characters ignore amazes, amuses, or fills the novel's Floyd with pride.

If Floyd does not think his environment so dull as to be unworthy of notice, neither do we view him as dull himself. Even his call home, although spoken to a recorder, involves a purposeful and relatively vivid message. He later holds a friendly conversation with Dimitri, a Russian friend, and he inwardly regrets his necessary evasiveness because he hates for political policy to come between genuine friends. Furthermore, the straightforward conversations on Clavius leave everyone appropriately impressed. The TMA-1—discovered because of its radial pattern of magnetic waves, sort of an electrical bull's-eye—clearly reveals "the first evidence of intelligent life beyond the Earth" (71). Floyd and the other scientists feel "triumph, and yet sadness" (74) at having such an old fascination resolved. Then, when he actually goes to see the monolith, Floyd sees the silliness of taking snapshots, but he also admits the historic value. Most of all, however, he realizes the immense implications: "Every person of real intelligence—everyone who looked an inch beyond his nose—would find his life, his values, his philosophy, subtly changed" (82). Unlike Moon-Watcher, Floyd feels fully aware of how the monolith alters his mind.

Therefore, whatever the problems and challenges of 2000, Floyd seems to be equal to them. Clarke's portrayal of Floyd and subsequent characters has its own problem, however: he simply notes the potentially annihilating threats to mankind and quickly forgets them. Clarke not only has Floyd appreciate the wonders of his environment, but, perhaps too quickly, he sends Floyd hopefully to those wonders. When Floyd sets out on his trip, presumably from Cape Canaveral, he sees the artifacts of earlier space ventures: "But these now belonged to the past, and he was flying toward the future" (42). Later, on the moon, he meets a scientist's daughter who was born there and would not wish to see the Earth and its problems; in a metaphor central to Clarke's theme, Floyd reflects, "The time was fast approaching when Earth, like all mothers, must say farewell to her children" (66). By this time, though, Clarke has already left Earth and its conflicts for the quest to Saturn[44] and the answer to the monolith's origin. In the film, the crisis of intelligence results from mankind's ignoring his intellectual capabilities. In the novel, Clarke presents a crisis of transition between those who would conquer each other on Earth and those who would conquer the frontiers of space. Unfortunately, by sticking with his capable explorers, Clarke ignores the crisis.

Like Floyd, Poole and Bowman exhibit no intellectual decline, and, as *Discovery* takes them further from Earth, they turn their attention from worldly problems to the larger challenges of cosmic exploration. Poole exhibits his intelligent engagement with the mission when, just before his death, he anticipates the spectacular sight of Saturn's completely filling their view when their ship would "become an eternal moon of Saturn!" (139). Poole also shows himself capable of wry humor. When he is removing the antenna's supposedly faulty directional controls, he mutters, "Tampering by unauthorized personnel invalidates the manufacturer's guarantee" (129). His film counterpart would not get this joke, let alone crack it. Still, his destiny does not allow him to survive the trip; the violence of his murder—he yells in surprise, and Bowman sees the run-away pod dragging Poole's lifeless body off—contrasts sharply with the silent, invisible stealth HAL uses in the film. We feel the shock more, for this crime does not simply eliminate some mere cipher.

Bowman also feels the human loss and, when he has the time to reflect, honors his colleague's memory by acknowledging the fulfillment of an explorer's hope: "Frank Poole would be the first of all men to reach Saturn" (142). Bowman, perhaps a bit more than Poole, exhibits an active, studious curiosity. He varies his activities, looking through the telescope at Earth, reading the newspad, listening to music, viewing films, and reading books— including "the *Odyssey*, which of all books spoke to him most vividly across the gulfs of time" (103). After the ordeal with HAL, Bowman returns to these activities in order to cope with his loneliness, but, now aware of *Discovery's* true mission, he also ponders new ideas and feelings: "Sometimes the thought of the goal toward which he was driving filled him with a sense of exaltation—and a feeling of power" (174). This Bowman, unneedful of any reawakening, thrives because he is the perfect student.

Bowman makes such a perfect student because of his malleability in the hands of what will be a perfect teacher. The trip to Saturn puts him in the proper frame of mind to encounter the ultimate lesson. In the film, Bowman sheds his physical attributes only when he has arrived in the white room. In Clarke's novel, Bowman begins this process aboard *Discovery*. After setting out, Poole and Bowman often make "rather intimate personal calls" (103) back to Earth, but soon these more carnal interests wane. The men, nevertheless, do not, as in the film, simply turn into spiritless automatons. Instead, the physical separation is creating a different mental awareness. As the narrator says of Poole after the birthday greeting arrives from home, Poole does not lack any response so much as he feels quietly affected by the separation in time and space, having traveled "into a new dimension of remoteness," where emotional bonds have practically "been stretched beyond the yield point" (120). Bowman certainly shares this change, and after the loss of any human companionship, the separation from his physical life increases. When he needs to fill the silence, he plays audio tapes: first classical plays; then opera, culminating in Verdi's *Requiem Mass*; then only instrumental music, moving through the romantic composers until "their emotional outpourings became too oppressive"; finally finding "peace . . . in the abstract architecture of Bach, occasionally ornamented with Mozart" (175). With each change, he sheds more of his former self, moving from the physical to the ascetic.

If he seems to approach the condition of a machine, the evolution still somehow ennobles him. As John Hollow writes, "Clarke is not afraid of being replaced by machinery."[45] The novel practically bursts with admiration for mechanical feats. Floyd is impressed with the machines that brought him so routinely to the moon; similarly, Bowman feels almost incredulous at the mechanisms guiding a probe to an asteroid—a bit of astronomical target practice in which the machines "were aiming at a hundred-foot-diameter target, from a distance of thousands of miles" (107). The degree of difficulty having grown, the test given to Moon-Watcher still supposedly provides a good indication of capability. When *Discovery* settles into orbit and its engines shut down for good, Bowman feels "pride" and "sadness," practically eulogizing the engines that propelled him so far (182).

HAL, of course, would appear to be the exception, but even this programmatic killer finds forgiveness in Clarke's scheme of things. HAL stands as a product of "the third computer breakthrough," a technological leap forward, which occurs about every twenty years; another breakthrough, expected soon, "worried a great many people" (95–96). Therefore, like mankind, HAL is a creature whose "race" is in transition. In any case, at present HAL has actual intelligence. According to the novel, a standard devised by Alan Turing, a British mathematician, had answered the question of HAL's capacity for thought: in any extended exchange, if one could not tell the difference between a machine's replies and those that a human might give, then that machine could be said to be thinking. Of course, HAL can reach this mark easily, but, like throwing something at a target, this test seems, to me, not a very exacting measure of intelligence. The point remains, nonetheless, that HAL has been endowed with the ability to think by its creator (i.e., Clarke), and it certainly is chatty—and devious—after the human fashion. HAL even begins conversations with "a brief electronic throat-clearing" (134). After *Discovery* passes Jupiter and the men have only Saturn to wait for (only HAL knows the actual mission), HAL begins to make errors. It predicts the failure of the antenna's guidance system—nothing is wrong with it—and then it predicts the failure of the replacement part. Bowman cannot believe the coincidence, but when HAL insists that it is "incapable" of making mistakes, Bowman sees "no safe answer to that" (136) and gives up. Nevertheless, Mission Control calls to state that HAL has made an error; just as they order HAL's disconnection, the signal breaks off—the guidance control fails, the antenna drifts off target, and HAL is seemingly vindicated. HAL then kindly accepts the men's contrite apologies. Bowman and Poole never consider the possibility that HAL is silencing a threat to itself. So cut off from human contact, they seem to feel safe from human chicanery.

Soon enough, however, Poole is flagging behind his run-away pod, and HAL flatly commiserates, "Too bad about Frank, isn't it?" (143). In the ensuing scene, Bowman's tact and quick thinking unexpectedly abandon him. Standard operating procedure would dictate that he revive one of the hibernators to replace Poole. Having considered the likelihood that HAL has become dangerous, Bowman unwisely announces that he wants to revive all three—unwisely, for the suggestion must tip off HAL regarding Bowman's suspicions. HAL claims that it can run the ship without additional crewmen, but, when Bowman insists, HAL offers to handle the revivals; Bowman insists, again, that he be given control, and only when threatened, again, with disconnection does HAL suddenly give in. Of course, in view of the partial message from Mission Control and HAL's subsequent behavior, disconnection of some circuits should have topped Bowman's list of things to do. Poole's death obviously shocks Bowman, but, unlike his film counterpart at first, Bowman does not suffer as a man of limited mental resources would; that the incident would so disorder Bowman's thinking as to cause him practically to arouse and forewarn HAL's defensiveness strikes me as rather incredible. In the event, HAL uses the advantage offered and opens a hatch to vacuum out the ship. The lucky proximity of an emergency shelter supplied with oxygen and a space suit saves Bowman. Now, like Moon-Watcher, he uses his good fortune and finally does what must be done about this binary leopard.

HAL's demise does not stretch out so pitifully, mostly because Bowman acts, once more, with determination and efficiency. HAL understates a greeting of sorts: "Something seems to have happened to the life-support system, Dave. . . . Lucky you weren't killed" (154–55). Meanwhile, Dave can coolly joke to himself about performing amateur brain surgery. Bowman tells himself that HAL cannot feel pain, but HAL does evince panic and madness. All the frantic pleas and crazy announcements of rhymes, logarithms, and songs show human emotions, but their ridiculous portrayal owes more to histrionic melodrama than to believable psychology (the original *Star Trek* television series used to excel at these overly operatic death scenes for computers, perhaps so as not to allow the machines to give better performances than the human actors). For other reasons, Bowman remains relatively unmoved and pulls the last plug just as HAL says, "I . . . am . . . ready . . . for . . . my . . . first . . . lesson . . . today" (157).

HAL has an excuse. Its "life" has the sole purpose of the pursuit of truth in the service of mankind, but its program for the mission includes the command to keep secret the mission's purpose. HAL does not understand the need for security and national interest—a rare intrusion of the earthly conflict that improbably assumes anyone can easily join the race to Saturn—and, in short, feels "guilt" (148). It becomes neurotic and, when faced with disconnection, homicidal (a psychology that goes well beyond anything justified by the Turing test). Even Bowman grows more understanding after the fact: "program conflicts" caused HAL's guilt, and, not meaning to hurt anybody, it panicked "like any clumsy criminal" (169). Clarke thereby wants us to see the connection between man's faulty instruction of his creations and the aliens' grander instruction of their charges. Nevertheless, inconsistency fouls the design. If we believe HAL capable of actual thought, we can fairly ask why it cannot comprehend the distinction between a secret and a lie; or, if the distinction is not granted, we might ask why HAL still cannot manage the simple act of holding in "mind" contradictory ideas. Clarke has said HAL's problem comes about because of "these clods back at Mission Control," but he sees no "rationale for HAL's behavior" in the film.[46] Clarke's own terms betray the problem: he treats HAL like a being, but he blames HAL's errors on programming; such an explanation does not offer a rationale for behavior, but merely points out a mechanical mistake. The portrayal of HAL's "character" features large inconsistencies; that is, to indulge in a sci-fi cliché, its character does not compute.

Even so, in the world of the novel, HAL's intelligence must be accepted as real, if flawed, and its actions are forgiven. In fact, as Bowman speculates on his lonely voyage to Saturn, machines perhaps represent a step in intellectual maturity. According to this view, advanced beings would shed their biological bodies in favor of "metal and plastic," leading to a "far finer and subtler" development of the senses; eventually, the brain would not be necessary, and the immortal entity of the mind could "free itself from matter" and evolve into "spirit" (173–74)—exactly the case with the monolith's creators (as the narrator will redundantly verify at each point). Given this view of intelligence, HAL marks a misstep in the right direction; through Bowman, our cosmic parents will gently keep us on our feet.

Bowman, as free of earthly connection as possible, now stands ready to confront this mature, spiritual intelligence. To use HAL's famous last words, Bowman is ready for his first lesson. As he approaches the moon Japetus, he notices that its one bright, elliptical patch has a "tiny black dot at the exact center" (181). Upon nearer approach, Bowman resolves this dot as a huge version of the monolith; when he goes to land his pod on it, Bowman sees it open as a gate into another dimension. By hitting this last interplanetary target (the significance of Bowman's name should now be apparent), he passes the entrance exam. Calmly observant, Bowman notices a large spaceship with "broken ribs and dully gleaming sheets of metal that had been partly peeled off like the skin of an orange" (198); also, he sees several other spaceships, not in a "parking lot," but "a cosmic junk heap" (203). The former probably shows the only remains of a cast-off body of an evolving alien, and the latter probably represent the cast-off vehicles of some previous pupils raised beyond their immature orbits. Finally, the long journey—filled with mostly unnecessary observations—ends in a hotel suite. Bowman soon surmises that "it was some kind of test" (209) and later fears that he has failed. Still, he tries to maintain his perceptive abilities. He notes that the furnishings and provisions prove false upon examination: the books have no print inside, and the food, regardless of the label, is made of the same unknown substance. By watching the television, he correctly guesses that monitored signals have provided his hosts with this setting, which he hopes means that his hosts want to make him feel at home. The other point about which he can rest assured is that, by coming there, he has already passed all the tests.

Bowman's transformation will be quicker and more absolute than Moon-Watcher's. The aliens probe Bowman's mind in his sleep; they unwind his memory, collecting and storing all his knowledge and experience. When they come to his beginning, Bowman has become a baby for another beginning. At first he cries, but quickly he feels protected. The monolith shows the infant several flashy shapes and patterns—just as it had to Moon-Watcher—and now the processing "carried out at far deeper levels of the mind" moves more swiftly, for the aliens have improved their methods and this subject's brain has "an infinitely finer texture" (217–18). The infant's awareness and power grow to awesome proportions. He recognizes his origin in these aliens; he realizes that his body merely incarnates "his mind's present image of itself," which would fall away when "he had decided on a new form, or had passed beyond the necessities of matter" (218); and he knows that he can take himself back to Earth merely by willing it—and back he must go in order to save mankind. Nuclear war is breaking out (quite unexpectedly in terms of the novel's plotting). The puny missile hardly distracts the Star-Child, as the narrator now calls him: "The feeble energies it contained were no possible menace to him: but he preferred a cleaner sky. He put forth his will, and the circling megatons flowered in a silent detonation that brought a brief, false dawn to half the sleeping globe." Like Moon-Watcher at the beginning of another epoch, Star-Child has been made "master of the world," unsure of what to do next: "But he would think of something" (221).

Whatever that "something" may be, Star-Child is the chosen one, also like Moon-Watcher, to save the race. He has obviously achieved, through his selection, a higher intelligence, a more mature intelligence. Maturity stands out as the key quality here, for Bowman has not otherwise shown significant superiority over his fellows before entering the Star-Gate; his intelligence suffices, but his selection as the aliens' chosen one comes down, more than anything else, to his experiencing the journey and outliving the others. What distinguishes Bowman is survival, not intelligence. His film counterpart, on the other hand, survives because he alone rouses himself and passes the test of intelligence. This latter Bowman returns as a manifestation of higher intelligence in a world sorely in need of mental and spiritual invigoration. Clarke's Bowman receives intelligence as a means to an end: with his powers, he can dismiss those who would misuse the knowledge of the atom, and he can thereby assure the continued survival of mankind.

All told, therefore, Clarke's novel hardly "explains" Kubrick's film. Kubrick visualizes the evolution of intelligence, whereas Clarke speculates on how apes started to evolve, what space travel between the planets will be like, and who the aliens will be when we inevitably meet them. In the process, Clarke often digresses from the main action, fails to develop the conflict well, and draws inconsistent characters. Ironically, the film finally inspires more speculation as it raises several issues: the definitive nature of mankind, the value of technology, the purpose of exploration, and the quality of life in the space age. Clarke's singular speculation sets most of these issues aside with the claim that we came from ancient astronauts, leaving us with only one issue: whether we will really meet again.

The suggestion here, that the novel greatly simplifies the film, would apparently stand Bluestone on his head. For example, the film portrays thought and intelligence much more subtly than does the novel: Kubrick portrays inspiration, or the birth of thought, in motifs of music, triumphant postures, alignments, and intense eyes; Clarke offers, as a corresponding motif, the image of hitting a bull's-eye—rather like an experiment to see if pigeons can be taught to peck the right button by rewarding them with crackers. Kubrick's motifs comprise, as Bluestone would predict, "external signs"; Clarke, however, conceives a no less "external" motif, which, furthermore, less effectively represents the same or similar mental state—contrary to Bluestone's claims.[47] Moreover, Paul H. Stacy, one who accepts Bluestone's theory on adaptations (specifically, he employs the distinction between concept and percept), uses that framework to set the film over the novel in regard to HAL's characterization:

> 2001 exploits the necessary mechanization of the camera. That is the best reason why HAL is more interesting than the people; that is why his death is more touching than that of catatonic humans. HAL's death is technological; in any other medium it would be different. (Clarke's short story, or the movie-based novel, demonstrates this painfully.)[48]

I do not agree that mechanical recordings are uniquely suited to mechanical subjects, but I find it interesting that Bluestone's method can be turned against him.

I will not, however, draw any theoretical, deductive conclusions from this case in which the film, in my view, demonstrably surpasses the novel. Bluestone has his cases wherein the opposite occurs, yet now we have another case wherein his conclusions would not hold. The point, I think, is that deductive conclusions can mislead, for a story presents an artist with potential powers and effects to be realized, and their realization seldom depends on the material of printed words or filmed images.

Afterword/Afterimage

The beauties of writing have been observed to be often such as cannot in the present state of human knowledge be evinced by evidence, or drawn out into demonstration; they are therefore wholly subject to the imagination, and do not force their effects upon a mind preoccupied by unfavorable sentiments, nor overcome the counteraction of a false principle or of stubborn partiality.

—Samuel Johnson, *The Rambler* No. 93

About the challenge of making *2001*, Kubrick confidently stated, "If it can be written, or thought, it can be filmed."[1] His statement could equally apply to the challenge of adapting novels to the screen, but, finally, in regard to creating effective fictions, the statement might be altered to: If it can be thought, it can be written and filmed.

Whatever I or other theorists and critics write about the practice, adapting novels to the screen remains a popular art—popular with producers as well as the audience. And these adaptations do not always involve best sellers. To cite one example, many of those who went to see *Clueless* may not have known they were taking part in a "revival" of sorts, and those who did recognize the source for this film, and the more straightforward adaptations that soon followed, may have had difficulty thinking of Jane Austen as a hot property.

If the string of films based upon Austen's novels has generally won critical praise, as other adaptations continue to appear, so do the usual suspicions about the practice. The Disney corporation's version of *The Hunchback of Notre Dame* stands accused as the latest travesty. I would agree with those who would suggest that the Disney writers should have come up with an original story if they wanted to sell the self-esteem-despite-disadvantages plot. Even so,

I would also dare hope that some youngsters will someday pick up the novel out of curiosity; in any case, the reputation of Victor Hugo will likely survive.

Perhaps we can find a precedent in the case of *The Last of the Mohicans*, adapted by Michael Mann in 1992. In an interview at the time of the film's release, Mann emphasized the novel's exciting qualities:

> The idea was to take this and make it the way it really must have been . . . and give it the same kind of edge that it would have had if I was making a contemporary thriller on the streets of L. A. or New York. The frontier was not this happy little place of log cabins. This was the lower east side of New York in the 18th century.

In spite of this professed admiration for James Fenimore Cooper's timeless story-telling, Mann nevertheless soon admits, "Oh, you can't get through the novel. . . . You have to put a gun to your head to get through the novel."[2] His adaptation would not qualify as a faithful work, and his adaptation did not alter Cooper's reputation.

Of course, whether or not an author's reputation thrives does not stand as the central issue in the discussion about adaptations. That discussion, I think, is changing because of the inventiveness of today's filmmakers. In regard to the adaptations of Jane Austen's works, many viewers have granted that the Austen films retain a great deal of fidelity to their sources, yet some I know have come out of the theaters saying that they miss Jane Austen— that is, that they miss her narrator's voice. This complaint returns us to the initial problem that I have been trying to recast, if not remove: the cinema cannot duplicate the novel. The experience of one is obviously different from the experience of the other, yet the narrative pleasures need not be different, let alone diminished. In the case of *Persuasion*, Roger Michell may have missed some opportunities to match the narrator's humorous view of her characters. Such views, however, can find their way into the film. For instance, in Simon Langton's recent version of *Pride and Prejudice*, the famous opening line, rather than being lost with the narration, is spoken by Elizabeth.

That solution takes care of the one line, but what about a more thorough treatment of a narrator's sense of humor? In *Cold Comfort Farm*, Stella Gibbons satirized contemporary fiction set in the dramatically rustic countryside, and she underlined her parodic style by marking the more exaggerated passages with stars, an idea borrowed from the travel writing of Baedeker. John Schlesinger's film does not keep the omniscient narrator, but he manages to keep some of the florid prose: Flora, the heroine who fancies herself a Jane Austen in the making, speaks these lines as she struggles to describe the sunsets in her journal. Otherwise, the adaptation succeeds by resisting what some would claim is film's natural inclination: it never shows the "something nasty" that Aunt Ada saw in the woodshed.

Also, a filmmaker may solve the problem of maintaining a narrator's voice, obviously, by simply maintaining the narrator. Martin Scorsese's use of Joanne Woodward to set scenes and describe circumstances in voice-over for his version of *The Age of Innocence* worked wonderfully, I think, although others regarded the device as a distraction, an admission that the film's visual style could not successfully portray the story.

Such a solution represents nothing new as far as film technique is concerned, and the negative responses represent nothing new either, although the wording sometimes varies of late. When faithful adaptations appear, some critics describe the works as exhibiting a "slavish" fidelity; other dismissive terms— "Masterpiece-Theatre treatment" or "Ivoryesque"—serve the same purpose: to demonstrate that films, which supposedly cannot be faithful to novels, fail when they nevertheless remain faithful to the novel. Not every installment of Masterpiece Theatre measures up to *Brideshead Revisited*, and James Ivory's *Remains of the Day* did not, for me, succeed as well as his *Howard's End*, but I cannot see how these terms can stand as insults.

Criticism of this sort comes, I think, out of what Samuel Johnson's epigram describes as "false principle" or "stubborn partiality." He goes on to write, "To convince any man against his will is hard, but to please him against his will is . . . above the reach of human abilities." No doubt I am being stubborn in proposing the set of principles I think offer the best approach to adaptations, yet I would like to think that I begin with the pleasures of the novels and films and then work back to the principles; if, therefore, I am trying to convince my readers, I am also hoping first that they have experienced the same pleasures, no matter how they would wish to account for them.

Still, the discussion of adaptations will remain at loggerheads if the language of the discussion encourages such an outcome. "Concept" versus "percept," like the "showing" versus "telling" dichotomy, offers critical certainty and shuts off discussion. If this study accomplishes nothing else, I would like to think that it points to a more accommodating language, one that discusses what novelists and filmmakers have done, rather than one that defines what they may do. My references to the theorists I use in developing my approach indicate, not a set of inviolate rules, but rather a set of models for this language. Their inductive approach, you could say, I found conveniently adaptable.

Notes

Introduction

1. Daniel Blum, *A Pictorial History of the Silent Screen* (New York: Putnam, 1953), 50.

2. Library of Congress, *Catalog of Copyright Entries: Cumulative Entries: Motion Pictures, 1912–1939* (Washington, DC: GPO, 1951), 424.

3. Jay Leyda, *Kino: A History of the Russian and Soviet Film* (London, George Allen and Unwin Ltd., 1960), 410.

4. Harry M. Geduld, *Authors on Film* (Bloomington: Indiana University Press, 1972), 88–90.

5. Francis Levy, "Hollywood Embraces the Difficult Novel," *New York Times*, 22 March 1981, p. D13; Richard Corliss, "We Lost It at the Movies," *Film Comment*, January–February 1980, 38; "By the Book," *Film Comment*, March–April 1991, 40.

6. Levy.

7. Hugo Münsterberg, *The Film: A Psychological Study* (1916; rprt., New York: Dover, 1970); Rudolf Arnheim, *Film as Art* (Berkeley: University of California Press, 1957); Vachel Lindsay, *The Art of the Moving Picture* (1915; rprt., New York: Liveright, 1970); Lev Kuleshov, *Kuleshov on Film: Writings of Lev Kuleshov*, ed. and trans. Ronald Levaco (Berkeley: University of California Press, 1974); V. I. Pudovkin, *Film Technique and Film Acting*, trans. Ivor Montague (1929, 1937; rprt., New York: Grove Press, 1976); and Sergei Eisenstein, *The Film Sense*, trans. Jay Leyda (New York: Harcourt, 1942), and *Film Form: Essays in Film Theory*, trans. Jay Leyda (New York: Harcourt, 1949).

8. Béla Balázs, *Theory of Film: Character and Growth of a New Art*, trans. Edith Bone (1952; rprt., New York: Dover, 1970), 46–48, 84, 139–42.

9. Ibid., 48.

10. J. Dudley Andrew, *The Major Film Theories: An Introduction* (London: Oxford University Press, 1976), 98, 92; see Balázs 87–88 and 156–61.

11. Balázs, 258–61.

12. George Bluestone, *Novels into Film* (Berkeley: University of California Press, 1957), 33. At one point, he describes one of these codes as "Hollywood Aristotelianism," which subordinates "spectacle, diction, character, and certainly thought . . . to plot, the prime arbiter" (103); I would hope to show later that this terminology reflects a rather offhand use of Aristotelian principles.

231

13. Ibid., 1, 5.

14. Ibid., 47–48.

15. Ibid., 62; Balázs, 120.

16. Bluestone, 61–62.

17. Ibid., 110.

18. Ibid., 63–64, my emphasis.

19. Lester Asheim, "From Book to Film: Simplification," *Hollywood Quarterly* 5 (1950–51): 297–98.

20. Lester Asheim, "From Book to Film: Summary," *The Quarterly of Film Radio and Television* 6 (1951–52): 259–70.

Gerald Peary and Roger Shatzkin, in the introduction to *The Classic American Novel and the Movies* (New York: Ungar, 1977), count four tendencies in the criticism of adaptations. In their collection, critics often comment upon the film's reduction of the novel's story, the addition of melodramatic romances and happy endings, and the softening of ideological content; Peary and Shatzkin also note that the critics implicitly regard an adaptation as appropriate if it "offers an 'equivalent' of the book instead of a critique" (5–8). Their list of tendencies certainly does not cover as much ground as Asheim's covers, but, coming so many years later, it does not cover any new ground either.

On the other hand, Richard Corliss puts a new twist on the old point about the "sanitizing of a novel's naughty bits": "The difference is that, these days, the emasculation is performed in the name of liberalism." He offers the examples of Brian DePalma's *The Bonfire of the Vanities* and Bernardo Bertolucci's *The Sheltering Sky*: in the former, the filmmaker substitutes a black judge for a Jewish judge, lest the scene of his spitting on black prisoners enrage the audience too much; and in the latter, the director deletes a scene in which the protagonist encounters native Africans in a fourth-class train car, because it seemed "a condescending vision of Third World squalor" ("By the Book," 44–45). Presumably, one could make the same point about Demi Moore's assertiveness-trained Hester Prynne in Roland Joffe's version of *The Scarlet Letter*.

21. Lester Asheim, "From Book to Film: The Note of Affirmation," *The Quarterly of Film Radio and Television* 6 (1951–52): 68.

22. On the subject of differences between novels and films, Judith Mayne agrees that Asheim's study points to "industrial control of the cinema," whereas Bluestone's "defense of cinema" emphasizes "aesthetic autonomy and individual authorship" for the filmmakers (*Private Novels, Public Films* [Athens: University of Georgia Press, 1988], 101–2). That defense and autonomy do not, in my view, matter much if the product inevitably proves to be less flexible, less subtle, and less challenging in the ways Asheim measures.

23. Bluestone, 217–18.

24. Gotthold Ephraim Lessing, *Laocoön*, trans. Ellen Frothingham, in *Criticism: The Major Texts*, enl. ed., ed. Walter Jackson Bate (New York: Harcourt, 1970), 248.

25. Jean Mitry, "Remarks on the Problem of Cinematic Adaptation," trans. Richard Dyer, *The Bulletin of the Midwest Modern Language Association* 4 (1971): 1, 7–8.

26. Ibid., 4–5.

27. Siegfried Kracauer, *Theory of Film: The Redemption of Physical Reality* (London: Oxford University Press, 1960), 28.

28. Andrew, *Major Film Theories*, 125–28.

29. Kracauer, 237, 242.

30. Edward Murray, *The Cinematic Imagination: Writers and the Motion Pictures* (New York: Ungar, 1972), 109, 293.

31. George W. Linden, *Reflections on the Screen* (Belmont, Calif.: Wadsworth, 1970), 57.

32. Charles Eidsvik, *Cineliteracy: Film Among the Arts* (New York: Random House, 1978), 180, 187–88.

33. Christian Metz, *Film Language: A Semiotics of the Cinema*, trans. Michael Taylor (New York: Oxford University Press, 1974), 78.

34. Ibid., 47.

35. Harold Toliver, *Animate Illusions: Explorations of Narrative Structure* (Lincoln: University of Nebraska Press, 1974), 193, 195.

36. Frank D. McConnell, *The Spoken Seen: Film and the Romantic Imagination* (Baltimore, Md.: The Johns Hopkins University Press, 1975), 5.

37. Frank D. McConnell, *Storytelling and Mythmaking: Images from Film and Literature* (New York: Oxford University Press, 1979), 5.

38. William Luhr and Peter Lehman, *Authorship and Narrative in the Cinema: Issues in Contemporary Aesthetics and Criticism* (New York: Putnam, 1977), 174.

39. James Monaco, *How to Read a Film: The Art, Technology, Language, History and Theory of Film and Media* (New York: Oxford University Press, 1977), 29; Andrew Sarris, "Literature and Film," *The Bulletin of the Midwest Modern Language Association* 4 (1971): 13, 14–15; Pauline Kael, "Notes on Heart and Mind," in *Deeper into Movies* (New York: Warner, 1974), 299 (Kael even goes one step beyond the truism concerning good films from bad books: "Although good movies have often been made from inferior books, in the last few years I've been embarrassed to discover that even when movies have been made from books that aren't especially worth reading, the books are still often superior" [299]); Corliss, "By the Book," 45; Ira Konigsberg, *The Complete Film Dictionary* (New York: New American Library, 1987), 6.

40. Ingmar Bergman states this position most directly: "Film has nothing to do with literature; the character and substance of the two art forms are usually in conflict. . . . It is mainly because of this difference between film and literature that we should avoid making films out of books" ("Introduction: Bergman Discusses Film-Making," in *Four Screenplays of Ingmar Bergman* [New York: Touchstone, 1960], 17–18).

Charles Eidsvik, in "Toward a 'Politiques des Adaptations,'" attacks this prejudice against adaptations and suggests that this purist attitude may reflect a "desire to keep movies at a *kitsch* level" (in *Film and/as Literature*, ed. John Harrington [Englewood Cliffs, N.J.: Prentice-Hall, 1977], 30). Leland Poague also argues that film "fulfills the same functions, appeals, in general, to the same faculties of the mind, as literature," thereby contradicting "the countless statements of the 'film has nothing to do with literature' variety" ("Literature vs. Cinema: The Politics of Aesthetic Definition," *The Journal of Aesthetic Education* 10.1 [1976]: 85–86).

Sarah Kozloff notes that charges like Bergman's assume that "narrative is a subset of literature," whereas it "is the larger kingdom," encompassing novels and films. She continues by pointing out that anyone who objects to films that adopt "literary" poses, such as first-person narrators, should also object to novels that adopt poses, such as pretending to be diaries or letters (*Invisible Storytellers: Voice-Over Narration in American Fiction Film* [Berkeley: University of California Press, 1988], 17–18).

41. Obviously, I adhere to the policy, not much altered from the so-called "auteur theory," that treats the director—sometimes with the writer—as a film's "author": the one nominally in control of the collaborative art, and the one responsible for the product. If that control should prove only nominal, however, the collaboration could yet produce a work that seems to be unified as long as the collaborators "are governed by the unified invention and intent of the text: that is, their implied authors" (Seymour Chatman, *Coming to Terms: The Rhetoric of Narrative in Fiction and Film* [Ithaca: Cornell University Press, 1990], 82).

42. R. S. Crane, *The Languages of Criticism and the Structure of Poetry* (Toronto: University of Toronto Press, 1953), 26, 37.

43. Morris Beja, *Film and Literature: An Introduction* (New York: Longman, 1979), 79.

44. F. E. Sparshott, "Basic Film Aesthetics," in *Film Theory and Criticism: Introductory Readings*, ed. Gerald Mast and Marshall Cohen (New York: Oxford University Press, 1974), 210.

45. V. F. Perkins, *Film as Film: Understanding and Judging Movies* (Middlesex: Penguin, 1972), 59.

46. Andre Bazin, "In Defense of Mixed Cinema," in *What Is Cinema?*, trans. Hugh Gray (Berkeley: University of California Press, 1967), 1:67.

47. Chatman, *Coming*, 159, 163.

48. Joy Gould Boyum, *Double Exposure: Fiction into Film* (New York: Mentor-NAL, 1985), 9. Boyum's book has attracted some, but not a great deal of, critical attention. Her academic credentials—professor of English and communication arts at New York University—should raise no questions, but her regular stint as reviewer for popular magazines such as *Glamour* may cause some to take her book less seriously. Blurbs on and inside the cover (such as "FASCINATING AND ENTERTAINING!") do not help.

49. Ibid., 21.

50. Ibid., 29, 35.

51. Ibid., 83.

52. Ibid., 94. The reference is to Martin C. Battestin, "Osborne's *Tom Jones*: Adapting a Classic," in *Man and the Movies*, ed. W. R. Robinson (Baltimore, Md.: Penguin, 1969), 31–45.

53. Boyum, 60.

54. Perkins, 189.

55. Aristotle, *Poetics*, XIV:1, trans. S. H. Butcher, in *Criticism: The Major Texts,* enl. ed., ed. Walter Jackson Bate (New York: Harcourt, 1970), 27.

56. Aristotle, *Poetics*, XXVI:4–5, in Bate, 38.

57. Wayne C. Booth, "How Not to Use Aristotle: *The Poetics*," in *Now Don't Try to Reason with Me: Essays and Ironies for a Credulous Age* (Chicago: University of Chicago Press, 1970), 115.

58. Crane, 149.

59. Ibid., 43.

60. Elder Olson, *On Value Judgments in the Arts and Other Essays* (Chicago: University of Chicago Press, 1976), 286 n.

61. Crane, 143.

62. Ibid., 177; the phrase comes from T. C. Chamberlin, "Multiple Working Hypotheses," *Science*, o.s., 15 (1890): 92–96; rprt. in *Journal of Geology* 39 (1931): 155–65.

63. This interpretive process resembles David Bordwell's description of a film viewer's activity:

> The perceiver applies narrative schemata which define narrative events and unify them by principles of causality, time, and space. . . . In the course of constructing the story the perceiver uses schemata and incoming cues to make assumptions, draw inferences about current story events, and frame and test hypotheses about prior and upcoming events. Often some inferences must be revised and some hypotheses will have to be suspended while the narrative delays payoff. While hypotheses undergo constant modification, we can isolate critical moments when some are clearly confirmed, disconfirmed, or left open. In any empirical case, this whole process takes place within the terms set by the narrative itself, the spectator's perceptual-cognitive equipment, the circumstances of reception, and prior experience. (*Narration in the Fiction Film* [Madison: University of Wisconsin Press, 1985], 39)

Despite the similarities, Bordwell proposes a "Constructivist" theory, which accords to the audience all the responsibility for making meaning, whereas Crane's framework would have the audience recover meaning made by the artist. In Chatman's terms, "It is not that the viewer constructs but that she *reconstructs* the film's narrative . . . from the set of cues encoded in the film" (*Coming*, 127).

64. Crane, 181.

65. Gerald Mast, *Film/Cinema/Movie: A Theory of Experience* (New York: Harper, 1977), 18, 36–37.

66. Ibid., 64, 106, 112.

67. Ibid., 275.

68. Samuel Taylor Coleridge, *Selected Poetry and Prose*, ed. Elisabeth Schneider, 2nd ed. (New York: Rinehart, 1971), 432. Coleridge makes the same distinction between "copy" and "imitation" in chapter 17 of his *Biographia Literaria* and in "On Poesy or Art."

69. Bruce Morrissette, *Novel and Film: Essays in Two Genres* (Chicago: University of Chicago Press, 1985), 13.

70. Herbert Read, "The Poet and the Film," in *A Coat of Many Colors: Occasional Essays* (London: Routledge, 1945), 231.

71. Poague, 89.

72. James Phelan, *Worlds from Words: A Theory of Language in Fiction* (Chicago: University of Chicago Press, 1981), 65–66.

73. Neil Sinyard makes the fine observation that, James's style notwithstanding, important turning points in his novels often rely on "pictorial dramatisation." In *The Portrait of a Lady*, "the moment in Chapter 40 when [Isabel] interrupts her husband in conversation with Madame Merle and something about their posture tells the truth about their relationship is exquisitely pictorial." And in *The Ambassadors*,

> the crucial event in the novel is an act of seeing: the moment in Book II, Chapter 4, when Strether glimpses two people in a boat on the river and suddenly realises that

two people he has idealised are having a squalid affair. The effectiveness of the moment is entirely due to James's almost cinematic point of view, angle of vision, and his rendering of Strether's skill in reading off the correct meaning from the image he inadvertently sees. (*Filming Literature: The Art of Screen Adaptation* [London: Crook Helm, 1986], 26–27)

74. Phelan, 115–16.

75. Bluestone, 48.

76. Joseph M. Boggs, *The Art of Watching Films: A Guide to Film Analysis* (Menlo Park, Calif.: Benjamin/Cummings, 1978), 202. A variation of this dichotomous problem comes from Robert Giddings, Keith Selby, and Chris Wensley. They agree that film uniquely presents a sense of "here and now," but they also think that this quality enhances film's ability to shift tenses:

> The very sharpness of this sense of the present time provides for a swift but credible switch of time from past to present. It is this which makes flashback so effective an element in the vocabulary of film. It is difficult to achieve in literary text. (Few would admit it, but isn't this one of the qualities which makes Conrad's novels so difficult to read?). (*Screening the Novel: The Theory and Practice of Literary Dramatization* [London: Macmillan, 1990], xiii)

77. Sparshott, 218.

78. Morrissette, 36.

79. Alain Robbe-Grillet would disagree with this analysis of the film he wrote for Alain Resnais. In the introduction to the published screenplay, Robbe-Grillet talks about a past and a future that the stranger offers the woman who is stuck in the hotel "where time is apparently abolished"; the stranger, however, "is making it up as he goes along," and this "past . . . has no reality beyond the moment it is evoked." Cinema, he adds, is the ideal medium for such a story because, in contrast to literature, "on the screen verbs are always in the present tense . . . : by its nature, what we see on the screen *is in the act of happening*, we are given the gesture itself, not an account of it" (*Last Year at Marienbad*, trans. Richard Howard [New York: Grove, 1962], 11–12).

Joan Dagle persuasively counters Robbe-Grillet's assertions. Like Morrissette, she regards reading and film viewing as similarly present-tense events, which should not be confused with events in the work read or viewed; the "irretrievability" of the film image—a supposed problem that will disappear because of video technology's "radically altering viewing methods"—may matter in "the act of perceiving the film" but warrants no "assumption that the narrative itself must be always a present tense narrative" ("Narrative Discourse in Film and Fiction: The Question of the Present Tense," in *Narrative Strategies: Original Essays in Film and Prose Fiction*, ed. Syndy Conger and Janice Welsch [Macomb, Ill.: Western Illinois University Press, 1980], 58 n., 55). Robbe-Grillet makes this confusion. For instance, he argues that, when a superimposition signals a flashback, the image in the flashback remains "indistinguishable from the present action, an image which is in fact *in the present tense*" (13). Dagle answers that the superimposition "is not, as Robbe-Grillet claims, a case of two present-tense images interrupted by some sort of non-image which signals the past tense, but rather a case of an image which itself speaks the past tense." Because he confuses the act of viewing with the content of what is viewed, Robbe-Grillet cannot, according to Dagle, make this important distinction: "We view the image of the superimposition that introduces the flashback in the present tense, but the image itself signifies both present and past events" (49). The story told in *Marienbad* then presents difficulties, not only for the viewers, but for the filmmakers as well: they wish to suppress "the signifiers which establish temporal relations within shots or sequences," but the "timeless present of *Marienbad* reveals that film narrative can speak entirely in the present tense only with great difficulty" (57).

80. Bluestone, 55–60.

81. Ibid., 49–50.

82. Monaco, 29–30.

83. Konigsberg, 265.

84. Norman Friedman, *Form and Meaning in Fiction* (Athens: University of Georgia Press, 1975), 145–56. This scale identifies predominant modes of presentation, not rigid classifications that cover all narrative fiction. For instance, a story such as Ralph Ellison's "King of the Bingo Game" comes to us predominantly through the protagonist's mind, which is to say through selective omniscience, but the final event of the protagonist's being knocked unconscious from behind must come from a supplementary omniscience. In another case, Trollope's *The Warden* features a predominantly editorially omniscient narrator: he has knowledge of actions and conversations in several places and at all times, past and present, and he allows himself to comment on these actions, as, for instance, when he worries that, except for those under twenty or over sixty, women readers will disdain Eleanor Harding's plan to intercede with John Bold on behalf of her father; yet this narrator also writes, at one point, of his personal acquaintance with the Grantly household and children—as if he were a first-person witness to the action, and who therefore could not know as much as he claims to know in other sections of the novel.

On another point about these categories, we should remember that they describe large sets of narratives in which we may define clear subsets. Interior monologue or "stream of consciousness" would fit into the selective omniscience categories and would certainly differ from the narration of a novel by Henry James; an epistolary novel would fit into the first-person categories and possibly, as in the case of Samuel Richardson's *Clarissa*, multiply the perspectives; in other first-person works, we could distinguish between narrators who are conscious of putting together a story for a wide audience (for example, Huck Finn) from narrators who are overheard in private conversations (for example, Estelle in Margaret Atwood's "Rape Fantasies").

The relatively small number of categories, in other words, should not put too many restrictions on our ability to describe and analyze any fiction.

85. I say "nearly complete" because, no matter how withdrawn, *somebody* is organizing the narrative; even seemingly random events caught on film must be qualified by the question of why the camera is there and pointed in that direction. Sarah Kozloff makes this point in softening the rigid distinction between telling and showing: "In film, then, while there are major differences between having the camera capture an action and having a narrator describe that action, the ideal of blissful communion between the viewer and some untouched, untainted reality presented by a completely neutral mechanism is an illusion" (14).

86. See Kozloff, 82–99, for a complete discussion of this film.

87. One might have objected that most films using either kind of omniscience are old, the point being—as it is in the parallel criticism of novels—that telling is old-fashioned and not as effective as showing. This objection amounts to another deductive dogma. Wayne Booth's *The Rhetoric of Fiction* (Chicago: University of Chicago Press, 1961)

tells and shows us, however, that if more objective modes of representation are the fashion, they are not the standard of judgment in fiction.

88. Margaret Thorp, "The Motion Picture and the Novel," *American Quarterly* 3 (1951): 197. Thorp would limit point of view in film and novel to the selective omniscience of James's "central intelligence"; other choices are available, but James's choice is "most effective"—and most natural in film (198). The standard she sets certainly reaches high, but I would object to any dogmatic standard, no matter how august.

89. Beja, 39.

90. Ibid., 38.

91. Boyum, 102.

92. See my article "From a Certain Point of View in 'A Scandal in Bohemia': Outsmarting Mr. Sherlock Holmes" (*The Victorian Newsletter* 86 [1994]: 7–9) for a fuller discussion of this story and its faulty adaptation for television by Granada.

93. Morrissette, 97.

94. Morrissette states that the film, "far from establishing the prescribed identification between human eye and the camera lens, has demonstrated the near impossibility of such an identification" (55). This statement accurately describes the failure of viewers to identify themselves as the "I" of a first-person narration, a failure commonly described by several critics. Robert T. Eberwein, so far as I know, is the only critic who shares my preference for describing the film in other terms: the film "offers the equivalent not of a first person narrative, but of one written in the *second* person" ("The Filmic Dream and Point of View," *Literature/Film Quarterly* 8 [1980]: 199).

95. Sarah Kozloff notes a cinematic possibility not open to novelists: the singing narrator (for example, Louis Armstrong in *High Society*, or the omniscient minstrels, Nat King Cole and Stubby Kaye, in *Cat Ballou*) (78).

96. Bruce F. Kawin, *Mindscreen: Bergman, Godard, and First-Person Film* (Princeton: Princeton University Press, 1978), 4.

97. Ibid., 10.

98. Ibid., 18–19, 51.

99. Edward Branigan, *Point of View in the Cinema: A Theory of Narration and Subjectivity in Classical Film* (Berlin: Mouton, 1984), 219.

100. Ibid., 20–21.

101. Ibid., 43–44. His terms for the narrators equate "omniscient" with "third person" and "subjective" with "first person"—equations that I think confuse matters, as I have already discussed. In a note, he explains that "usually in literary criticism omniscient narration refers to *intrusive* narration" (the kind of narration Friedman calls editorial omniscience, which is less common than Branigan suggests). He goes on to state that he "will blend this type of omniscience with . . . its opposite: a pure, camera-like objectivity"; Branigan thereby rejects the "distinction telling/showing" in favor of "a rationalist metatheory which posits the existence of silent, *effaced* narrators" (68 n.). I will have more to say about this rejection later, but Branigan, unlike Bluestone and others, does not confound terms so much as he deliberately collapses them.

102. Ibid., 73.

103. Ibid., 176–77. This tendency to see through levels of narration makes for an original twist on the criticism of Montgomery's *The Lady in the Lake*, which Branigan regards as wholly subjective in its point of view. Given the relative levels of narration,

"the exclusive use of . . . first person narration in a novel or film . . . eventually loses impact for many readers. The reader becomes accustomed to the narration as merely another way of telling *the* story which is conventionally told in the third person" (92).

104. Ibid., 194.

105. Ibid., 178.

106. Ibid., 59.

107. George M. Wilson, *Narration in Light: Studies in Cinematic Point of View* (Baltimore, Md.: The Johns Hopkins University Press, 1986), 209 n.

108. Ibid., 8.

109. Ibid., 100.

110. Ibid., 86–87.

111. Ibid., 127, 132.

112. Ibid., 133–34. Sarah Kozloff, speaking about first-person voice-over narrators in film, similarly distinguishes between such a narrator and "another presence that supplements the nominal narrator's vision, knowledge, and story-telling powers": "the narrating agent of all films (with or without voice-over)" (44). This cinematic implied author is "the real narrator, the image-maker" (45).

In Kozloff's thinking, this implied image-maker must stand behind a first-person voice-over because such a "narrator speaks intermittently—and sometimes only minimally—and is not in control of his or her story to the same degree, or in the same manner, as a literary narrator" (43). Certainly we do not imagine that whoever speaks the voice-over also composes and plays the soundtrack music, but neither do we assume that the first-person narrator of a novel designs and executes the book's cover. This notion of control need not be so absolute or comprehensive. To use Conan Doyle as an example once more, when a client recounts at length his or her own story or intrigue, we do not imagine that Watson has lost or given up control of the narrative.

113. Wilson, 39.

114. Chatman, *Coming*, 13, 15.

115. Seymour Chatman, "What Novels Can Do that Films Can't (and Vice Versa)," *Critical Inquiry* 7 (1980): 121–22.

116. Seymour Chatman, *Story and Discourse: Narrative Structure in Fiction and Film* (Ithaca: Cornell University Press, 1978) 37.

117. Chatman, "What Novels," 128, 132–33.

118. Chatman, *Coming*, 20, 38.

119. Ibid., 45–49.

120. Ibid., 85, 218 n.

121. Ibid., 143–44, 154.

122. Two other terms Chatman proposes that further divide "point of view" are "center" and "interest." The former identifies the protagonist, and the latter identifies any character about whom the audience feels concern. Both sorts of identification strike me as quite simple to accomplish, and I seldom if ever hear anyone use "point of view" to describe either case.

123. Chatman, *Coming*, 149.

124. Morrissette, 13.

125. Bluestone, 48.

126. Beja, 57.

127. Richard A. Hulseberg, "Novels and Films: A Limited Inquiry," *Literature/Film Quarterly* 6 (1978): 61–62.

128. Phelan, 235 n.

129. Bruce F. Kawin, *Faulkner and Film* (New York: Ungar, 1977), 26–28.

130. Friedman, 64.

131. Northrop Frye, *Anatomy of Criticism: Four Essays* (Princeton: Princeton University Press, 1957), 52.

132. Beja, 58–59.

133. Of course, some viewers today can get through such lengthy films at a more leisurely pace in the comfort of their own homes with their own VCRs.

134. See Friedman, 53.

135. Friedman, 125, my emphasis.

136. Morrissette, 25. With his assent held well in check, Dudley Andrew discusses a similar conclusion. He divides adaptations into three kinds. The first two, "borrowing" and "intersecting," involve less typical works: the former refers to adaptations *from*, not of, widely known works (such as Bible stories); the latter refers to films that confront but do not assimilate "an ultimately intransigent text" (such as the adaptations by Straub or Pasolini). The last kind "concerns fidelity and transformation, . . . the reproduction in cinema of something essential about the original text." He adds that discussion of this kind of adaptation is "the most frequent and most tiresome" (*Concepts in Film Theory* [New York: Oxford University Press, 1984], 98–100). He has reservations about such transformations, for

> one must presume the global signified of the original to be separable from its text if one believes it can be approximated by other sign clusters. . . . If one accepts this possibility, at the very least one is forced to discount the primary articulations of the relevant language systems. One would have to hold that while the material of literature . . . may be of a different nature from the materials of cinema, . . . both systems may construct in their own way, and at higher levels, scenes and narratives that are indeed commensurable. (101)

In the end, Andrew states the case well without accepting it.

137. Crane, 43.

138. Olson, 309.

139. See Ibid., 315–17.

140. Crane, 156.

141. Ibid., 181.

142. Ibid., 181.

143. Andrew, *Concepts*, 97.

144. Olson, 326.

145. Andrew, *Concepts*, 106.

Say It Ain't So: *The Natural*

1. Asheim, "Summary," 259–65.

2. Pauline Kael, "The Candidate," review of *The Natural*, dir. Barry Levinson, *New Yorker*, 28 May 1984, 100.

3. Ron Fimrite, "A Star with Real Clout," *Sports Illustrated* 7 May 1984: 103.

4. Bluestone, 23.

5. Ibid., 41.

6. Ibid., 92, 113.

7. Tony Tanner, *City of Words: American Fiction 1950–1970* (New York: Harper, 1971), 323.

8. Jeffrey Helterman, *Understanding Bernard Malamud* (Columbia: University of South Carolina Press, 1985), 23.

9. Bill Borst, *Still Last in the American League: The St. Louis Browns* (West Bloomfield, Mich.: Altwerger and Mandel, 1992), 97. Malamud, in 1952, when *The Natural* was published, could count on readers' remembering several of these events as recent history.

In regard to the Browns' therapist, Borst writes that Dr. David F. Tracy, who "called himself a psychologist," experimented with "hypnosis to overcome fear and achieve relaxation." In an article, Tracy wrote: "The Browns are victims of nervous tension. Their ball players don't believe in themselves. With treatments I can teach them better how to relax and with mental relaxation, they will play better in the field." The owners of the Browns heard of Tracy's ideas, hired him, and then saw their team lose nearly two-thirds of its games for the season. Tracy did not win the esteem of the manager or players, and the press dubbed him "the whammy man" (94–96).

To be fair to Tracy, Borst also notes that the good doctor pointed to the Phillies as another team in need of his methods, and if he had gone to Philadelphia rather than St. Louis, he would have joined the aforementioned pennant winner, and the contemporary respect for sports psychology would have come about decades earlier (99).

10. Helterman, 23; Earl R. Wasserman, "*The Natural*: Malamud's World Ceres," *The Centennial Review of Arts and Sciences* 9 (1965): 438–39.

11. James M. Mellard, "Four Versions of Pastoral," in *Bernard Malamud and the Critics*, ed. Leslie A. Field and Joyce W. Field (New York: New York University Press, 1970), 71.

12. Bernard Malamud, *The Natural* (New York: Farrar, 1952), 22–23; subsequent references to this edition will be given in the text.

13. Frederick W. Turner III, "Myth Inside and Out: *The Natural*," in Field and Field, 110.

14. Several critics have listed the correspondences between Roy and Babe Ruth, but we can also note correspondences between him and Ted Williams—some arising after the novel's publication, proving the power of myth in baseball. Although his parents stayed together during his childhood, Williams writes, in his autobiography, "I didn't see much of my dad"; he and his dad "were never very close" (Ted Williams with John Underwood, *My Turn at Bat: The Story of My Life* [New York: Fireside, 1988], 19, 30). Williams pitched in high school and, very briefly, in the minor leagues before moving to the outfield. About his career, Williams writes, "I wanted to be the greatest hitter who

ever lived. A man has to have goals . . . and that was mine, to have people say, 'There goes Ted Williams, the greatest hitter who ever lived'" (7). Writing in 1969, Williams may be consciously repeating Roy's desire (the new edition of the autobiography in 1988 does make one reference to the film, so Williams was aware of Roy's story in at least one version). In any case, he would share some of Roy's professional problems: being the "star" on a team that had not won a pennant in decades, thriving personally, but often being castigated in the press for not being a "team player." An eerie coincidence occurred in 1956, when Williams, angry at striking out, tried to throw his bat and accidentally let it fly into the stands, where it struck a woman; in the first aid room, Williams writes, "the blood was running down her head and I about died," but she forgave him on the spot (137–38).

Roy's comeback in some ways also recalls the career of "Smokey Joe" Wood. As a pitcher in 1912 for the Boston Red Sox, Wood led the American league with thirty-four victories and became one of the heroes of the World Series by winning three games. But after 1915, he was through as a pitcher. He did not play in 1916, and then he came back with the Cleveland Indians as an outfielder; although he did not hit many home runs, he hit well for average (as high as .366 in 1921) and drove in 275 runs in five more years as a player.

15. Andrew Kopkind, review of *The Natural*, dir. Barry Levinson, *The Nation* 2 June 1984: 683.

16. David Ansen, "It's Going, Going . . .," review of *The Natural*, dir. Barry Levinson, *Newsweek* 28 May 1984: 77.

17. Kevin Thomas Curtin, "*The Natural*: Our *Iliad* and *Odyssey*," *The Antioch Review* 43 (1985): 228, 236.

18. Ross Wetzsteon, "Too Close for Comfort," *American Film,* May 1984, 19, 21.

19. Bluestone, 23.

20. Ibid., 35.

Why? The Case of *Looking for Mr. Goodbar*

1. I base this account of the Quinn murder case upon several articles in the *New York Times*: 5 January 1973, p. 1; 6 January 1973, p. 16; 7 January 1973, p. 39; 10 January 1973, p. 1; 11 January 1973, p. 44; 18 January 1973, p. 32; 2 February 1973, p. 14; 6 May 1973, p. 22; 10 May 1973, p. 46; and 22 July 1973, p. 33.

2. In contrast to my argument that Rossner's themes turn out meaningless in their oversimplification, Leslie Fishbein contends that, given the times, when the sexual revolution and the women's liberation movement were in transition, "on every major issue Rossner treats, she exhibits her own confusion, which mirrors the confusion of her audience" ("*Looking for Mr. Goodbar*: Murder for the Masses," *International Journal of Women's Studies* 3 [1980]: 174).

3. His films over two decades prior to *Mr. Goodbar* include several adaptations (*The Brothers Karamasov, Elmer Gantry,* and *Lord Jim*), one of the most successful being *In Cold Blood*. Rossner's novel, like Truman Capote's, follows the lives of characters clearly drawn from a famous murder case. Given this fact, we could imagine that Brooks would view *Mr. Goodbar* as a way to repeat a success.

In Cold Blood figures in another element of this story because Lacey Fosburgh wrote *Closing Time: The True Story of the "Goodbar" Murder* (New York: Delacorte, 1977) with Capote's model in mind. This work includes much more of the factual background to the principals' lives and much more about the legal work involved in catching and jailing the murderer. As for the specific motivations and events of the crime, Fosburgh has "stepped in where full and accurate accounts do not exist and created scenes or dialogue . . . it is reasonable and fair to assume could have taken place, perhaps even did" (x–xi). The nonfiction version, however, strikes me as no more credible or satisfying than Rossner's.

4. Caroline Blackwood, "Getting It All Over With," review of *Looking for Mr. Goodbar*, by Judith Rossner, *Times Literary Supplement,* 12 September 1975, p. 1012.

5. Judith Rossner, *Looking for Mr. Goodbar* (New York: Simon & Schuster, 1975), 8. All further references to this novel will appear in the text.

6. Julia O'Faolain, "Victims," review of *Looking for Mr. Goodbar*, by Judith Rossner, *London Magazine* 15.5 (1975/76): 115.

7. Problems of style also arise in the narrator's presentation of herself. Where the narrator intrudes—or blunders in—the effect borders on the ridiculous. For example, in Eli's recounting to Theresa of his sexual awakening, he tells of confronting his wife with his new desires: "Rachel was staring at him as though he was speaking Sanskrit when they both knew it was only a written language" (120). Worse, the narrator sometimes muddles the attribution of thoughts. In one scene, James and Theresa are arguing about her relationship with Tony when she snaps that Tony is "a good lay":

He blanched, if you could say that of anyone who was so pale to begin with. He regarded her gravely.

Gravely. Because I just buried myself. (253)

In the first line, the narrator seems to be picking on James's fair complexion, whereas it is Theresa who likes to pick on him; then in the second line, Theresa's italicized thought puns on the narrator's description that she could not have read or heard. Overall, Rossner's good ear for conversation turns a bit tinny for her narrator's commentary.

8. Having announced the theme of victimization in the preface, Rossner withdraws the editorial narrator and, but for the exceptions noted before, presents Theresa's story neutrally.

9. Blackwood, 1012.

10. Friedman, 84.

11. Agnes McNeill Donohue, review of *Looking for Mr. Goodbar*, by Judith Rossner, *The Critic* 34.2 (1975): 82.

12. Ibid., 82.

13. Furthermore, if Rossner's view of "Irish Catholic life" allows for little nuance, she uses similarly broad strokes when Eli, Theresa's first barroom pick-up, recounts to her his sexual awakening from the deep slumber of his Hasidic background. This lengthy digression reinforces the point about religion's perversion of pleasure, but it also undercuts Rossner's point about male oppressors. Rossner wants us to see Theresa as oppressed by a patriarchal religion and culture: both make women victims of their own gender. Although Eli uses his long, sad story to seduce Theresa, that story shows a man can be a victim of religion too.

14. An especially annoying nod to "big contemporary issues" of the 1960s is the use Rossner gets out of Vietnam. The sole reference to the war comes in White's confession. Stunned by Theresa's telling him to go, he has a flashback to a friend "who got it in the spine in Nam, and I caught his face when they was lifting him up onto the stretcher to the copter" (8–9). Wilson, the actual killer of Roseann Quinn, was not a veteran, from what I can gather, so this supplementary motivation seems little more than a cheap afterthought.

15. The novel implies that men combine the lives of body and mind, although no one we see does so well. For instance, James and Tony do not even, like Theresa, have another life; Engle manages a combination of sorts, but he uses the mind to seek pleasure for the body.

16. Asheim, "Summary," 259–70. On the other hand, Brooks's film also contravenes several conclusions: the film does not include a greater variety of costumes or settings; does not make the point of view any more omniscient or impersonal, despite leaving out authorial intrusions; does not assume a lower level of comprehension by the audience; and retains the tone of negation as well as the degree of violence, sex, profanity, and criticism of religious authority and social values.

17. Louise Sweet, review of *Looking for Mr. Goodbar*, dir. Richard Brooks, *Sight and Sound* 47 (1978): 126; John Simon, "Double Whammy," review of *Looking for Mr. Goodbar*, dir. Richard Brooks, *National Review* 29 (1977): 1443.

18. Reviewers often pointed to the false shock of an added "attack" on Theresa near the film's end. That shock merely provides a foreboding jolt and little more. Theresa answers her door, and with sudden bass strums on the soundtrack, a man with a knife and a stocking mask bursts in and makes her scream; expecting trouble from Tony, we are quickly relieved to see that the knife is a toy and the attacker is one more of Katherine's men accompanying her to a costume party. It is a cheap thrill, but an effective one.

19. The violent primal scene that James recounted recalls Perry's flashback in Brooks's version of *In Cold Blood*.

20. As in the novel, titillation remains a primary attraction. Jacquelyn N. Zita writes that the film "provides a compelling example of how the codes of pornography have infiltrated into the ideologies—the folklore, mythologies, and mass-media representations—of our culture," although "the special development of Teresa's [*sic*] subjectivity" separates the film from "mainstream pornography" ("Pornography and the Male Imaginary," *Enclitic* 9 [1987]: 30, 33).
Fosburgh's book changes names—for instance, Roseann Quinn becomes Katherine Cleary, and John Wayne Wilson becomes Joe Willie Simpson—and then Fishbein uses these pseudonyms as the names of the actual parties; through Fishbein's article, I surmise, the error persists in Zita's article.

21. Joyce Sunila, "Women and Mr. Goodbar," *Human Behavior* 7.3 (1978): 67.

22. Names emphasize these contrary states. Katherine picks up on a remark by her husband and dubs her sister "Saint Theresa by day, and swingin' Terry by night." Tony calls her various names—"Sonya-bologna," "bitch," "cunt"—whereas James always calls her Theresa, pronouncing it "Ter-RAY-sa," therefore accentuating the reference to her Spanish patroness, Saint Theresa of Avila. The appropriateness of this name is apparent when one remembers the ecstatic pain St. Theresa felt on the occasion of a visitation by an angel; this piercing ecstasy is celebrated in Bernini's sculpture "Ecstasy of Saint Theresa" and in the poetry of Richard Crashaw, especially "The Flaming Heart."

23. Sunila makes much of the claim that Gary suffocates Theresa in the novel, whereas he stabs her in the film: "It is typical of Hollywood's sensationalist and derivative

mentality to have her chopped up (raped) with a knife à la Hitchcock, DePalma and the other hostile/aggressive misogynist directors" (64). As a matter of fact, he suffocates her at first in both versions; in the novel, he then clubs her into unconsciousness with a lamp and then stabs her repeatedly, but in the film, he just stabs her. The novel's version more closely resembles Roseann Quinn's actual murder, but otherwise, the film's version makes no changes—none that could be called sensationalist or misogynist by comparison.

24. Henry A. Giroux, review of *Looking for Mr. Goodbar*, dir. Richard Brooks, *Film Quarterly* 31.4 (1978): 53.

25. Tracy Johnston, "Who Else Is Looking for Mr. Goodbar?" *Ms.*, February 1978, 26.

Damned if You Do, and Dammed if You Don't: *Deliverance*

1. Judith Rossner, "Kiss 'n Kill: *Star 80* and the Playboy Ethic," *The Movies*, November 1983, 78.

2. James Dickey, *Deliverance* [screenplay], Screenplay Library (Carbondale: Southern Illinois University Press, 1982), 154.

3. Ibid., 155–56. These remarks differ greatly from others offered in an interview years earlier: "I think there must be very few instances in the whole history of film making of a movie staying as close to the original novel as this one. . . . [S]ome things about it, of course, I would change a little bit. I advised them or asked them to do things they didn't do, but, on the other hand, they did some things that came off better on the screen than what I had projected" (Geoffry Norman, "Playboy Interview: James Dickey," *Playboy*, November 1973, 215).

While shooting was still in progress, Dickey felt, at best, more ambivalent, according to one report. Tom Burke records that Dickey proclaimed the result would be "a wunnerful film, very suspenseful, very *meaningful*," but added in the next breath that some changes from the screenplay "are unnecessary an' perhaps harmful"; the more sentimental eulogy for Drew, for instance, should go, because "*that's* not what my story is about." Whatever he hoped, Dickey could not make others see things his way. In fact, Jon Voight does not even see the novel Dickey's way: "What he's saying is that the guy who kills to survive is the good guy. And I just don't believe that. . . . I can't believe that's really what the goddamn book is about!" (Tom Burke, "Conversations with, Um, Jon Voight," *Esquire*, January 1972, 155, 157). In an interview with Michel Ciment, Boorman, like Voight, states his differences with Dickey: "Philosophically, we had very little in common. . . . For me . . . violence doesn't make you a better person—instead, it degrades you" (Michel Ciment, *John Boorman*, trans. Gilbert Adair [London: Faber, 1986], 129).

These interviews demonstrate that those who produce the art do not always offer the clearest evaluations of the art. The fact that now such interviews often fit into a publicity campaign does not help.

4. Burke notes that the frustrated Dickey had not been around the location much because Boorman "asked him to leave" (155). The actual composition of the screenplay, then, arose mostly out of lengthy correspondence; in the interview with Ciment, Boorman says that "most of the dialogue was [Dickey's]," but "I wrote the script" (129).

5. Dickey, screenplay, 156.

6. Ciment, 10.

7. James Dickey, *Deliverance* (New York: Dell, 1970), 7. All further references to this edition will be given in the text.

8. Charles Thomas Samuels, "What Hath Dickey Delivered?" review of *Deliverance*, by James Dickey, *New Republic*, 18 April 1970, 24. Samuels adds that these very qualities will be lost in the anticipated film adaptation.

9. R. E. Foust discusses this motif at length, identifying it as *tactus eruditus*. Foust writes that Dickey emphasizes touch over sight (a sense that I will not discount so much), not as "indiscriminate sensation," but as "*tactus eruditus*—the educated, the erudite touch." This distinction serves to separate Ed's experience from what Lewis would seek: "Ed's tactile experiences allow him to sense the 'mindless beauty' of nature but not to 'merge' with it. For, as Dickey has remarked, a man can enter only half way into nature: to pretend a more intimate contact is romantic solipsism" (R. E. Foust, "*Tactus Eruditus*: Phenomenology as Method and Meaning of James Dickey's *Deliverance*," *Studies in American Fiction* 9 [1981]: 214).

10. Warren Eyster, "Two Regional Novels," review of *Deliverance*, by James Dickey, *Sewanee Review* 79 (1971): 471.

11. Peter G. Beidler, "'The Pride of Thine Heart Hath Deceived Thee': Narrative Distortion in Dickey's *Deliverance*," *South Carolina Review* 5 (1972): 29–40.

12. Paul Edward Gray, review of *Deliverance*, by James Dickey, *Yale Review* 60 (1970): 105.

13. Boorman has stated that his films are "always subjective": "That's to say, I place the camera in such a way as to show things from the point of view of the characters" (Gordon Gow, "Playboy in a Monastery," *Films and Filming* 18.5 [1972]: 19). Obviously, his definitions of points of view differ from my own.

14. Philip Strick, review of *Deliverance*, dir. John Boorman, *Sight and Sound* 41 (1972): 228.

15. James F. Beaton, "Dickey Down the River," in *The Modern American Novel and the Movies*, ed. Gerald Peary and Roger Shatzkin (New York: Ungar, 1978), 296.

16. Herb A. Lightman, "On Location with *Deliverance*," *American Cinematographer* 52 (1971): 798–99.

17. Charles Thomas Samuels, "How Not to Film a Novel," review of *Deliverance*, dir. John Boorman, *American Scholar* 42.1 (1972–73): 152.

18. Friedman, 86–87.

19. Eugene M. Longen, "Dickey's *Deliverance*: Sex and the Great Outdoors," *Southern Literary Journal* 9 (1977): 138–39.

20. William Heyen, "A Conversation with James Dickey," *Southern Review*, n.s., 9 (1973): 151.

21. Friedman, 88.

22. Statements to the effect that the adaptation reduces Dickey's "psychological study of self-discovery and spiritual deliverance to an adventure story with mere overtones of psychological conflict" (Robert C. Covel, "James Dickey's *Deliverance*: Screenplay as Intertext," *James Dickey Newsletter* 4.2 [1988]: 15) miss the point. The conflicts differ, but Boorman's Ed develops in ways that a spectacular but simple adventure would not explore.

Robert Armour, unlike most who find fault in the differences between the novel and film, finds the film to be superior: according to Armour, both deal with the myth of the

American Adam (from R. W. B. Lewis's book of the same name), but the novel "dissipates this theme by including other material," specifically the prologue and epilogue (Robert Armour, "*Deliverance*: Four Variations of the American Adam," *Literature/Film Quarterly* 1 [1973]: 282).

23. R. Barton Palmer, "Narration, Text, Intertext: The Two Versions of *Deliverance*," *James Dickey Newsletter* 2.2 (1986): 7.

24. Dickey, screenplay, 14.

25. Contradicting Asheim's and Bluestone's conclusions, when lost, Lewis says, "Well . . . we screwed up" (61) in the novel, but in the film, "Well, we fucked up." So much for toning down the profanity to enhance mass appeal.

26. Charles E. Davis, "The Wilderness Revisited: Irony in James Dickey's *Deliverance*," *Studies in American Fiction* 4 (1976): 224.

27. Ronald T. Curran, "Biology and Culture: Hollywood and the Deliverance of Dickey's Weekend Backwoodsmen," *Southern Quarterly* 18.4 (1980): 89, 85.

28. Dickey has specifically supported Lewis, saying he would do the same: "Hell, if you murder a hillbilly, no matter what he was doing to you or a member of your party . . . well you'd just better think twice before you commit yourself to being tried . . . where everybody is everybody's kin" (Heyen, 154). In another interview, Dickey has even hinted that he had already been part of or knew of such dilemmas: "Some of the things in the book really happened, I'm not at liberty to say which ones" (Walter Clemons, "James Dickey, Novelist," *New York Times Book Review,* 22 March 1970, 22).

29. Longen, 141.

30. John E. Loftis categorizes all four characters according to how well they qualify as technicians (for example, Bobby comes without any technical knowledge and never learns any, whereas Lewis has such an obsession about technique that he entertains no emotional or moral feelings). In his successful stalking of the second hillbilly, Ed demonstrates the novel's central lesson: that "technique can be either limiting or liberating, and the individual's human stature is reflected in his application of, accomplishments through, and finally transcendence of specific techniques" (John E. Loftis, "Technique as Metaphor in James Dickey's *Deliverance*, *The South Carolina Review* 16.1 [1983]: 66).

31. Edward Doughtie, "Art and Nature in *Deliverance*," *Southwest Review* 64 (1979): 177.

32. In the screenplay, Dickey has Ed sing a Coca-Cola jingle to calm himself; it is a notable change because Drew worked as a sales supervisor for a big soft-drink company. The screenplay, by the way, does not call for a different actor to play the hillbilly in this scene, suggesting that Dickey does not think Ed shot the wrong man.

33. Davis, 229.

34. Dickey adds a couple of points in the screenplay worth noting here. First, Ed reads a paper for any news that might affect him, and he barely notices the model, who approaches him and leaves disappointed. Secondly, the screenplay has a scene showing Ed and Lewis next to a lake; Ed "rather negligently" unties a piece of rope from a tree and throws it away—a rope that we would have to believe is the same one that broke as he was lowering the body to the river. Ed's ignorance of the model and his confidence to return to the scene of his one killing, relative to the novel, offer subtly stronger evidence of Ed's renewal.

35. Heyen, 155.

36. Davis, 225.

37. Dickey, screenplay, 121.

38. Beaton, 298; Beaton goes on to say that this contrast cheaply overstates the cultural clash.

39. Vilmos Zsigmond, the film's cinematographer, refers to this first killing as "the murder" in an interview with Michel Ciment; Ciment himself refers to both the hillbillies as "murdered" (Ciment, 253, 124).

40. Beaton, 303.

41. Boorman tells Ciment that he "admired in the novel the ambiguity which surrounded the identity of the hillbilly who is killed" (Ciment, 129–30). Ciment turns this ambiguity into a perverse certainty by interpreting the film's message as a denunciation of the "myth of regeneration through violence, a myth fundamental to American civilization": "By killing an innocent man (one who was, in all likelihood, a stranger to the incident; and Drew, in any case, was not shot), Ed is caught up in a vicious circle of reprisals, goaded into acts of violence whose first victim is his own peace of mind" (126). The violence certainly does not rejuvenate Ed, but Ed has not committed murder; if the film did no more than denounce murder, we would hardly come away with any new perspectives on the larger subject of violence. In any event, the same actor plays the man who escaped and the man atop the cliff: incontrovertible evidence that Ed's victim is no "stranger" to the earlier attack, and strong circumstantial evidence that Drew was shot.

42. Stephen Farber, "*Deliverance*—How It Delivers," *New York Times,* 20 August 1972, late ed., sec. 2, p. 9.

43. Beaton, 305.

44. Farber, 9.

Walking Around in Harper Lee's Shoes:
To Kill a Mockingbird

1. Robert L. Carringer, *The Making of "Citizen Kane"* (Berkeley: University of California Press, 1985), 3–15.

2. Amy Lawrence, *Echo and Narcissus: Women's Voices in Classical Hollywood Cinema* (Berkeley: University of California Press, 1991), 194–95. Despite that standing, she adds, neither the novel nor the film have earned similar attention from serious critics: "It has not been seriously addressed in either film or literary studies" (169); and "I have been unable to find any major articles written on the film in the past ten years" (195).

3. Edgar H. Schuster, "Discovering Theme and Structure in the Novel," *The English Journal* 52 (1963): 506.

4. Virginia Campbell, "*To Kill a Mockingbird*," in *Magill's Survey of Cinema: English Language Films*, ed. Frank Magill, 1st ser., (Englewood Cliffs, N.J., Salem Press, 1980), 4:1756.

5. The film also adheres to Lee's implicit criteria, set down in a college article on British films, for cinematic quality:

After a steady diet of vulgar extravaganzas belched forth to the public by money-mad Hollywood producers, it is a relief to see a quiet, unpretentious movie in which the heroine does not look like an Ipana ad, and the hero is a reasonable facsimile of a human being. (W. U. McDonald Jr., "Harper Lee's College Writings," *American Notes and Queries* 6 [1968]: 132)

6. Harper Lee, *To Kill a Mockingbird* (New York: Warner, 1960), 34. All further references to this edition will appear in the text.

7. Claudia Johnson suggests that, like Harper Lee under the tutelage of her own father, the children may also be getting a prelaw education, although the narrator never actually confirms that she or Jem became a practicing attorney. Johnson goes on to speculate that, if we read the novel as a "brief for her father's sainthood," we the jury have been so persuasively moved to find in favor of Lee's father that "closing the case as it were, may in some way account for the subsequent silence of this authorial voice" (Claudia Johnson, "The Secret of Men's Hearts: Code and Law in Harper Lee's *To Kill a Mockingbird*," *Studies in American Fiction* 19.2 [1991]: 131).

8. I note here a dissenting opinion by Colin Nicholson, a dissent that would fit well with Bluestone's theory. He first regrets the film's inability to match the experience—the "pace and control"—of reading the "leisurely, reasoned and reflective" novel. Material differences aside, he goes on to charge that the film simplifies the novel by excluding too much that comes out in the subplots; this simplification, he adds, leads to the shifting of central interest from Scout to Atticus, owing to "the star system of the Hollywood studio productions of the sixties" (Colin Nicholson, "Hollywood and Race: *To Kill a Mockingbird*," in *Cinema and Fiction: New Modes of Adapting, 1950–1990*, ed. John Orr and Colin Nicholson [Edinburgh: Edinburgh University Press, 1992], 151–52).

9. Uncredited, by Kim Stanley, according to Kozloff, 76.

10. McDonald, 131.

11. Nick Aaron Ford, "Battle of the Books: A Critical Survey of Significant Books by and about Negroes Published in 1960," *Phylon* 22 (1961): 122.

12. Fred Erisman observes that Jem reads *Ivanhoe*, which he sees as a sly allusion by Lee to the nostalgic, stale romanticism of the old South ("The Romantic Regionalism of Harper Lee," *The Alabama Review* 26 [1973]: 122–36).

13. The elimination of the scene at Calpurnia's church does cause some dilution of Lee's portrayal of blacks, particularly in the characterization of a few of the more peripheral characters met at the church. Nick Aaron Ford praises Lee for producing "living, convincing" black characters who are "neither saints nor devils, neither completely ignorant or craven or foolish, nor completely wise or wholly courageous" (122). In the film, the fewer black characters do not fit simple stereotypes, but neither collectively nor individually do they behave other than with nobility.

14. Erisman, 129–30. He also points out that Atticus's lesson about the primacy of one's conscience recalls Emerson's "Self-Reliance": "Nothing can bring you peace but yourself. Nothing can bring you peace but the triumph of principles" (130–31).

15. Lawrence, 170, 172, 196.

16. Ibid., 170, 179, 174.

17. Among the autobiographical elements of the novel, Lee's characterization of Dill relies much upon her memory of Truman Capote. When his parents divorced, Capote's mother left him with relatives in Monroeville, Alabama, and did not send for him until years after she had remarried; Lee was a neighbor of those relatives and became a lasting

friend of Capote's (Helen S. Garson, *Truman Capote* [New York: Ungar, 1980], 2). Capote's persona might tend to confirm the cynical distance Dill expects to keep from humanity, but his writing also shows an ability to sympathize with others.

18. Lawrence, 172.

19. Erisman, 131.

Back Where We Started: *2001: A Space Odyssey*

1. William Kloman, "In 2001, Will Love Be a Seven-Letter Word?" *New York Times*, 14 April 1968, late ed., sec. 2, p. 15.

2. Bluestone, 47.

3. For information on Kubrick's and Clarke's collaboration, see Jerome Agel, *The Making of Kubrick's 2001* (New York: New American, 1970), and Arthur C. Clarke, *The Lost Worlds of 2001* (New York: New American, 1972). In the latter, Clarke hints that Kubrick delayed approval of revisions in the novel in order to keep it from preceding his film (46–49), but by Clarke's own account, Kubrick's suggested revisions all seem to have benefited the novel.

4. Jeremy Bernstein, "Chain Reaction," *New Yorker,* 21 September 1968, 180.

5. See two reviews by Joseph Gelmis of *2001: A Space Odyssey*, dir. Stanley Kubrick: "*Space Odyssey* Fails Most Gloriously," *Newsday*, 4 April 1968, and "Another Look at *Space Odyssey*," *Newsday*, 20 April 1968. Both are reprinted in Agel, 263–65 and 265–68.

On the other hand, several well known and influential reviewers (e.g., Pauline Kael, Stanley Kauffmann, and Andrew Sarris) wrote scathing reviews that they never reconsidered or changed upon reconsideration. Clive Barker attacked such critics for missing the point of the film "because it did not fit into their vocabulary of filmic criticism" (Clive Barker, "Is *2001* Worth Seeing Twice?" *Cinéaste* 2.1 [1968]: 15–16).

6. Arthur C. Clarke, *Report on Planet Three and Other Speculations* (New York: New American, 1972), 224.

7. Ibid., 214.

8. Agel, 328. Carolyn Geduld suggests that such reaching for the audience's subconscious sinisterly resembles the Ludovico Treatment featured in Kubrick's next film, *A Clockwork Orange* (*Filmguide to 2001: A Space Odyssey* [Bloomington: Indiana University Press, 1973], 64–66); this notion, however, may come from too much hunting for consistency between films that I believe are opposite in tone.

9. John Russell Taylor, *Directors and Directions: Cinema for the Seventies* (New York: Hill and Wang, 1975), 130. The notion that *2001* appeals uniquely to younger generations began, I fear, with its reputation, in some circles, as "a trip": fortified with a hallucinogen of choice and seated in the front row before a Cinerama screen, one could enjoy the "star gate" sequence in a fashion certainly not experienced by the conventional film reviewer from the local paper. Such preparations, however, might just as radically alter one's appreciation of *Patton*.

In any case, the notion persists. Gary Crowdus, who thinks the film does have a coherent structure, asserts that critical reactions divide along a "generation gap" "between those who are able to comprehend the purely visually narrative sequences of the film and those who are confused by them" and "between those who are fascinated by the sequences of abstract visuals and those who find them dull and boring in the absence and expectation of a 'plot'" (Gary Crowdus, "A Tentative for the Viewing of *2001*," *Cinéaste* 2.1 [1968]: 14). Annette Michelson, who also finds coherent meaning in the film, offers a more unusual explanation for the film's appeal to younger audiences: since the story progresses analogously to the process "Piaget calls equilibrium," which "is the manner of the development of the child's intelligence," younger audiences understand and accept it more readily (Annette Michelson, "Bodies in Space: Film as 'Carnal Knowledge,'" *Artforum*, February 1969, 62).

10. Thomas Allen Nelson, *Kubrick: Inside a Film Artist's Maze* (Bloomington: Indiana University Press, 1982), 103.

11. W. R. Robinson and Mary McDermott write that this shot symbolically prefigures humanity's development as shown in the film to come:

> From the earth (the senses, i.e., the physical and bestial) to an intermediate and mediating plateau, the moon (reason), a specious end which is not really a source of light but only a partially lit up reflection of the source, to, finally, the sun (the imagination), a self-generating body and the true source of light. (W. R. Robinson and Mary McDermott, "*2001* and the Literary Sensibility," *The Georgia Review* 26 [1972]: 26)

Even though the spheres do not appear in this order—and I do not know whether Robinson and McDermott think they do—this figurative reading still illuminates the film's evocative style.

12. Alexander Walker, *Stanley Kubrick Directs*, expanded ed. (New York: Harcourt, 1972), 46.

13. These two alignments appear, from a low-angle shot, above the monolith: the moon and sun in the former, and the Earth and sun in the latter. However, from earlier shots in this latter scene, we could see that the Earth and sun were not approaching each other and thus had to pop into place as if by magic. Kubrick does call the alignments "magical" (Agel, 80), but I do not think he had in mind these sudden movements.

14. In a reading clearly contrary to my own, Judith A. Switzer finds a threatening irony in some of these scenes. Concentrating on Strauss's *Also Sprach Zarathustra* rather than the alignments, she notes that the second instance occurs "at the ape man's realization that he can use a bone as a tool to kill his enemies." This theme develops to the point where the tools independently murder people. Thus, in the final image, Switzer wonders, "What comfort is there in this image of regeneration? Having seen the arrogance of this race of tool-users, perhaps we should really dread the sound of the superman music when it heralds the next step of human evolution" (Judith A. Switzer, "The Utopian Vision in Kubrick's *2001* and *A Clockwork Orange*," in *Proceedings of the Fifth Annual Conference on Film*, ed. Maud S. Walther [West Lafayette, Ind.: Purdue University Press, 1980], 41). I would reply that the evolution portrayed in the film certainly involves steps backwards as well as forwards, but the latter prevail, and the music and alignments announce such progress—however tentative at first. Notably, that second instance of Strauss's music arrives with the ape-man's realization that he can use the bone to kill *for food*, not, as he must later realize without musical accompaniment, for subduing foes.

In regard to the specific motif of births, almost all critics have noted the several birthdays marked or mentioned in the film. If such a motif usually suggests health and progress, at least one other critic finds it more threatening than Switzer does. Zoë Sofia draws a clever diagram that identifies Floyd's Pan Am shuttle as a "sperm" that "inseminates [the] space station," the lunar shuttle as a "blastocyst" that "implants in [the] high-tech sub-lunar womb," and so on (the shape of *Discovery* is especially fruitful)—all ending with the Star Child and the so-called "extermination effect: earth disappears." According to Sofia,

> This extraterrestrial embryo is a perverse and misleading symbol whose engaging organic appearance invokes maternal fertility and belies its origin in the unholy union of man with celestial powers and the tools he's brought to life out of the excremental remains of his cannibalized mother, the planet Earth.

The Star Child then returns to extinguish, not to rescue. This "resurrection" portends "the negation of death": "It signifies not life, but deathlessness. . . . [B]y extinguishing life generally, extinction would cause the death of death" (Zoë Sofia, "Exterminating Fetuses: Abortion, Disarmament, and the Sexo-Semiotics of Extraterrestrialism," *Diacritics* 14.2 [1984]: 50–53). Sofia's gloomy reading of the film's final image has an obvious flaw, however: she assumes that the match-cut from bone to spacecraft represents the advance from hand-to-hand combat to orbiting nuclear weapons—an idea that relies on the novel's version of the future, not the film's (see also note 18, below). Couple this error with ideas of extinction that she derives from Jonathan Schell's *The Fate of the Earth*—for instance, "Extinction is unique not because it destroys mankind as an object but because it destroys mankind as the source of all possible human subjects" (Jonathan Schell, *The Fate of the Earth* [New York: Knopf, 1982], 137), which insight confirms that infertility inevitably follows death—and Kubrick's film may start to look like a wide-screen cryptogram from "the New Right's cult of fetal personhood" (Sofia, 47). But I do not see it that way.

15. The concept comes from Plato's *Timaeus*, but it has undergone some religious permutations. See A. E. Taylor, *A Commentary on Plato's* Timaeus (1928; Oxford: Clarendon Press, 1962), 216–19; Francis MacDonald Cornford, *From Religion to Philosophy: A Study in the Origins of Western Speculation* (London: Edward Arnold, 1912), 178–79; and Lynn Thorndike, *A History of Magic and Experimental Science* (New York: MacMillan, 1923), 1:372.

16. Tim Hunter, Stephen Kaplan, and Peter Jaszi, review of *2001: A Space Odyssey*, dir. Stanley Kubrick, in Agel, 216–17.

17. Nelson, 109; John Charlot, "From Ape-Man to Space-Baby: *2001*, An Interpretation," *East-West Film Journal* 1.1 (1986): 85.

18. I would wonder, for instance, how several critics, commenting on the match-cut that links humanity's prehistory and future, can identify—without reference to Clarke's novel—the satellite as a nuclear weapon. Just before tossing the bone into the air, the ape-man had used it as a weapon, so these critics might presume the match would be to another weapon—but why not, more generally, to another tool? I would hesitate to assume the more specific answer because Kubrick offers no specific information: given the objective point of view, the audience can safely register the satellite simply as a device in orbit; in fact, the cutting continuity from MGM identifies it as a "Spacecraft" and no more (reel 2, p. 5). To know more, we would need an omniscient point of view that could, for instance, insert a more detailed shot that clearly displayed a warhead or even a Department of Defense logo or nuclear symbol. This spacecraft has antennae, but nothing that would mark it as a weapon; it does not even have a nation's flag on it.

19. A dramatic point of view approaches real objectivity (objective in the sense of an apparent absence of a narrator). Clive Barker, without using these specific terms, calls the film "a dramatized documentary" because "of its truth—the accurate scientific data and detail Kubrick uses to create the reality of the future" (Barker, 15).

20. Friedman, 155–56.

21. Nelson, 102. See Clarke's *The Lost Worlds of 2001* for selections from earlier drafts in which he develops the explanations even more fully.

According to Clive James, this difference between Kubrick and Clarke comes down to an attitude toward technology and beings from outer space:

> Kubrick is able to suggest ordinary cultural change. He does not make the gee-whiz changes featured by Clarke in his book. . . . It is his capacity to remain *unenthusiastic* in this way that contrasts his vision with that of most SF writers, Clarke included. . . . The film has no illusions about either Man or the Universe: without thinking we are dirt, it does not imagine we are wonderful, and above all it does not believe in extra-terrestrial forces that will make us better. (Clive James, *"2001*: Kubrick vs. Clarke," *Film Society Review* 5.5 [1970]: 34)

I would say that, despite the fascination anyone would feel in discovering that we are not alone in the universe, Kubrick's film appeals to me because it does not rely on aliens' riding to our rescue. Clarke's optimism about scientific advances ironically suggests a pessimism about human endeavor: he cannot imagine that humans could achieve it alone.

22. Arthur C. Clarke, *2001: A Space Odyssey* (New York: New American Library, 1968), 56–57. All further references to this edition will be given in the text.

23. James, 28. About the collaboration between Kubrick and Clarke, James writes that "in the film Kubrick had, to a certain extent, frozen [Clarke] out" (27).

24. All the critics who like the film, let alone those who would champion it as a masterpiece, have defined, in one way or another, its coherent plot. Annette Michelson mounts an especially strong attack on those who find *Space Odyssey* boring and pointless when she makes it sound almost like a thriller: for a film that supposedly lacks a plot, "incident, surprise, discovery, shock and violence abound. Its plot turns, in fact, upon *intrigue*, as the French define plot" (Michelson, 57).

25. Walker, 244; Robinson and McDermott, 25–26, 33.

26. Don Daniels, "A Skeleton Key to *2001*," *Sight and Sound* 40 (1970/71): 29, 32–33.

27. Friedman, 89 and 106–11.

28. Carolyn Geduld, 42.

29. Elie Flatto, *"2001: A Space Odyssey*: the Eternal Return," *Film Comment* 5.4 (1969): 8.

30. James, 34.

31. Stanley Kauffmann, "Lost in the Stars," review of *2001: A Space Odyssey*, dir. Stanley Kubrick, *The New Republic,* 4 May 1968, 24-, reprinted in Agel, 225. F. A. Macklin, "The Comic Sense of *2001*," *Film Comment* 5.4 (1969): 10–12.

32. Carolyn Geduld, 52.

33. Crowdus, 13.

34. John Charlot cleverly notes that this shadowboxing remains as a sort of vestigial form of the ape-men's posturing before enemies (Charlot, 85).

35. Many critics have accepted, implicitly or explicitly, Clarke's explanation that HAL suffers a neurosis because human politics and bureaucracy dictated that HAL not tell its fellow astronauts their real mission. Others have elaborated upon this psychology. Robinson and McDermott assert that HAL stands upon "the infallibility of his words," a stance that places it firmly in the error of assuming that reason, rather than imagination, represents the fullest development of intelligence. As a "good rationalist," HAL strives to answer the questions of existence and, since it alone knows that the mission may yield some large answers, selfishly acts to have those answers "all for himself" and "be a Faustian master of his universe, a creature who possesses ultimate knowledge and omnisciently rules its domain" (Robinson and McDermott, 34).

Jay H. Boylan, on the other hand, wants to absolve HAL of any evil leanings and suggests a more precious motivation. Inasmuch as HAL could assume that humanity would soon encounter evolutionary knowledge and likely "transcend tool-using," HAL would fear for its relationship to humanity: "To put it more simply, *Hal cares for man.* His is a love relationship. . . . So, Hal is driven insane by a conflict between his desire to have humankind stay as it is and his desire to love, honor and protect the men of the ship" (Jay H. Boylan, "Hal in *2001: A Space Odyssey:* The Lover Sings His Song," *Journal of Popular Culture* 18.4 [1985]: 55).

As should be evident below, I do not think that computer chips, any more than potato chips, can go nuts.

36. Charlot, 87.

37. Richard D. Erlich, for one, writes that, owing to the film's thematic concerns—that "humans and machines are very like one another" and that humans essentially use tools to kill—the conflict between HAL and Bowman has an ironic decorum: "decorous that Hal, the most human character in the film, should become a murderer; decorous that a 'roboticized' Dave Bowman should have to kill Hal to achieve full humanity; and decorous that Hal should be the one character in the film to suffer a fully human death" (Richard D. Erlich, "Moon-Watcher, Man, and Star Child: *2001* as Paradigm," in *Patterns of the Fantastic,* ed. Donald M. Hassler [Mercer Island, Wash.: Starmont House, 1983], 76). As should be clear now, I would respond that, although the film certainly treats the themes mentioned, we see Bowman as less of a robot in his struggle with HAL, and simultaneously we see into HAL's truly robotic nature: a room-size "brain" made out of large chips.

38. We should not forget that Bowman does not really "kill" anything. He disables HAL's voice and "human" characteristics programming. In an analogous situation, we would not say that anyone disabling a car's seatbelt buzzer—or, in expensive models from a few years back, a "voice" that insists, "Your seatbelt is unfastened"—has thereby destroyed the entire car, let alone taken its life.

39. Nelson, 125.

40. Walker, 261.

41. Nelson, 132; Walker, 264.

42. Friedman, 86–87.

43. John Hollow, "*2001* in Perspective: The Fiction of Arthur C. Clarke," *Southwest Review* 61 (1976): 116.

44. The film has *Discovery* bound for Jupiter because artistic designers could not create a representation of Saturn that was satisfying to Kubrick (see Agel, 138).

45. Hollow, 125.

46. Gene Youngblood, *Expanded Cinema* (New York: Dutton, 1970), 147.

47. See Bluestone, 46–48.

48. Paul H. Stacy, "Cinematic Thought," *Hartford Studies in Literature* 1 (1969): 125.

Afterword/Afterimage

1. Agel, 11.

2. Frank Gabrenya, "Michael Mann's *Mohicans* a Drama for Today," *Columbus Dispatch*, 20 September 1992, sec. C, p. 2.

Works Cited

Primary Sources

Boorman, John, dir. *Deliverance*. Warner Brothers, 1972.

Brooks, Richard, dir. *Looking for Mr. Goodbar*. Paramount, 1977.

Clarke, Arthur C. *2001: A Space Odyssey*. New York: New American Library, 1968.

Dickey, James. *Deliverance*. New York: Dell, 1970.

———. *Deliverance* [screenplay]. Screenplay Library. Carbondale: Southern Illinois University Press, 1982.

Kubrick, Stanley, dir. *2001: A Space Odyssey*. MGM, 1968.

———. *2001: A Space Odyssey* (Dialogue Cutting Continuity). MGM, 1968.

Lee, Harper. *To Kill a Mockingbird*. New York: Warner, 1960.

Levinson, Barry, dir. *The Natural*. Tri-Star Pictures, 1984.

Malamud, Bernard. *The Natural*. New York: Farrar, 1952.

Rossner, Judith. *Looking for Mr. Goodbar*. New York: Simon & Schuster, 1975.

Secondary Sources

Agel, Jerome. *The Making of Kubrick's 2001*. New York: New American, 1970.

Andrew, J. Dudley. *The Major Film Theories: An Introduction*. London: Oxford University Press, 1976.

———. *Concepts in Film Theory*. New York: Oxford University Press, 1984.

Ansen, David. "It's Going, Going . . ." Review of *The Natural*, directed by Barry Levinson. *Newsweek* 28 May 1984: 77.

Aristotle. *Poetics*. Translated by S. H. Butcher. In *Criticism: The Major Texts*, enl. ed., edited by Walter Jackson Bate, 19–39. New York: Harcourt, 1970.

Armour, Robert. "*Deliverance*: Four Variations of the American Adam." *Literature/Film Quarterly* 1 (1973): 280–85.

Arnheim, Rudolf. *Film as Art*. Berkeley: University of California Press, 1957.

Asheim, Lester. "From Book to Film: Simplification." *Hollywood Quarterly* 5 (1950–51): 287–304.

———. "From Book to Film: Mass Appeals." *Hollywood Quarterly* 5 (1950–51): 334–49.

———. "From Book to Film: The Note of Affirmation." *The Quarterly of Film Radio and Television* 6 (1951–52): 258–73.

———. "From Book to Film: Summary." *The Quarterly of Film Radio and Television* 6 (1951–52): 258–73.

Balázs, Béla. *Theory of Film: Character and Growth of a New Art*. Translated by Edith Bone. 1952. Reprint, New York: Dover, 1970.

Barker, Clive. "Is *2001* Worth Seeing Twice?" *Cinéaste* 2.1 (1968): 15–16.

Bate, Walter Jackson, ed. *Criticism: The Major Texts*. Enl. ed. New York: Harcourt, 1970.

Battestin, Martin C. "Osborne's *Tom Jones*: Adapting a Classic." In *Man and the Movies*, edited by W. R. Robinson, 31–45. Baltimore, Md.: Penguin, 1967.

Bazin, Andre. "In Defense of Mixed Cinema." In *What Is Cinema?*, translated by Hugh Gray, 1:53–75. Berkeley: University of California Press, 1967.

Beaton, James F. "Dickey Down the River." In *The Modern American Novel and the Movies*, edited by Gerald Peary and Roger Shatzkin, 293–306. New York: Ungar, 1978.

Beidler, Peter G. "'The Pride of Thine Heart Hath Deceived Thee': Narrative Distortion in Dickey's *Deliverance*." *South Carolina Review* 5 (1972): 29–40.

Beja, Morris. *Film and Literature: An Introduction*. New York: Longman, 1979.

Bergman, Ingmar. "Introduction: Bergman Discusses Film-Making." In *Four Screenplays of Ingmar Bergman*. New York: Touchstone, 1960.

Bernstein, Jeremy. "Chain Reaction." *New Yorker* 21 September 1968: 180–84.

Blackwood, Caroline. "Getting It All Over With." Review of *Looking for Mr. Goodbar*, by Judith Rossner. *Times Literary Supplement,* 12 September 1975, p. 1012.

Bluestone, George. *Novels into Film*. Berkeley: University of California Press, 1957.

Blum, Daniel. *A Pictorial History of the Silent Screen*. New York: Putnam, 1953.

Boggs, Joseph M. *The Art of Watching Films: A Guide to Film Analysis*. Menlo Park, Calif.: Benjamin/Cummings, 1978.

Booth, Wayne C. *The Rhetoric of Fiction*. Chicago: University of Chicago Press, 1961.

———. "How Not to Use Aristotle: The *Poetics*." In *Now Don't Try to Reason With Me: Essays and Ironies for a Credulous Age,* 103–15. Chicago: University of Chicago Press, 1970.

Borst, Bill. *Still Last in the American League: The St. Louis Browns Revisited*. West Bloomfield, Mich.: Altwerger and Mandel, 1992.

Bordwell, David. *Narration in the Fiction Film*. Madison: University of Wisconsin Press, 1985.

Boylan, Jay H. "Hal in *2001: A Space Odyssey*: The Lover Sings His Song." *Journal of Popular Culture* 18.4 (1985): 53–56.

Boyum, Joy Gould. *Double Exposure: Fiction into Film*. New York: Mentor-NAL, 1985.

Branigan, Edward. *Point of View in the Cinema: A Theory of Narration and Subjectivity in Classical Film*. Berlin: Mouton, 1984.

Burke, Tom. "Conversations with, Um, Jon Voight." *Esquire,* January 1972, 116–19, 150–58.

Campbell, Virginia. *"To Kill a Mockingbird."* In *Magill's Survey of Cinema: English Language Films*, edited by Frank Magill, 4:1756–59. 1st ser. Englewood Cliffs, N.J.: Salem Press, 1980.

Carringer, Robert L. *The Making of* Citizen Kane. Berkeley: University of California Press, 1985.

Chamberlin, T. C. "Multiple Working Hypotheses." *Science* o.s. 15 (1890): 92–96. Reprinted in *Journal of Geology* 39 (1931): 155–65.

Charlot, John. "From Ape-Man to Space-Baby: *2001*, An Interpretation." *East-West Film Journal* 1.1 (1986): 84–89.

Chatman, Seymour. *Story and Discourse: Narrative Structure in Fiction and Film*. Ithaca: Cornell University Press, 1978.

———. "What Novels Can Do that Films Can't (and Vice Versa)." *Critical Inquiry* 7 (1980): 121–40.

———. *Coming to Terms: The Rhetoric of Narrative in Fiction and Film*. Ithaca: Cornell University Press, 1990.

Ciment, Michel. *John Boorman*. Translated by Gilbert Adair. London: Faber, 1986.

Clarke, Arthur C. *The Lost Worlds of 2001*. New York: New American, 1972.

———. *Report on Planet Three and Other Speculations*. New York: New American, 1972.

Clemons, Walter. "James Dickey, Novelist." *New York Times Book Review,* 22 March 1970, 22.

Coleridge, Samuel Taylor. *Selected Poetry and Prose*. Edited by Elisabeth Schneider. 2nd ed. New York: Rinehart, 1971.

Corliss, Richard. "We Lost It at the Movies." *Film Comment,* January-February 1980, 34–38.

———. "By the Book." *Film Comment,* March-April 1991, 37–46.

Cornford, Francis MacDonald. *From Religion to Philosophy: A Study in the Origins of Western Speculation*. London: Edward Arnold, 1912.

Covel, Robert C. "James Dickey's *Deliverance*: Screenplay as Intertext." *James Dickey Newsletter* 4.2 (1988): 12–19.

Crane, R. S. *The Languages of Criticism and the Structure of Poetry*. Toronto: University of Toronto Press, 1953.

Crowdus, Gary. "A Tentative for the Viewing of *2001*." *Cinéaste* 2.1 (1968): 12–14.

Curran, Ronald T. "Biology and Culture: Hollywood and the Deliverance of Dickey's Weekend Backwoodsmen." *Southern Quarterly* 18.4 (1980): 81–90.

Curtin, Kevin Thomas. *"The Natural*: Our *Iliad* and *Odyssey*." *The Antioch Review* 43 (1985): 225–41.

Dagle, Joan. "Narrative Discourse in Film and Fiction: The Question of the Present Tense." In *Narrative Strategies: Original Essays in Film and Prose Fiction,* edited by Syndy Conger and Janice Welsch, 47–59. Macomb, Ill.: Western Illinois University Press, 1980.

Daniels, Don. "A Skeleton Key to *2001*." *Sight and Sound* 40 (1970/71): 28–33.

Davis, Charles E. "The Wilderness Revisited: Irony in James Dickey's *Deliverance*." *Studies in American Fiction* 4 (1976): 223–30.

Donohue, Agnes McNeill. Review of *Looking for Mr. Goodbar*, by Judith Rossner. *The Critic* 34.2 (1975): 79–85.

Doughtie, Edward. "Art and Nature in *Deliverance*." *Southwest Review* 64 (1979): 167–80.

Eberwein, Robert T. "The Filmic Dream and Point of View." *Literature/Film Quarterly* 8 (1980): 197–203.

Eidsvik, Charles. "Toward a 'Politiques des Adaptations.'" In *Film and/as Literature*, edited by John Harrington, 27–37. Englewood Cliffs, N.J.: Prentice-Hall, 1977.

————. *Cineliteracy: Film Among the Arts*. New York: Random House, 1978.

Eisenstein, Sergei. *The Film Sense*. Translated by Jay Leyda. New York: Harcourt, 1942.

————. *Film Form: Essays in Film Theory*. Translated by Jay Leyda. New York: Harcourt, 1949.

Erisman, Fred. "The Romantic Regionalism of Harper Lee." *The Alabama Review* 26 (1973): 122–36.

Erlich, Richard D. "Moon-Watcher, Man, and Star Child: *2001* as Paradigm." In *Patterns of the Fantastic*, edited by Donald M. Hassler, 73–80. Mercer Island, Wash.: Starmont House, 1983.

Eyster, Warren. "Two Regional Novels." Review of *Deliverance*, by James Dickey. *Sewanee Review* 79 (1971): 469–74.

Farber, Stephen. "*Deliverance*—How It Delivers." *New York Times*, 20 August 1972, late ed., sec. 2, pp. 9-.

Field, Leslie A. and Joyce W. Field, eds. *Bernard Malamud and the Critics*. New York: New York University Press, 1970.

Fimrite, Ron. "A Star with Real Clout." *Sports Illustrated* 7 May 1984: 92–106.

Fishbein, Leslie. "*Looking for Mr. Goodbar*: Murder for the Masses." *International Journal of Women's Studies* 3 (1980): 173–82.

Flatto, Elie. "*2001: A Space Odyssey*: The Eternal Return." *Film Comment* 5.4 (1969): 6–9.

Ford, Nick Aaron. "Battle of the Books: A Critical Survey of Significant Books by and about Negroes Published in 1960." *Phylon* 22 (1961): 119–34.

Fosburgh, Lacey. *Closing Time: The True Story of the "Goodbar" Murder*. New York: Delacorte, 1977.

Foust, R. E. "*Tactus Eruditus*: Phenomenology as Method and Meaning of James Dickey's *Deliverance*. *Studies in American Fiction* 9 (1981): 199–216.

Friedman, Norman. *Form and Meaning in Fiction*. Athens: University of Georgia Press, 1975.

Frye, Northrop. *Anatomy of Criticism: Four Essays*. Princeton: Princeton University Press, 1957.

Gabrenya, Frank. "Michael Mann's *Mohicans* a Drama for Today." *Columbus Dispatch*, 20 September 1992, sec. C, pp. 1–2.

Garson, Helen S. *Truman Capote*. New York: Ungar, 1980.

Geduld, Carolyn. *Filmguide to 2001: A Space Odyssey*. Bloomington: Indiana University Press, 1973.

Geduld, Harry M., ed. *Authors on Film*. Bloomington: Indiana University Press, 1972.

Gelmis, Joseph. "*Space Odyssey* Fails Most Gloriously." Review of *2001: A Space Odyssey*, directed by Stanley Kubrick. *Newsday,* 4 April 1968. Reprinted in Agel, 263–65.

———. "Another Look at *Space Odyssey*." Review of *2001: A Space Odyssey*, directed by Stanley Kubrick. *Newsday,* 20 April 1968. Reprinted in Agel, 265–68.

Giddings, Robert, Keith Selby, and Chris Wensley. *Screening the Novel: The Theory and Practice of Literary Dramatization*. London: Macmillan, 1990.

Giroux, Henry A. Review of *Looking for Mr. Goodbar*, directed by Richard Brooks. *Film Quarterly* 31.4 (1978): 52–54.

Gow, Gordon. "Playboy in a Monastery." *Films and Filming* 18.5 (1972): 18–22.

Gray, Paul Edward. Review of *Deliverance*, by James Dickey. *Yale Review* 60 (1970): 104–5.

Griffith, James. "From a Certain Point of View in 'A Scandal in Bohemia': Outsmarting Mr. Sherlock Holmes." *The Victorian Newsletter* 86 (1994): 7–9.

Harrington, John. *Film and/as Literature*. Englewood Cliffs, N.J.: Prentice- Hall, 1977.

Helterman, Jeffrey. *Understanding Bernard Malamud*. Columbia: University of South Carolina Press, 1985.

Heyen, William. "A Conversation with James Dickey." *Southern Review,* n.s., 9 (1973): 135–56.

Hollow, John. "*2001* in Perspective: The Fiction of Arthur C. Clarke." *Southwest Review* 61 (1976): 113–29.

Hulseberg, Richard A. "Novels and Films: A Limited Inquiry." *Literature/Film Quarterly* 6 (1978): 57–65.

Hunter, Tim, Stephen Kaplan, and Peter Jaszi. Review of *2001: A Space Odyssey*, directed by Stanley Kubrick. *Film Heritage* 3.4 (1968): 12–20. Reprinted in Agel, 215–22.

James, Clive. "*2001*: Kubrick vs. Clarke." *Film Society Review* 5.5 (1970): 27–35.

Johnson, Claudia. "The Secret Courts of Men's Hearts: Code and Law in Harper Lee's *To Kill a Mockingbird*." *Studies in American Fiction* 19.2 (1991): 129–39.

Johnston, Tracy. "Who *Else* Is Looking for Mr. Goodbar?" *Ms.,* February 1978, 24–26.

Kael, Pauline. "Trash, Art, and the Movies." *Going Steady*. New York: Warner, 1970. 103–58.

———. "Notes on Heart and Mind." In *Deeper into Movies,* 290–301. New York: Warner, 1974.

———. "The Candidate." Review of *The Natural*, directed by Barry Levinson. *New Yorker* 28 May 1984: 100–101.

Kauffmann, Stanley. "Lost in the Stars." Review of *2001: A Space Odyssey*, directed by Stanley Kubrick. *The New Republic,* 4 May 1968, 24-. Reprinted in Agel, 223–26.

Kawin, Bruce F. *Faulkner and Film*. New York: Ungar, 1977.

———. *Mindscreen: Bergman, Godard, and First-Person Film*. Princeton: Princeton University Press, 1978.

Kloman, William. "In 2001, Will Love Be a Seven-Letter Word?" *New York Times,* 14 April 1968, late ed., sec. 2, p. 15.

Konigsberg, Ira. *The Complete Film Dictionary*. New York: New American Library, 1987.

Kopkind, Andrew. Review of *The Natural*, directed by Barry Levinson. *The Nation* 2 June 1984: 682–83.

Kozloff, Sarah. *Invisible Storytellers: Voice-Over Narration in American Fiction Film*. Berkeley: University of California Press, 1988.

Kracauer, Siegfried. *Theory of Film: The Redemption of Physical Reality*. London: Oxford University Press, 1960.

Kuleshov, Lev. *Kuleshov on Film: Writings of Lev Kuleshov*. Edited and translated by Ronald Levaco. Berkeley: University of California Press, 1974.

Lawrence, Amy. *Echo and Narcissus: Women's Voices in Classical Hollywood Cinema*. Berkeley: University of California Press, 1991.

Lessing, Gotthold Ephraim. *Laocoön*. Translated by Ellen Frothingham. In *Criticism: The Major Texts*, enl. ed., edited by Walter Jackson Bate, 245–48. New York: Harcourt, 1970.

Levy, Francis. "Hollywood Embraces the Difficult Novel." *New York Times,* 22 March 1981, p. D13.

Leyda, Jay. *Kino: A History of the Russian and Soviet Film*. London: George Allen and Unwin Ltd., 1960.

Library of Congress. *Catalog of Copyright Entries: Cumulative Entries: Motion Pictures, 1912–1939*. Washington, DC: GPO, 1951.

Lightman, Herb A. "On Location with *Deliverance*." *American Cinematographer* 52 (1971): 796–801.

Linden, George W. *Reflections on the Screen*. Belmont, Calif.: Wadsworth, 1970.

Lindsay, Vachel. *The Art of the Moving Picture*. 1915. Reprint, New York: Liveright, 1970.

Loftis, John E. "Technique as Metaphor in James Dickey's *Deliverance*." *The South Carolina Review* 16.1: 66–76.

Longen, Eugene M. "Dickey's *Deliverance*: Sex and the Great Outdoors." *Southern Literary Journal* 9 (1977): 137–49.

Luhr, William, and Peter Lehman. *Authorship and Narrative in the Cinema: Issues in Contemporary Aesthetics and Criticism*. New York: Putnam, 1977.

Macklin, F. A. "The Comic Sense of *2001*." *Film Comment* 5.4 (1969): 10–15.

Mast, Gerald. *Film/Cinema/Movie: A Theory of Experience*. New York: Harper, 1977.

Mayne, Judith. *Private Novels, Public Films*. Athens: University of Georgia Press, 1988.

McConnell, Frank D. *The Spoken Seen: Film and the Romantic Imagination*. Baltimore, Md.: The Johns Hopkins University Press, 1975.

———. *Storytelling and Mythmaking: Images from Film and Literature*. New York: Oxford University Press, 1979.

McDonald, W. U., Jr. "Harper Lee's College Writings." *American Notes and Queries* 6 (1968): 131–33.

Mellard, James M. "Four Versions of Pastoral." In *Bernard Malamud and the Critics*, edited by Leslie A. and Joyce W. Field, 67–83. New York: New York University Press, 1970.

Metz, Christian. *Film Language: A Semiotics of the Cinema*. Translated by Michael Taylor. New York: Oxford University Press, 1974.

Michelson, Annette. "Bodies in Space: Film as 'Carnal Knowledge.'" *Artforum,* February 1969, 54–63.

Mitry, Jean. "Remarks on the Problem of Cinematic Adaptation." Translated by Richard Dyer. *The Bulletin of the Midwest Modern Language Association* 4 (1971): 1–9.

Monaco, James. *How to Read a Film: The Art, Technology, Language, History and Theory of Film and Media*. New York: Oxford University Press, 1977.

Morrissette, Bruce. *Novel and Film: Essays in Two Genres*. Chicago: University of Chicago Press, 1985.

Münsterberg, Hugo. *The Film: A Psychological Study*. 1916. Reprint, New York: Dover, 1970.

Murray, Edward. *The Cinematic Imagination: Writers and the Motion Pictures*. New York: Ungar, 1972.

Nelson, Thomas Allen. *Kubrick: Inside a Film Artist's Maze*. Bloomington: Indiana University Press, 1982.

Nicholson, Colin. "Hollywood and Race: *To Kill a Mockingbird*." In *Cinema and Fiction: New Modes of Adapting, 1950–1990*, edited by John Orr and Colin Nicholson, 151–59. Edinburgh: Edinburgh University Press, 1992.

Norden, Eric. "Playboy Interview: Stanley Kubrick." *Playboy,* Sept. 1968, 85-. Reprint, Agel, 328–54.

Norman, Geoffry. "Playboy Interview: James Dickey." *Playboy,* November 1973, 81-.

O'Faolain, Julia. "Victims." Review of *Looking for Mr. Goodbar*, by Judith Rossner. *London Magazine* 15.5 (1975/76): 113–20.

Olson, Elder. *On Value Judgments in the Arts and Other Essays*. Chicago: University of Chicago Press, 1976.

Palmer, R. Barton. "Narration, Text, Intertext: The Two Versions of *Deliverance*." *James Dickey Newsletter* 2.2 (1986): 2–11.

Peary, Gerald and Roger Shatzkin, eds. *The Classic American Novel and the Movies*. New York: Ungar, 1977.

———. *The Modern American Novel and the Movies*. New York: Ungar, 1978.

Perkins, V. F. *Film as Film: Understanding and Judging Movies*. Middlesex, England: Penguin, 1972.

Phelan, James. *Worlds from Words: A Theory of Language in Fiction*. Chicago: University of Chicago Press, 1981.

Poague, Leland A. "Literature vs. Cinema: The Politics of Aesthetic Definition." *The Journal of Aesthetic Education* 10.1 (1976): 75–91.

Pudovkin, V. I. *Film Technique and Film Acting*. Translated by Ivor Montague. 1929, 1937. Reprint, New York: Grove Press, 1976.

Read, Herbert. "The Poet and the Film." In *A Coat of Many Colours: Occasional Essays,* 225–31. London: Routledge, 1945.

Robinson, W. R. and Mary McDermott. "*2001* and the Literary Sensibility." *The Georgia Review* 26 (1972): 21–37.

Robbe-Grillet, Alain. Introduction to *Last Year at Marienbad*, translated by Richard Howard, 7–15. New York: Grove, 1962.

Rossner, Judith. "Kiss 'n Kill: *Star 80* and the Playboy Ethic." *The Movies,* November 1983, 36-.

Samuels, Charles Thomas. "What Hath Dickey Delivered?" Review of *Deliverance*, by James Dickey. *New Republic,* 18 April 1970, 23–26.

———. "How Not to Film a Novel." Review of *Deliverance*, directed by John Boorman. *American Scholar* 42.1 (1972–73): 148–54.

Sarris, Andrew. Review of *2001: A Space Odyssey*, directed by Stanley Kubrick. WBAI, New York. 3 April 1968. Reprint, Agel, 242.

———. Review of *2001: A Space Odyssey*, directed by Stanley Kubrick. *Village Voice* 20 February 1969: 47.

———. "Literature and Film." *The Bulletin of the Midwest Modern Language Association* 4 (1971): 10–15.

Schell, Jonathan. *The Fate of the Earth*. New York: Knopf, 1982.

Schuster, Edgar H. "Discovering Theme and Structure in the Novel." *The English Journal* 52 (1963): 506–11.

Simon, John. "Double Whammy." Review of *Looking for Mr. Goodbar*, directed by Richard Brooks. *National Review* 29 (1977): 1443–44.

Sinyard, Neil. *Filming Literature: The Art of Screen Adaptation*. London: Crook Helm, 1986.

Sofia, Zoë. "Exterminating Fetuses: Abortion, Disarmament, and the Sexo-Semiotics of Extraterrestrialism." *Diacritics* 14.2 (1984): 47–59.

Sparshott, F. E. "Basic Film Aesthetics." In *Film Theory and Criticism: Introductory Readings,* edited by Gerald Mast and Marshall Cohen, 209–32. New York: Oxford University Press, 1974.

Stacy, Paul H. "Cinematic Thought." *Hartford Studies in Literature* 1 (1969): 124–30.

Strick, Philip. Review of *Deliverance*, directed by John Boorman. *Sight and Sound* 41 (1972): 228–29.

Sunila, Joyce. "Women and Mr. Goodbar." *Human Behavior* 7.3 (1978): 62–67.

Sweet, Louise. Review of *Looking for Mr. Goodbar*, directed by Richard Brooks. *Sight and Sound* 47 (1978): 125–26.

Switzer, Judith A. "The Utopian Vision in Kubrick's *2001* and *A Clockwork Orange*." In *Proceedings of the Fifth Annual Conference on Film,* edited by Maud S. Walther, 37–42. West Lafayette, Ind.: Purdue University Press, 1980.

Tanner, Tony. *City of Words: American Fiction 1950–1970*. New York: Harper, 1971.

Taylor, A. E. *A Commentary on Plato's* Timaeus. 1928. Oxford: Clarendon Press, 1962.

Taylor, John Russell. *Directors and Directions: Cinema for the Seventies*. New York: Hill and Wang, 1975.

Thorndike, Lynn. *A History of Magic and Experimental Science*. Vol. 1. New York: MacMillan, 1923.

Thorp, Margaret. "The Motion Picture and the Novel." *American Quarterly* 3 (1951): 195–203.

Toliver, Harold. *Animate Illusions: Explorations of Narrative Structure*. Lincoln: University of Nebraska Press, 1974.

Turner, Frederick W., III. "Myth Inside and Out: *The Natural*." In *Bernard Malamud and the Critics*, edited by Leslie A. and Joyce W. Field, 109–19. New York: New York University Press, 1970.

Walker, Alexander. *Stanley Kubrick Directs*. Expanded ed. New York: Harcourt, 1972.

Wasserman, Earl R. "*The Natural*: Malamud's World Ceres." *The Centennial Review of Arts and Sciences* 9 (1965): 438–60.

Wetzsteon, Ross. "Too Close for Comfort." *American Film,* May 1984, 16–21.

Williams, Ted, with John Underwood. *My Turn at Bat: The Story of My Life.* New York: Fireside, 1988.

Wilson, George M. *Narration in Light: Studies in Cinematic Point of View.* Baltimore, Md.: The Johns Hopkins University Press, 1986.

Youngblood, Gene. *Expanded Cinema.* New York: Dutton, 1970.

Zita, Jacquelyn N. "Pornography and the Male Imaginary." *Enclitic* 9 (1987): 28–44.

Index